D1585196

BYZANTINE ARCHITECTURE
AND DECORATION

1 Santa Sophia, Constantinople

BYZANTINE ARCHITECTURE
AND DECORATION

By

J. Arnott Hamilton
M.A., B.D., Ph.D., Hon. F.R.I.A.S.

With a Foreword by

PROFESSOR D. TALBOT RICE
M.B.E., M.A., B.Sc., D.Litt., F.S.A.

London
B. T. BATSFORD LTD

"Then too the pillar'd Dome, magnific, heav'd
Its ample Roof; and Luxury within
Pour'd out her glittering Stores."

THOMSON, *The Seasons* (*Autumn*)

First published, 1933
Second Edition, 1956

Printed and bound in Great Britain by Jarrold and Sons Ltd
London and Norwich for the Publishers
B. T. BATSFORD LTD
4 Fitzhardinge Street, Portman Square, London, W.1

DEDICATED TO THE MEMORY OF MY
MOTHER, WITH THE THOUGHT OF MANY VISITS
PAID TOGETHER TO
BYZANTINE CHURCHES
(b. 12 January 1854; d. 31 January 1948)

FOREWORD

BY D. TALBOT RICE, M.B.E.

Professor of Fine Art in the University of Edinburgh

THE problems of origins, of when domes were first used on a
large scale over a square base, of where the pendentive was
invented, and of how vaults were built in different regions,
have exercised the minds of numerous scholars since the early
years of this century, and a very great deal has been written on
the subject. But though the preoccupation with origins has been
considerable, not very much has been written about the developments consequent upon them, and the history of the Byzantine
domical style has by most writers been referred to only in very
broad outline. Yet, between the completion of Justinian's Sancta
Sophia in 537 and the building of the most recent traditionally
Byzantine church, there were more than a thousand years of
extensive building activity. And if the period was long, the area
over which churches of a Byzantine character were set up was
even more extensive, for builders over the whole area from
Mesopotamia to the south of France and from Egypt to Central
Russia were the heirs of the Byzantine tradition. Each area
boasted its own local traditions, and these influenced both technique and style, often very considerably, but even if the species
were different, the genus remained the same. And it is with the
genus that Dr. Hamilton is concerned.

Apart from such basically architectural features as domes,
vaults and the actual plan, the decoration formed an intrinsic
part of every Byzantine church. Mosaics, frescoes, carvings in low
relief, were all essential parts of the whole. Without them the
true nature of the building is hardly comprehensible; without the
building to frame it, the decoration remains incomplete. It is
thus essential that the two should be treated together, and
Dr. Hamilton has throughout treated the two as corollaries; hence
the dual title of his book. But architecture is his main theme.
Articles or books dealing with architecture in particular regions are
fairly numerous; it is works of this type that have brought our
knowledge up to date. But since the first edition of Dr. Hamilton's

book went out of print there has been no convenient general survey. That first edition has now been brought up to date; the results of research in numerous fields since it was first published in 1933 have been incorporated, and the text has been completely revised from beginning to end. The work was always useful; in its new form it will prove even more valuable. Now that tours and cruises include as often as not Byzantine as well as Classical monuments in their programmes, it will be of the greatest help to tourists. The specialist at his desk will find it an invaluable guide to research in fields kindred to his own. Even the lacunae in the story are useful, for on the one hand they will serve to indicate fields in which further detailed inquiry is most necessary, and on the other the records of certain lovely churches which have disappeared in recent times, like that of the Assumption of the Virgin at Nicaea, will serve to remind us that at best the story is inevitably an incomplete one, for so much that was fine, so much that was vital, has disappeared.

In completing this new edition of *Byzantine Architecture and Decoration* Dr. Hamilton has performed a very useful service. It is a pleasure to introduce the book to the reader. But it is the book, not the introduction, that is valuable, for it constitutes a thorough and all-embracing survey, of the problems of origin and development on the one hand, and of the distribution of the monuments and the character of the developed style on the other. No similar survey is available, either in English or any other language.

PREFACE

THIS book was first published twenty-three years ago, and I feel very grateful at being able, after so considerable a lapse of time, to issue a second edition.

The generous appreciation given to the first edition and the steady demand for it throughout the years encourage me to feel that a second was justified.

The whole book has been revised and re-written. While many passages have undergone little alteration, a great many others have been expanded considerably and much additional matter has been introduced into the text. Much more is said about the historical and cultural background and about the aesthetic qualities and religious significance of Byzantine Architecture and Art. The descriptions of the dome, the squinch and the pendentive have been more fully developed in the light of recent research. A new chapter has been inserted on the domed churches of Aquitaine as a result of a visit to that part of France.

It is my earnest hope that this enlarged edition will prove of interest and value to its readers and will lead many of them to further study. References in footnotes would have added too much to its price, but it is hoped that the Bibliography will be a sufficient guide.

I desire to express my most grateful thanks to Mr. James R. Blair, C.I.E., M.A., for so kindly reading over my typescript to me and inserting my corrections, to Mr. R. Butchart, Hon.M.A., for his careful work in compiling the Index and reading the proofs, and to Professor Talbot Rice for his constant encouragement and his goodness in contributing the Foreword.

I also thank Messrs. B. T. Batsford Ltd., and especially Mr. Brian Batsford and Mr. Anthony Harding, for all the care they have taken in producing this volume and in collecting the illustrations, most of which are new to this edition.

J. A. H.

Edinburgh
July 1956

CONTENTS

CONTENTS

ACKNOWLEDGMENT

THE author and the publishers wish to record their gratitude to the following for supplying illustrations and for their permission to reproduce them in this book:

Fratelli Alinari, Florence, for figs. 6, 18, 28, 48, 49, 51, 52, 55, 57–60, 117, 118, 152, 153, 157–9; Caisse Nationale des Monuments Historiques, Paris, for fig. 77; the Exclusive News Agency Ltd., for figs. 3, 27, 29, 30, 33, 37–9, 68, 71, 75, 89, 97, 102, 122, 137, 145, 149, 150 and 156; L. Franzio, Athens, and the Department of Information of the Greek Government, London, for fig. 125; the Department of Information of the Greek Government, London, for fig. 46; the Hellenic Society, for figs. 19, 69, 70 and 74; the Italian State Tourist Department, for figs. 4, 25 and 161; A. F. Kersting, F.R.P.S., for figs. 8 and 126; the Mansell Collection, for fig. 36; Spyros Meletzis, Athens, and the Department of Information of the Greek Government, London, for fig. 121; Jasper More, for fig. 62; Picture Post Library, for figs. 7 and 139; Paul Popper Ltd., for figs. 1, 2, 5, 40, 56, 83, 84, 90, 115 and 124; the Royal Institute of British Architects, for figs. 95 and 96; Editions René, Périgueux, for figs. 163 and 164; the Legation of the Rumanian People's Republic, London, for fig. 134; Sezione Edizioni d'Arte, Rome, for figs. 147 and 155; the Soviet Embassy, London, for figs. 141–4; the Staatliche Bildstelle, Berlin, for figs. 98, 100, 105–7, 116 and 120; Cecil Stewart, D.A.(Edin.), F.R.I.B.A., for figs. 91 and 92; Jan Vandermeulen, Adelaide-Kaap, South Africa, for figs. 17, 26, 32, 35, 47, 50, 53, 123, 127, 129–32 and 135; the Trustees of the Victoria and Albert Museum, for fig. 76; Editions d'Art Yvon, Paris, for figs. 167 and 170.

LIST OF ILLUSTRATIONS

*The numerals in parentheses in the text refer to the
figure numbers of illustrations*

7

9

11

LIST OF ILLUSTRATIONS

CHAPTER I

The Byzantine Scene

BYZANTINE Architecture was evolved in the East Roman or Byzantine Empire in the centuries which followed the foundation of Constantinople in the year 330 of the Christian era. It reached maturity in the sixth century and flourished within the changing frontiers of the Eastern Empire till the capture of Constantinople in 1453 by the Ottoman Turks. It long survived the conquest of the city, fashioning the structure and dictating the plan of eastern churches until the present day. Nor was it confined within the limits of the Empire: both before and after the conquest it spread far beyond them, and it was radiated over a vast expanse which stretched from the plains of northern Russia to the deserts of Egypt and from the mountains of Armenia to the meadows of Aquitaine.

Through many centuries the survival and the expansion of the Byzantine style were due, above all, to the power and prestige of Constantinople, proud capital of the Christian Empire of the East, a wonderful city of fabulous renown. For more than a thousand years Constantinople was a great cultural centre, absorbing and refashioning the ideas which men brought to its shores from many lands, and disseminating far and wide its formulated thoughts. It was a rich and splendid city, the richest and most splendid in the world: it contained the great palaces of the Emperor, where, surrounded by an army of court functionaries and officers of state, he dwelt in a legendary magnificence; it was the seat of a patriarch who wielded authority over innumerable souls as ecclesiastical guardian of the Orthodox faith. It possessed churches of outstanding fame and beauty, whither came hosts of devotees to venerate the miraculous relics which they enshrined: it contained monasteries whose total inmates formed a population in themselves; it was the centre of a large and flourishing commerce to which traders came from every part of the known world to buy and sell in its crowded markets. Above all else, Constantinople, in spite of natural corruption and recurrent weakness, stood forth

13

as the champion and bulwark of Christian civilisation in the East. Time and time again it successfully repelled invasion. Fruitlessly did the barbarian hordes hurl themselves against its impregnable walls. It was only the weakness which followed the Crusaders' occupation of the city in the thirteenth century which led to its final downfall before the Turkish onslaught.

In so rich and favourable an environment scholarship and art found many followers. The works of classical antiquity were prized and studied in the university and schools. Historians and poets, theologians and scientists, jurists and grammarians, wrote down their thoughts and gave them to mankind. The painter, the sculptor, the worker in ivory or precious metal were always active in the service of the Church, the Court and the private patron. The fame of Constantinople had spread to the most distant places and craftsmen flocked to it from east and west to absorb its culture and exercise their talents. Works of Byzantine craftsmanship, ivories and silks and jewelled caskets, were carried back by visitors to be treasured and imitated in their native lands. It is a matter for no surprise that the influence of so celebrated a city on the formation and course of Byzantine Art was profound and lasting. It was Constantinople that gave to Byzantine architecture and art both the impetus to burst into living growth and the power to expand and to endure.

In founding his new capital on the site of the ancient Greek colony of Byzantium, the Emperor Constantine chose a position of incomparable beauty and of supreme commercial and strategic value. As the traveller, having passed through the Dardanelles, is crossing the Sea of Marmora, he beholds in front of him, emerging every instant more clearly on their hilly promontory, the domes and minarets of Istanbul. The scene is one of vivid animation and enchanting loveliness. The broad expanse of sunlit sea is enlivened with the craft of every type and clime: the mosques and houses of the city, elevated above the waters, stand out distinct in the pellucid air and the waves beat gently on the hoary walls which fringe the rocky shore. Just beyond the city opens the narrow Bosphorus running between the picturesque and wooded banks of Europe and Asia, until it reaches the wide desolation of the Euxine. Set in the midst of so much beauty, Istanbul, as Constantinople is now officially designated, with all the proud record of its storied past, ranks inferior to none of the great historic cities of the world.

2   CONSTANTINOPLE AND THE GOLDEN HORN

3   CONSTANTINOPLE: the Walls

4 EMPEROR JUSTINIAN MOSAIC, S. VITALE, RAVENNA

5 VIRGIN AND EMPERORS
MOSAIC OF SANTA SOPHIA,
CONSTANTINOPLE

It is built on a hilly trilateral projection of land which juts out into the Bosphorus and the Sea of Marmora. Its southern shore is washed by the waters of that sea and its northern flanked by the Golden Horn, an inlet which curves deep into the land and forms a secure and commodious harbour(2). The short eastern side of the promontory faces Asia. The western or landward side was protected by ranges of massive walls, which for centuries repelled the rapacity of the barbarian and are the pensive glory of the town today.

In the centuries which followed its foundation, Constantinople attracted a vast population of citizens, who lived in stately palaces or were crowded together in the narrow streets which climbed the seven hills. Through the centre of the city there ran a broad thoroughfare called the Mese, flanked by fine shops, stately public buildings and long arcades. Statues and groups of statuary were a witness to the pride or gratitude of wealthy citizens. In the public or private gardens the leaping waters of the fountain cooled the air and the shade of the plane trees gave refuge from the sun. Stately forums like the Forum of Constantine inter-rupted the highway, which was terminated at the Augusteum, a wide square fronting the senate-house and the main entrance to the palace. The beauty of the city was enhanced by the classic statues which Constantine brought from the cities of antiquity and which so profusely adorned the courts and porticoes of his new metropolis.

Fire and sword and slow decay have destroyed almost all the splendours of Constantinople, but one incomparable building— the Church of Santa Sophia(1)—and several other monuments of interest or beauty have survived to attest its majesty and its opulence. On the site of the Hippodrome can still be seen three famous memorials of the past. One of them is an Egyptian obelisk brought there by the Emperor Theodosius. The fourth-century sculptures on its marble base depict the monarch and his court watching the games: he gazes at the chariots as they race around, or holds the laurel wreath which is to be presented to a victor. Another monument is the venerable Serpent Column, which had been erected at Delphi to commemorate the Greek victory over the Persians at Plataea; its three heads have long since been broken off. The third monument is an obelisk called the Colossus. Not far away is the porphyry column of Constantine—the so-called "Burnt Column" so often scorched by fire. Erected by Constantine to commemorate the foundation of the city, it was the scene of an annual service of remembrance.

The Hippodrome was a favourite centre of life for the crowds of citizens. Situated near the Sacred Palace, it was curved at one end and was divided down the middle by the spina, which seems to have been made up of monuments, including some of the choicest statues of antiquity. The chariot races, the athletic contests and the acrobatic shows agitated the wild enthusiasm of a dense throng of spectators, while political meetings held in the same wide arena incited them to turbulence and riot. The Hippodrome was also the scene of triumphal processions when, in the presence of a victorious Emperor, a train of captive barbarians and the rich spoils of plundered cities gratified the pride of the citizens. Only about a hundred years after the fall of Constantinople the traveller Gyllius lamented the disappearance of the Hippodrome, of which he saw some columns still erect. Within the last thirty years excavations have been undertaken on the site.

Byzantine administration circled round the holy person of the Emperor, and his palace must needs reflect such august majesty. The Sacred Palace was not a single stately edifice but a whole cluster of buildings set almost haphazard in a wide garden at the eastern end of the peninsula. Constantine began the work and other emperors added to the series. Stately halls and audience-rooms, sumptuous sleeping-chambers, churches, terraces and porticoes were scattered throughout the spacious gardens, whence a magnificent prospect extended across the sea to the Asiatic shore. Broad flights of marble stairs led from one level to another, and the gardens were beautified with trees and flowers. The buildings were of different shape, rectangular, octagonal, cruciform, and some of them were roofed with the Byzantine dome.

The Emperor Constantine VII (Porphyrogenitus) has described the magnificence of the palace in his *Book of the Ceremonies*, and the splendour of its decoration evoked an amazed and universal admiration. The walls were panelled with polychrome marble; ranges of porphyry and marble columns upheld the roofs; gay hunting scenes in glittering mosaics spread themselves around the rooms; pavements charged with eagles and peacocks formed the floors; cupolas and ceilings gleamed with golden tesserae. There was a terrace whose golden roof rested on fifteen columns of Phrygian marble. There was a bronze fountain with a golden pineapple and bronze lions spouting water from their mouths.

16

Thousands of candelabra lit the spacious halls when darkness fell, revealing all the details of the rare brocades and tapestries.

Hardly anything has survived of the great Palace of the Emperors at Constantinople.

Beside the Sea of Marmora not far from the Church of SS. Sergius and Bacchus there rest the remains of a building which has been called the "House of Justinian". It is said to have been the residence of that monarch before his accession, but, though of the Byzantine era, is of much later date. There were four doors opening out on to a balcony which faces the sea, and there were vaulted rooms inside. Near by was the Bucoleon, an addition to the Sacred Palace which was enlarged and fortified by the Emperor Nicephorus Phocas and which was the scene of his assassination. It received its name from the statue of a bull and a lion which adorned its quay, whence the Emperors were rowed in state in the imperial barge to visit sacred shrines upon or near the shore. William of Tyre in the twelfth century wrote with admiration of the statues of animals and the stately staircases and the marble quay. Excavations undertaken at the Sacred Palace within recent years have uncovered a magnificent mosaic pavement which is one of the most important discoveries of Byzantine archaeologists.

The Sacred Palace was the habitation of the Emperor, and every method was adopted to surround him with glamour and mystery. He was the supreme autocrat, the arbiter of destiny, the vicegerent of God, "the equal of the Apostles". A great army of functionaries, designated with grandiloquent titles, formed his court. Their costumes were of silk and other costly fabrics, appropriate for the long elaborate ceremonies which constantly took place. Perhaps it was the reception of foreign ambassadors which afforded the best occasion for display. The sovereign, clad in his imperial robes, stiff with cloth of gold and glittering with jewels, sat on his golden throne in the apse at the end of the great apartment. Near him was a golden plane tree on which mechanical birds were perched. Two golden lions crouched beside the throne and two gryphons flanked its sides. The rarest treasures were exhibited in the alcoves. In their rich embroidered robes the court dignitaries, ranged in order of etiquette, awaited the entrance of the envoy. As he entered the mechanical birds on the plane tree began to sing and flutter: the lions roared and the notes of an organ pealed. The ambassador prostrated himself on the floor.

When he looked up he beheld the throne suspended in the air with the Emperor clad in a different but equally magnificent robe. The throne which had been carried through an aperture in the roof descended slowly to the floor. The ceremony will seem trivial to the modern mind, but it can well be imagined how it would astound the envoy of some barbaric nation whose mind had already been dazzled beyond conception by all the opulence of the imperial palace.

The reverence accorded to the Emperor was not derived solely from his position as autocrat of an extensive realm. He was also the favoured of God, the defender of Christianity, the ruler of the Church, the champion of Orthodoxy. In his portraits his sacred head was encircled with the halo, emblem at first of power and later of sanctity. The attitude of approach towards him was one of worship. There is in the Library of S. Mark at Venice a psalter of the eleventh century containing a miniature which perfectly illustrates the Byzantine conception of the imperial person. In front of a rich gold background the Emperor Basil II stands erect upon a jewelled footstool. Haloed and bearded he looks sternly before him. He grasps a spear and is protected by a golden cuirass. His feet are shod in the scarlet buskins of imperial rank, and his purple tunic is fringed with gold. One angel has placed the golden diadem upon his brow and another grasps his spear. In the sky above, Christ clasps the Gospels and holds out a golden circlet. Below the footstool, on a green background, eight robed figures prostrate themselves in the obligatory attitude of obeisance.

The aura of pomp and grandeur which enveloped the sacred person of the Emperor spread most naturally into the realm of art. The oriental conception of Christ as expressed in the majestic picture of Him as the Pantocrator, the Almighty, accorded with the attitude adopted towards the Emperor. Religious art was animated by the spirit of ceremonialism which permeated the life of the Court and which was reflected in the elaborate ordinances of the Church. Angels, clad in stiff bejewelled raiment and bearing the imperial insignia of labarum and orb, surrounded the Pantocrator like high dignitaries of the Emperor(7). The costumes of certain saints reproduced those worn by the soldiers of the royal guard: the gestures and genuflections of courtly etiquette were imitated in such scenes as the Adoration of the Infant Christ by the Wise Men of the East. The whole interiors of the churches with their revetment of mosaics and multi-coloured marbles

18

paralleled the splendour of Byzantine Imperialism as it shone forth in the halls of the palaces.

Of course it was only the minority of churches which could afford such an outlay of magnificence. The humbler churches had to be contented with paintings in fresco secco, but even in these paintings the spirit of Byzantine court splendour is evident: the rich-robed angels still adore the powerful Christ; the attitudes of obeisance are still preserved.

It must be said, however, that these traits are combined with others of a more popular appeal, due to the influence of the monastic artist. The monastery was often in close contact with the people, and its church the active centre of social work. It is recorded how in Asia Minor adjacent buildings connected with churches included almshouses, hospices, infirmaries and even provision for supplying water to the villages. As the Church by its activities catered for the immediate spiritual and bodily needs of the people, so in its art it made a direct appeal to their natural emotions. The miraculous played a profound part in their thoughts and the stories of the saints exercised a profound influence over their imagination. The walls of village churches were therefore painted with compositions more direct and popular in their appeal and, especially in later days, scenes from the apocryphal gospels and the lives of the saints supplied the demand for the marvellous.

The commercial and industrial importance of Constantinople played no little part in the development of her architecture and art. The most precious and beautiful materials were conveyed to her markets and her wharves. The opulence of her wealthy citizens incited the erection of stately buildings and the creation of all manner of artistic and expensive ornaments. There was a constant flow of overland commerce, and the seaborne trade was extensive. From Sicily, Thrace and Egypt came the grain which was needed to feed a great population. From the Morea and the Cyclades the vessels sailed through the Dardanelles "laden with amber grapes and Chian wine". Olives and fruit were ferried from the Asiatic shore. Caravans laden with gems and spices and aromatic gums wended their way to Antioch in Syria or Trebizond on the Black Sea coast, whence their precious freight was shipped to the Golden Horn. The mines of Africa supplied the gold which was minted into the Byzantine coins of such high reputation. The ivory of the Asiatic forests was fashioned into coffers and diptychs, exquisitely carved.

The houses in Constantinople were mainly made of wood and the churches of brick, but marble was lavishly used for decorative purposes. White marble which was sculptured into the beautiful Byzantine capitals was quarried in the mines of Paros and Pentelicus. The Prinkopo Islands in the Sea of Marmora and quarries in Thessaly and elsewhere supplied pink and green and other coloured marbles to panel the churches and palaces with a glowing polychrome revetment. Lovely white marble came from the Marmora Islands. Timber was floated down the broad rivers of Russia to the Black Sea, and metals from Macedonia entered the capital across the plains of Thrace. Silks and fabrics were poured into the city from the East, and the fantastic Oriental designs with which they were embroidered were copied by the sculptors of Constantinople on their marble slabs. The export resembled the import trade in its extent. Constantinople was a great centre of distribution and it dispatched many of its imports to the West. It was also an important industrial centre. All the ordinary needs of the inhabitants of a large city had to be supplied, and men sat in their open booths at the potter's wheel, or made articles in wood and copper for domestic use. Even more lucrative was the trade in luxuries which were provided in great quantities for export to the West and to other parts of the Empire or for the gratification of the citizens themselves. The Church was a great patron. Bishops and priests must perform the liturgy in rich embroidered vestments. The venerated relics of a saint must rest in a reliquary flashing with silver and jewels. The furnishings of a church—the altar, the ambo, the icon-frames, the hanging lamps—must be precious and worthy adornments of the House of God.

The officials of the court demanded an equal splendour, for the imperial etiquette required elaborate and distinctive robes for the innumerable dignitaries who thronged the palace and paraded their grandeur with ostentatious vanity. The wealthy citizens filled their palaces with jewelled ornaments and gay tapestries, while the services of the calligrapher were in demand to provide manuscripts for the scholar and the jurist.

Wealth and patronage encouraged the development of the arts in Constantinople, but they could never have flourished so enduringly without security. For hundreds of years the great metropolis was inviolate. Its security was due to the mighty walls which stretched from the Sea of Marmora to the Golden Horn, and which stand with the melancholy of departed glory in their abandoned state(3).

The first walls were built by Constantine who is believed himself to have traced their line; and when an attendant expressed his amazement at their extent, he is said to have replied that he followed an invisible guide. But the city soon spread beyond the walls of Constantine to the west. The historian Sozomen declared that the population had exceeded that of Rome. The orator Themistocles says that by the time of Theodosius I, Constantinople's "beauty was not as formerly dispersed in patches but that it covered the complete site", like a garment woven to the fringes. The former edge of the city, which glittered with porphyry and gold, had now become its centre. So in the reign of Theodosius II a new range of walls was built about a mile to the west of the old ones which had been erected by Constantine.

Battered and restored in many places, with creepers trailing down their weather-beaten stones, and with flowers growing in the crenellations of their massive towers the Theodosian walls remain as a majestic memorial of the power and glory of the Byzantine Empire. The Theodosian walls consisted of an outer and inner wall separated by a *peribolos* or terrace. The inner wall, 15 feet thick, was battlemented and flanked on the outside with ninety-six bold projecting towers. The outer wall was of lesser thickness but was also furnished with towers. Beyond it stretched a broad terrace and deep moat. The walls were made of limestone blocks relieved with courses of brick. Prominent among the gates was the "Porta Aurea", the "Golden Gate", a triple entrance of marble which seems originally to have been an isolated triumphal arch built in imitation of those at Rome. Bright with gilding, it was adorned with scenes in relief from classical mythology and bore a cross upon its summit. Through it the Emperors were wont to pass in triumph in celebration of a victorious campaign; in his gorgeous robes, with crown on head and sceptre in hand, he would move slowly upon his way, while the crowd of spectators sang hymns to God, the bestower of victory. At a later date frescoes of the Crucifixion and Last Judgment were painted on the Golden Gate.

The road spanned by the Gate of the Pege or Spring led to a sacred well, which was a favourite place of pilgrimage and a locality of much natural beauty, diversified with trees and flowers. The Emperor Basil I built a magnificent palace by this delectable site, where he resorted to worship in the Church of the Fountain and bathe in the miraculous waters.

Later Emperors added to the walls in the area towards the Golden Horn, enclosing within the city's limits the suburb of Blachernae with the Palace of the same name. Other walls ran round the sea-front, where they rise grandly and picturesquely from the shore with the blue waters of the Sea of Marmora lapping their base.

So for centuries the great city dwelt safe within its circuit of fortifications. Truly has it been said that the walls of Constantinople were the guardian of Christian civilisation against the invaders who otherwise might have swept over Europe from the East.

It cannot be too strongly emphasised that Constantinople was a Christian city and that the Byzantine Empire was the champion of the Christian faith. Of course, evil and superstition abounded, but the Empire had chosen Christianity as its official creed and held to it with a passionate devotion. Religion permeated the whole life of the city and affected the attitude of its citizens towards time and towards eternity. The discourses of famous preachers and the record of charitable institutions are a testimony to its ethical persuasion and practical results. The visible signs of religion met one at the corner of every street and were welcomed into every home. Constantinople was a city of churches, ranging from the vast and magnificent Cathedral of Santa Sophia to humble little shrines. The dome of a church must have diversified the outline of almost every street: Ruy de Clavijo, a Spanish traveller of the fifteenth century, was amazed at the abundance of churches which the city contained. Most splendid of all was the Cathedral of Santa Sophia, where the ritual was chanted in the presence of the Emperor amid surroundings of marvellous splendour and with the most gorgeous ceremonial. The cathedral and the other remaining churches are described in later chapters, but many more have perished. Some were parish churches; some were attached to monasteries; some were little shrines through whose open doors the passer-by would enter to pay his devotion before a holy picture in the midst of his daily work. The thought of the eternal entered in a very tangible way into everyday life. The sacred icon was cherished in the home; the coins of the realm might be stamped with the head of Christ; the games were opened with prayers and the Cross was carried before the armies in battle.

The prestige of the Church in Constantinople was enhanced by the residence of the Patriarch, who exercised authority over the numerous bishops and priests of far-flung regions. He held a position second only to that of the Emperor. Church and State were closely linked together in the Empire: the Emperor, sanctified by divine authority, was supreme in Church as well as State, but the Patriarch could often guide him in national affairs. He dwelt in a palace of many rooms and halls, richly adorned with mosaics.

The religious atmosphere of the city was still further increased by many monasteries inhabited by monks from all parts of the Empire. In the verdant vale of the little River Lycus and among the shady groves near the walls these monasteries abounded. Schools, hospices, infirmaries might combine with the church and monastic dwellings to form the complex of the monastery, and thousands of monks, in their black dress and tall cylindrical hats, prayed and worked in these quiet habitations. Their influence on the life of the capital was profound. Held in the utmost veneration by pious Christians, they exercised a sway over the minds of the citizens which was of paramount importance.

Finally in briefly assessing the religious importance of Constantinople account must be taken of the great influx of pilgrims which flowed without ceasing from every quarter of the Christian world. They were attracted by the prestige of the Christian metropolis and by the splendour of its churches, but even more were they drawn towards it by the innumerable relics which it contained. Emperors and bishops had collected in the city all the precious relics they could obtain. The bones of a holy anchorite, the garment or shroud of a saint, a dim icon painted by S. Luke, the spear of a holy warrior, the nails and wood of the Cross itself—these and many other relics preserved in costly caskets enriched with gold and jewels attracted multitudes of pilgrims to their shrines. Through their medium it was believed that diseases could be cured and calamities averted, and the chroniclers declare they were more precious than silver and gold. To Constantinople they drew their votaries from far and near, and the pilgrims returned home full of tales of wonder about the splendid city whose mysterious fame was spread throughout the known world.

THE PROGRESS OF BYZANTINE ART

Constantine's patronage of the Christian religion gave an immediate impetus to Christian Art. In the second decade of the fourth century he had granted toleration to Christianity, and after the foundation of his new capital he favoured it and supplied it with buildings for worship. His contributions to church architecture, though doubtless exaggerated by his eulogists, were important and considerable. "A mighty luminary and a most distinct and powerful herald of genuine piety . . . he gave costly benefactions to the churches of God, both enlarging and heightening the sacred edifices and embellishing the most august sanctuaries of the Church with abundant offerings." Of his churches in Constantinople that of the Holy Apostles seems to have been specially distinguished. It is declared to have been of great height and to have been covered with slabs of coloured marble. Its ceiling was of finely fretted work overlaid with gold. It was splendidly conspicuous in the middle of an open court surrounded by porticoes.

As time went on, the ecclesiastical authority of Constantinople steadily increased. The second Oecumenical Council, which was held there in A.D. 381, decreed that the Bishop of Constantinople had a dignity second to that of Rome "because Constantinople is New Rome". Constantinople soon became the mistress of ecclesiastical affairs in the East. Alexandria was long her proud rival, but in the fifth century the Coptic Church fell into heresy and schism, and a shattering blow was dealt at the waning influence of the Egyptian city. Soon Constantinople rivalled the ancient capital on the Tiber and exceeded Rome in power.

For many years two Emperors ruled over the Roman Empire, one in the East at Constantinople, the other in the West at Rome, Milan or Ravenna. But the victorious myriads of the barbarians from the north eventually put an end to the old western empire in 476. Meanwhile a succession of Emperors followed Constantine the Great in the East. They consolidated their frontiers and strove to keep the barbarians at bay, until, with the advent of the great Justinian (527–565), a brief but brilliant period of power and vast expansion followed. It was in the reign of Justinian that Byzantine Art blossomed into perfect flower. Not only in Constantinople but in all parts of his vast dominions, Justinian strove to perpetuate his glory by building. It is recorded that many of his churches were so large and magnificent that "a person beholding any one of them would imagine it to have been his only work and that he had spent the whole period of his life in adorning it alone".

Several important churches erected by Justinian in Constantinople have long since disappeared, but fortunately Santa Sophia, the greatest of them all, has been preserved until this day. Of the vanished churches the most notable was that of the Holy Apostles, which was destroyed by the Turks but which had already left its imprint on the plan of S. Mark at Venice. A five-domed cruciform church, it was furnished with antique columns and sumptuously adorned with mosaics and marble.

The period which followed the death of Justinian brought difficulty to the Empire, which was engaged in a constant conflict with Avars, Persians or Arabs. Byzantium saw the eighth century opening in anarchy and disintegration. Little survives of the art or architecture of this era, which, however, cannot have been a period of absolute stagnation. Justinian II attempted building on the grand scale and the seventh and early eighth centuries witnessed the production of Byzantine mosaics in Rome and a brilliant architectural activity in Armenia.

The accession to the Byzantine throne in 717 of Leo III, the Isaurian, led to a long-continued dispute which occupies an important place in the history of East Christian Art. This dispute is known as the Iconoclastic Controversy and had to do with the permissibility of rendering divine and holy persons in icons or sacred pictures and in other works of art. It finally came to an end in 842 and will be described in a later chapter.

With the accession in 867 of Basil I, Byzantine Art entered upon a new and brilliant phase. As the era of Justinian was designated by M. Charles Diehl the first, so the Basilian era was called by him its second "Golden Age". Plans were further developed and elevations were treated with a new refinement. Interiors came to be decorated after an iconographical scheme in accordance with which the pictures in mosaic or fresco were assigned to those parts of the building which best suited or symbolised their individual themes. It follows that the pictorial decoration of a Byzantine church is closely bound up with the architecture. The "golden age" of the Basilian dynasty was prolonged into that of the Comneni which began in 1081. From the Basilian and Comnenian epochs a number of interesting churches survive in Constantinople, though all but one of them have long since been turned into mosques. From the capital a powerful influence radiated to the frontiers of the Empire and beyond: Greece possesses many churches of great charm, the majority of them small in size, but carefully and elegantly constructed; Venice preserves an imperishable monument of Byzantine genius in the domed and cruciform Cathedral of S. Mark; the Norman kings of Sicily built Byzantine churches which blended Norman and Saracenic elements; the Russian princes strove to emulate Byzantium in the style of their religious edifices; numerous churches were erected in Asia Minor and monasteries arose on the sacred slopes of Mount Athos; Armenia began for a second time to be marvellously prolific in architecture and according to some writers, persisted in controlling western regions by an influence which had long been potent.

In Constantinople a severe check was given to artistic development in 1204 when it was barbarously ravaged by the knights of the Fourth Crusade: but with the restoration in 1261, under the dynasty of the Palaeologi, Byzantine Art revealed its recuperative power, and in the shrunken dominions of the Empire it flourished anew. In other countries it developed under the inspiration of refugees who had fled from the capital on the Latin invasion. Constantinople has churches dating from the period of the Palaeologi which are characterised by much beauty and refinement. The mosaics of the Church of the Chora in Constantinople are of this time and are among the finest creations of Byzantine Art. Architecture and art flourished beyond the confines of the capital. Pious zeal continued to endow monasteries on Mount Athos where churches of good quality were erected long after the Turkish conquest. Salonica was enriched with rare examples of the builder's art: at Mistra, in the Morea, one of the few possessions of the Empire, churches were erected and adorned with frescoes that are among the choicest expressions of Byzantine painting. The Serbian monarchs covered their territory with churches distinguished for loftiness of outline and richness of decoration. A few curious churches exist at Trebizond on the south coast of the Black Sea, relics of the ephemeral Trapezuntine Empire. Architecture developed in Russia so as ultimately to form a separate style.

In the lands which were to fall under Moslem rule, the Byzantine Art of this epoch was the last splendour of a dying day. With the capture of Constantinople in 1453 the shadows fell. Numerous churches were changed into mosques. No longer could the Christians build costly and imposing shrines. The additions which were so often made to churches in Greece show the difference which the conquest made; whereas the original structures are of beautiful workmanship, the masonry of the additions is rough and rude (101).

Interiors were still decorated with frescoes, but these, though of considerable interest, are, with important exceptions, equally crude in execution.

For more than a thousand years Byzantine Architecture fulfilled its function, sometimes with magnificence, often with distinction, always with propriety. Moslem invasion arrested its development as a Christian style, but it had left to the world a legacy of grand and logical construction, of sensitive and refined detail, of exquisite craftsmanship, of wise and appropriate decoration and of rich and splendid colour. This legacy was inherited both by the West and the East: Byzantine sculpture and illumination had long since penetrated the western world; Byzantine Architecture was a source of inspiration both to the architects of Renaissance churches in Italy and to those of Turkish mosques in Istanbul.

CHAPTER II

The Byzantine Church

THE SIGNIFICANCE OF ITS STRUCTURE AND
ITS MURAL DECORATION

THE distinctive characteristic of a true Byzantine church is a dome covering a square space below. In the developed form the component parts of the building group themselves around the crowning dome, with their vaults extending to the outer walls like the equal arms of a cross, and with the angles of the cross filled in with chambers at a lower level. The church was therefore a central-planned structure, square in plan, cruciform at a higher level and crowned with a dome (8).

Why did the Eastern Christians adopt and cherish this type of building for their worship? In early days basilicas and simple hall-churches were common in the East. The former continued to be employed and the latter never ceased to be erected. But whenever possible their ideal church was built central-planned and covered with its dome. The reasons which induced the Eastern Church to prefer this plan are partly aesthetic, partly symbolic and partly practical.

The dome must have appealed to them for aesthetic reasons. When they found it could cover a square space, and was therefore suitable for their purpose, they saw that they could use it with great effect. It was a monumental feature, giving prominence and distinction to the edifice which was set apart for the worship of God. Noble and majestic, it was the culmination and completion of the sacred building. But the dome also attracted them by its symbolic significance. Sometimes architectural historians have made too much of symbolism as a reason for architectural forms. Yet the love of symbolism is so prevalent in the East that we can safely affirm that the symbolism of the dome made its appeal from the very first. The testimony of Christian writers shows that it soon took a permanent hold of the Byzantine mind. As the symbol of the vault of heaven, it was the fitting canopy for the place of worship, where in the centre of the dome Christ was most rightly portrayed blessing his followers from on high.

The cruciform superstructure, though evolved from structural necessity, made an equally powerful appeal to the Byzantine mind.

So much for the superstructure. The ground plan of the church is approximately square. The square plan of a Byzantine developed church is a marked contrast to the Romanesque or Gothic parish church of the West with its long narrow nave and aisles. The difference between the two plans must be explained by the differences in the Liturgy. In the Latin medieval church the priest with his attendants celebrated the Mass in the chancel, distant from the congregation in the nave: he and his acolytes remained within the ambit of the altar. There, within that prescribed area, he moved to and fro, offering up his prayers and consecrating the sacred elements. That altar was the focal-point of the church, and it was to the place of the altar that the gaze of the worshippers who were gathered within the nave was naturally directed. It was therefore clear that a long and fairly narrow nave was most suitable for worshippers at such a form of service: the more of them who could clearly see the ceremonial of the altar the more effective was the plan. In the Eastern Orthodox Church the ceremonial moves in a different way. A screen, the iconostasis, extends across the end of the church, shutting off the sanctuary from view. The priest comes out of the sanctuary by a northern door in the iconostasis; he passes through the central door into the altar space; he moves among the people censing them as he proceeds.

A great part of the service is hidden from the people, or from the great majority of them. The sacred acts are performed in the mystery of the concealed sanctuary. When the priest does make his appearance and moves before or among the congregation he is plainly seen by all. A church of square plan is thoroughly suited for such a type of service, and there is no need to sacrifice breadth to length. Another characteristic of the Eastern Church which is emphasised in the form of the building is its corporateness. Orthodox writers are never tired of laying stress on the communal sense which pervades the act of worship. The fellowship of believers in the church is a cardinal ideal and a supreme reality. The unbroken lines of the external walls and the compact nature of the edifice harmonise with this conception. The Byzantine church is not, say, like a Baroque rotunda with chapels radiating from the central area breaking the curve of the circle or ellipse, and each containing its altar. The walls of the nave in the Byzantine church are unbroken and there is the one altar—in the sanctuary. The corporate nature of this worship seems inherent in the plan. There is of course ample room for private devotion: the worshipper, whether he is alone in the empty church or whether he has come to attend a service, bows down in prayer before the individual icons.

But this does not lessen the sense of congregational corporateness conveyed by the general structure. Nor does the presence of side chapels, which are really separate rooms attached to the building entered as a rule by doors of their own, more or less walled off from the main structure.

Aesthetically, a typical Byzantine church of the developed type is distinguished by its compactness and unity of mass: externally the whole ensemble of the structure is presented immediately to the eye, and there is neither disassociation nor disorder in its several parts.

Yet at the same time there is a multiplicity within this unity, and a complexity within this simplicity. The dome is sustained by a subtle and balanced system of internal buttressing, and the result is that in the interior the unitary conception is combined with a more complex treatment of the space. As one stands beneath the dome and sees it rise above, as one looks to the four points of the compass and beholds the rounded vaults extending in equal proportions to the enclosing walls, the sense of harmony and unity prevails. But as one glances at the angle spaces, one feels the subtle and complex adjustment and the perfect equilibrium which maintains the structure as a whole. It all seems typical of the Byzantine mind. It is of the same nature as the solutions which the Greek Orthodox Fathers formulated in the Doctrines of the Trinity and the Person of Christ. In their solution of the Doctrine of the Trinity they maintained the distinction of the Persons: there were three equal Persons in the Godhead. But they also declared the Unity of the Nature: the Three were One. In their Christological discussions they clove to the dogma of divine and human natures in the One Person Christ; they rejected any confusion either in nature or in will. The same spirit animates the building, the idea of difference in unity, of balance and proportion, of harmony and equilibrium.

The Byzantine church was completed by being furnished with three apses which projected from the eastern end. These apses, as we shall see later, were necessitated by the requirements of the service; so also was the narthex, a vestibule along the western end.

With each part of it fulfilling its definite function in maintaining the fabric and meeting the liturgical demands the Byzantine church is strictly logical, and its appearance explains its construction. Its treatment gives it dignity or charm and its decoration closely knit to the architecture is appropriate and refined. The dome was later elevated on a high polygonal drum, but in the best churches appeared as integral to the understructure and was characterised by a firm elegance and distinction of line.

Byzantine mural painting and mosaic were closely associated with the architecture. For that reason a general description follows of the painted decoration of a Byzantine church. In the course of the volume, while any elaborate criticism is beyond its scope, mention will be made of the decoration in individual churches.

The roof and walls of a Byzantine interior were richly clad with pictures. The ample wall space was seen by the Church at an early date to afford an opportunity of instructing the ignorant and strengthening the faithful, and the principle adopted was elaborated as time went on.

Byzantine Art was a didactic art: controlled by ecclesiastical authority, its aim was to teach the events of sacred story and the dogmas of the Church. So the walls were clad with paintings which became an integral part of the edifice, delivering their silent message to every worshipper. By the time of Basil I the interiors had come to be decorated in accordance with an iconographical scheme, in accordance with which the various scenes were assigned to definite positions on the walls and vaults. To the Greek mind, different parts of the building had a symbolic significance and the pictures adorned the areas which most fittingly symbolised their respective themes. High up in the central dome, symbol of heaven, is the bust of Christ Pantocrator, the "Ruler of All". Surrounded by a rainbow, He holds the Book of the Gospels in His left hand and raises His right in benediction (7). He is surrounded by archangels and angels in rich imperial habiliments, by the All-blessed Virgin, and John the Baptist the Prodromos or Forerunner of the Lord. Below them, the drum which supports the dome is encircled with the prophets who foretold the Advent of the Messiah. The pendentives, the connecting links between dome and vaults, are appropriately occupied by the evangelists, whose gospels are the media through which the work of Christ is known. The sanctuary likewise symbolises the heavenly places, and so in the conch of the apse is seated the Virgin on her jewelled throne between Michael and Gabriel the archangels. Farther down is depicted the scene known as the "Divine Liturgy" in which Christ, clad in patriarchal robes receives a procession of angels bearing candles, censers and instruments of the Passion(9). Still farther down in the apse there is the "Communion of the Apostles" where Our Lord, doubly represented, gives the bread and wine to His apostles. In the apse are also to be seen the "Fathers of the Church", venerable figures in episcopal robes. Prototypes of the Sacrifice on Calvary, such as the story of Cain and Abel, and Daniel in the Lions' Den also have their place in the sanctuary, along with priestly prototypes of Christ, like Aaron and Melchizedek. The vaults and upper walls in the nave are reserved for the Twelve Great Festivals of the Church—the Annunciation, the Nativity, the Presentation in the Temple, the Baptism, the Transfiguration, the Raising of Lazarus, the Entry into Jerusalem, the Crucifixion, the Resurrection (usually the Descent into Hades), the Ascension, and the Death (or Falling Asleep) of the Virgin. The miracles and parables figure on the lower zones and in the lowest of all are figures of saints. Episodes from the Life of the Virgin and Lives of the Saints are often portrayed in the narthex. In general outline this scheme came to be followed out, though the shape and size of the church and local tradition produced many variations. The scheme had a definite liturgical connection, concentrating as it did on the Liturgy and on the Great Festivals of the Church, which by word or symbolic action are shown forth in that service; for the Liturgy is the symbolic drama of the saving work of Christ wrought in His Incarnation, Passion, and Resurrection. The application of the scheme became more and more rigid in course of time, and artists adhered closely to the minute rules in the manuals issued for their use. The best known of these guides to Western readers is the "Painters' Guide" by the monk Dionysius and discovered by Didron in a monastery on Mount Athos in the nineteenth century.

The impression which can be made on the mind by a worthy Byzantine church is both striking and profound. We have already spoken of its harmony, proportion and unity of mass. About its exterior there is also a feeling of dignity and assurance, of

6   BAPTISTERY, NAPLES: Squinch Mosaic

7   CAPPELLA
PALATINA,
PALERMO:
Dome Mosaic

8 ATHENS: the Small Cathedral

9 KAISARIANI, ATTICA: Fresco of the Divine Liturgy

completeness and finality. Here again it seems to show forth the spirit of Eastern Orthodoxy. The Orthodox Church holds fast with unflinching determination to the decisions of the General Councils, enacted in the first eight centuries of the Christian era. No development of, and no deviation from, the ancient faith is tolerated. It is convinced of the truth of its position and with absolute assurance it upholds its venerable dogmas. It may not be too fanciful to see this same spirit in the buildings where these dogmas are set forth. Not only have the general features of the plan persisted until the present day, but there seems to inhere in the structure that same spirit of completeness, of assurance, of self-contained assertion, of finality. The domes and vaults rest surely and firmly on a solid base, so different from the Gothic spire, tapering upwards to its point. Without projections, except for the apses, the plan is set forth in its clear square or rectangle.

But in the interior of the church another spirit also prevails. It is the spirit of the invisible and eternal. The Orthodox Eastern Church has always felt intensely the reality of the unseen world. Its ascetics renounced the earth and spent their lives in the contemplation of heaven. The miraculous and supernatural invaded the life of the populace at every turn. The communion of saints was a vivid reality, and the unseen world was ever present to the faithful. Such was the ideal, an ideal, of course not always, but yet often a power in the soul of the Orthodox believer. This mystical and supramundane spirit pervades the building. The dome and vaults are as the quiet canopy of heaven: behind the gilded iconostasis in the mysterious recesses of the apse Christ's presence becomes real; the nave, where the worshippers stand to watch the sacred drama, is part in shade and part illumined by the light of heaven. Everything combines to create the sense of the mystic and transcendental.

This supramundane quality is profoundly emphasised by the pictures which clothe the walls. In some churches it takes on the quality of splendour as well as mystery. The polished surfaces of green and purple marbles gleam with light. The blue and red and green of mosaics shimmer in the diffused light or sparkle in the sunbeams, and the figures of the saints shine forth mysteriously from their background of golden space.

The humbler shrines whose walls were covered with frescoes in various hues possess an equally haunting and unworldly beauty. There too the solemn gaze of Christ is directed down upon the worshippers below, the sacred story is unrolled upon the vaults, and the saints stand stiffly around the walls. The other-worldly sense is largely due to the method of treatment. The pictures are painted flat and, broadly speaking, without much attempt at strict naturalism: the landscapes and architectural backgrounds are schematised; the colours are often arbitrary; the human figure is neglected; and the draperies conceal the body in stiff folds. All this indifference to nature invests them with the other-worldly atmosphere. The saints are not of this earth but come from beyond. The gospel events are not merely famous episodes of long ago but are suffused with an eternal quality.

We are helped to understand the nature of Byzantine Art by contrasting it with an art to which it is poles apart—with Baroque. The Baroque artist was conscious also of the eternal. He filled his churches with sculptured cherubs, with flying angels, with saints overwhelmed in rapturous ecstasy, with the Virgin in the glory of Paradise, with Christ ascending to the skies. The dome over the church seems to dissolve into space and the worshipper, all barriers removed, gazes up into the celestial regions. But how different the treatment from that of Byzantine Art! The whole scene and its persons are naturalistic: the figures are modelled to resemble life; the landscapes are those of the world around; the draperies are tossed by the breeze; every art of perspective and foreshortening is used to enhance the reality of the illusion.

Yet the Baroque artist is dealing with religion and the immortal. The difference between the Baroque and Byzantine artist lies in a fundamentally separate point of view, however similar their themes may be. The Baroque artist carries earth up to heaven, the Byzantine artist brings heaven down to earth: the Baroque artist carries the temporal into the eternal, the Byzantine artist brings the eternal into the temporal; the Baroque artist peoples heaven with human forms, glorified and radiant with the joy of Paradise, but yet human forms, the Byzantine artist peoples earth with the immortal and solemn denizens of the world beyond. And perhaps both styles of treatment have in religious art their rightful place.

Thus it is that the interior of a Byzantine church is permeated with the sense of the unseen. The Pantocrator for ever blesses from heaven: the Gospel scenes are eternal in quality and the spectator becomes a witness of the actual event; the saints stand in solemn order around the walls, strange ascetics of the desert, gazing perpetually with earnest eyes, hermits with old wrinkled faces and long flowing beards, warriors who were seen in battle long after they had died, physicians who wrought miracles throughout the generations. There they stand in long array, with scrolls in their hands, mysterious and distant figures, hieratic and austere, the colours of their robes fading with the years, and they seem like denizens of another world who have come down to visit the people of earth.

CHAPTER III

The Origins of Byzantine Art

IT has been said at the beginning of this book that Byzantine Architecture was evolved in the years which followed the foundation of Constantinople in 330, and that it reached maturity in that city in the sixth century. Something must now be said about the regions in which that evolution took place and the influences which combined to form the process. Some of the remarks in this section will anticipate what is said in later chapters in more detail, but a brief preliminary survey of those regions and influences may help to open up the scene. Now the area where Byzantine Architecture and Art were evolved comprises the countries round the Levant—Anatolia or Asia Minor, Syria, including Palestine, and Egypt. These countries were not self-contained. They were part of the great Roman Empire across which communication flowed for ever to and fro; they extended from Syria and Anatolia, into the wide hinterland of the Orient to Mesopotamia and Iran.

The problem of the area in which Byzantine Architecture was evolved is an exceedingly complex one, and has given rise to different and antagonistic theories. In older days it was believed that Byzantine Art was simply a development of that of Imperial Rome. Some authorities have given the chief credit to Asia Minor. Others placed the origins farther east in Armenia and Mesopotamia. In more recent years some have laid stress on the supreme importance of Syria, while others again have revived the cause of Rome itself.

The problem as has been said is extremely difficult, and the difficulties arise from many causes. The dates which have been assigned to particular monuments differ very widely. Disputes have arisen about the original appearance of half-ruined buildings. How exactly were they roofed? What to one authority seems conclusive evidence is to another no evidence at all. New discoveries are made which suggest a change of outlook. Yet many sites which might yield valuable information remain unexplored. It seems most reasonable to believe that the two areas which contributed most to the development were Anatolia and Syria. Along the shores of the eastern Mediterranean were flourishing centres of Hellenistic culture, chief of which were Ephesus, Antioch and Alexandria. Each of these populous and important cities had a port for an extensive hinterland and was in constant communication with both East and West. Into these cities and their adjacent regions Christianity found an early entrance. Antioch, the town where the disciples of Christ were "first called Christians", soon became a centre of the new faith. In Ephesus a church was founded by S. Paul, while in many districts of Asia Minor Christianity spread with wonderful rapidity. The churches which were founded by S. Paul and his followers gathered more and more adherents. Alexandria was associated with the name of S. Mark and could boast distinguished theologians in the early third century. They were all magnificent towns and before the full development of Constantinople occupied a pre-eminent place in the Mediterranean world. Gleaming white temples and stately public buildings adorned their broad streets. Baths, colonnades, amphitheatres, libraries, occupied important sites. Teeming populations were engaged in all manner of trade, and wealth abounded beside poverty and want. But behind these Hellenistic cities there stretched great hinterlands which in Syria and Anatolia extended far into the Middle East. From Iran and Mesopotamia came the caravans laden with all the precious products of the East. They carried the influence of the Orient into the heart of the Roman Empire and the ideas of the Hellenistic cities were permeated by these Oriental modes of thought.

After the official recognition of Christianity churches could be erected without fear and the devotees of the faith were not slow to signalise their triumph. The commonest type was the basilica with its nave terminating in an apse and separated by arcades from its aisles. It is not the purpose of this book to enter into any description of the basilica. Suffice it to say that while in Rome it had a wooden roof, in the East it was often vaulted in stone or brick. Excavations, standing ruins and literary allusions prove the existence of many basilicas in the Hellenistic East. But in these areas another type of church was prevalent—the central-planned—and it was covered by a dome. The origin of the dome in one form or another goes back long centuries before the Christian era. First made of mud and wattle to crown a circular hut, it was later employed to cover a round sepulchral monument or tomb. It was constructed of wood or of flat courses of brick or stone and seems early to have obtained a religious significance, symbolising the majesty of God and the vault of heaven.

Some time before the Christian era the hemispherical dome formed of radiating voussoirs was devised. This was employed to cover circular buildings but the essence of Byzantine Architecture was that the dome should cover a square. This idea originated in Persia and Mesopotamia, and was thence carried to Syria and Anatolia to form the essential feature of the central-planned church. The central-planned churches of Syria and Anatolia were of different types—octagons, octagons within circles, cruciform, rotunda, domed square. Then the domed square was combined with the basilica, to form what is known as the domed basilica. A fusion was effected between Hellenism and the Orient.

At the same time it would not be right to deny to Rome a part in the formation of Byzantine Architecture. These areas were a part of the Roman Empire and the influence of the capital was far-reaching and profound. It is possible that the monumental scale and proportions of Santa Sophia may have been derived from such buildings as the great halls of the Roman baths or the basilica of Constantine at Rome, and the idea of having a dome so large may have been suggested by the Pantheon. But for the architecture generally the credit must be given to Syria and Anatolia.

This fusion of Hellenistic and Oriental elements is characteristic of Byzantine Art as a whole and is very evident throughout the whole history of its mural painting.

The Hellenistic cities had practised a picturesque naturalistic and graceful art which had its source in Hellenism. But another influence mingled with the Hellenistic to form Byzantine Art. This other influence was the Syrian. Syrian art was realistic and deeply expressive of religious fervour. It neglected accurate representation of drapery or the human form, but in the faces strove to set forth solemn emotions of the soul.

Moreover, this Syrian art was affected by an art which flourished still farther east and which consisted of formal design and colour patterns, antagonistic to the representation of the human face and figure. Although the Church demanded an art which could teach its adherents by the portrayal of biblical scenes, its artists felt the impact of this decorative style. So the Syrian style was evolved in such a way that the figures were set out flat in a single plane, the subjects being treated approximately in two dimensions. Even the ascetic and religious emotion expressed on the faces was depicted in a rather conventional manner.

Thus it was that two influences mingled to form Byzantine Art, the Hellenistic and the Syrian. They were influences which lived throughout the whole course of Byzantine history, sometimes the one and sometimes the other exercising the more powerful sway.

Moreover, the purely decorative and non-representational art of the Orient affected Byzantine Art in a more direct way. Oriental patterns appear in its mosaic and fresco. Foliaceous, geometrical and animal motives from the East were much employed in the sculptured slabs of parapets and screens(38, 162) while in the ivories they are found alongside the representation of sacred scenes

10   Three types of dome construction

and persons. On the other hand, it is in some of these ivories that the Hellenistic influence is most noticeable and most conscious.

Byzantine Art is finely represented in these ivories and other small works of craftsmanship(77). Incidentally, in the course of the volume one or two of them will be spoken of. They include chalices and crosses fashioned in precious metals and rich with jewels, boxes delicately carved in ivory, vestments woven in costly fabrics and patterned with beautiful designs, and manuscripts enriched with glowing illuminations. Many of these objects repose now in the museums and libraries of Western Europe, a rare and precious heritage from the departed glory of Byzantium.

Byzantine Architecture is predominantly ecclesiastical. The examples of secular architecture which have survived are few in number and relatively unimportant. The walls of Constantinople have been mentioned already as well as the Palace of the Emperors. Chief among the secular remains at Constantinople are the great underground reservoirs which supplied the city with water. The most famous of them are Bin-bir-derek and Jere-batan-Serai. With their forests of marble columns, these great underground cisterns are audacious in construction and mysterious in effect.

CHAPTER IV

The Plan and Construction of the Byzantine Church

THE DOME UPON THE SQUARE

THE distinctive and characteristic feature of a Byzantine church, as we have seen, is a dome set out in such a way as to cover a space which is square. It is important to emphasise this fact at the outset: there are many churches to be found in the Christian East which do not possess the dome; though they may be Byzantine in their decoration and detail they are not Byzantine in their elevation or their plan. The dome that rises above a square is the essential and formative element in the true Byzantine church.

In placing a dome over a square the Byzantines faced a much more difficult problem than the Romans did in setting one over a circle. In the Pantheon at Rome, built by the Emperor Hadrian in A.D. 120, the great hemispherical dome rests directly upon the massive walls of the vast rotunda. In the fourth-century Church of Santa Costanza at Rome, famous for the early Christian mosaics of its ambulatory, a circular wall rests upon an inner ring of coupled columns. This circular wall supports the hemispherical dome, and is carried farther up to form a strong abutment and to support a higher roof.

It involved no special difficulties to erect a dome upon such a rotunda(10). It was a much more complex matter to effect a transition from a square on the ground-level to the circle on which the base of the dome must rest. At a very early period the system of dome-over-square had been used in the construction of the wooden huts which served as the dwellings of primitive tribes, and it seems reasonable to suppose that the wooden-domed hut formed the prototype for a similar building in brick or stone. In what region of the world this transition to a more durable material took place has long been a subject of great dispute. An equal matter of controversy has been the precise geographical direction which was followed by this system of construction—the dome-over-square—

until it became an element in the Christian church. For a long time the credit was given to Rome, and it was believed that Byzantine Architecture was a development of that of Imperial Rome. In more recent years the Italian scholar Rivoira upheld this point of view, and it has been revived in quite modern times by Professor E. H. Swift of New York. On the other hand there has existed since the beginning of this century a widespread body of opinion which places the origin of Byzantine dome construction in the East. This attitude is associated with the name above all of Professor Josef Strzygowski of Graz and Vienna, who published a series of learned and sumptuous volumes to support his case. At first, in *Kleinasien: ein Neuland der Kunstgeschichte*, he gave the credit to Asia Minor, but in subsequent volumes he extended his outlook still farther to the East until it rested on Iran.

According to Strzygowski Aryan invaders penetrating Iran from the north, brought with them their conception of the square wooden hut covered with a dome by means of planks set across the angles to effect the passage from square to circle. Iran was scarce in wood, and so the builders in that country imitated the domed wooden hut in unbaked brick and then in burnt brick. In Strzygowski's words, "The dome over the square is of purely Iranian origin." He then emphasised the fact that Christianity got a firm footing in Persia by the second century. Numerous churches were built in Mesopotamia at an early date, and the cities of Nisibis, Edessa and Amida with their surrounding territories played an important part in the development of the Christian faith. In Mesopotamia it was the barrel-vault which was the favourite form of roof. The use of the dome spread to Armenia, where many domed churches were erected in stone: thence the usage of the dome-over-square spread westwards, where bricks were employed; Armenia according to Strzygowski was the cradle of Byzantine Architecture.

Other authorities such as Professor Charles Diehl and M. Gabriel Millet, both of Paris, saw Asia Minor as the birth-place of the Byzantine church edifice. Following the opinions expressed by M. A. Choisy in the latter part of the nineteenth century, Diehl believed that the popularity of the dome in Anatolia was the result of constructing vaults in brick as favoured by the architects of the great Hellenistic cities of Asia Minor. We shall revert to this theory at a later point in this chapter.

In recent years there has been a tendency to regard Syria

(including Palestine) as the area where the dome-over-square edifice was first constructed in masonry and also as the area where the domed church had its origin. The names of Cresswell and Baldwin Smith are especially associated with this view. It has long been known that edifices of an early date still exist in Syria showing the dome covering a square. It is one of the purposes of this chapter to classify these structures and similar ones in other areas. Reference is made to them below. It may have been from these small buildings, mostly tombs, that the idea of using the dome-over-square system was borrowed for churches.

Which of these divergent and conflicting solutions deserves the greatest credence? It seems safe to infer that the domed square constructed in masonry was derived from a wooden prototype, but that this prototype existed and was imitated in different regions. The prevalence of the domed square as a house unit in the East at the present day may point back to a long tradition which persisted in widely separated areas.

The second question was where the dome over the square was first applied to the Christian church. Strzygowski, as we have seen, gives the credit to Armenia. Yet Syria and Anatolia have a worthy claim to pre-eminence. As we shall see, domed cruciform churches were not infrequent in those areas during the fourth and fifth centuries of the Christian era. Baldwin Smith has emphasised the importance of the symbolism of the dome in the martyrion— the church which contained the relics of a martyr or commemorated him. These martyria followed the elevation of pagan tombs. They were domed, for the dome had come to be charged with a deep mystic significance which appealed intensely to the heart of the Christian believer. Among the ideas which circled around the domed building was that of the ancestral shelter: the domed wooden hut with the dome in clay and wattle was the dwelling-place of remote ancestors. A reverence for the memory of the dome clung to the minds of men, and it therefore was an appropriate covering for the burial chamber, the place of rest for the spirits of the departed. The tomb became sanctified by the covering dome. The dome of the tomb was adopted for the martyrion, and then the martyrion dome was adopted for the congregational church, until it became a permanent feature of the place of worship. Many of the martyria were round or octagonal in plan, but others were square and the domed square could readily be expanded into a cruciform structure. Many of the

11 Dome construction: the transition from the square to the circle

domes in Syria were made of wood: the wooden dome could be constructed on an imposing scale and covered with glittering metal. Moreover, its symbolic significance lay not only in its relation to the "ancestral shelter": the domed building also possessed a "cosmic" significance. It was the pattern and symbol of the universe with its over-arching sky and the dwelling-place of God.

However uncertain some of the details of his argument may be, it is certain that Baldwin Smith has done right in drawing attention to the symbolic significance of the dome. Whatever may have been the reason which first led the early Christians to adopt it as a covering to the churches there is no doubt that the Eastern mind soon beheld in the domed church a vivid and appropriate symbol of the universe created by God, who was worshipped within its walls.

So much for the origin of the dome on the square and its adoption in the Christian church. Let us now consider constructional features of the Byzantine church and in particular the methods which were adopted to effect the transition from the square to the circle. Several methods were used to bring about the desired result. The simplest was to lay a flat slab or slabs across the angles of the square, corbelling them out so as to form an approximate circle as a base for the dome (11).

In Syria the method is to be found at the Kalybé of Omm-es-Zeitoun (12), which dates from A.D. 282 and consisted of a square-domed room with flanking wings. A kalybé was a shelter used for pagan religious rites and this one at Omm-es-Zeitoun bears an inscription, "Good Fortune: the community of the village and of the god built this sacred Kalybé. . . ." It was built of volcanic stone and by the time it was seen by the Comte de Vogüé, the mid-nineteenth-century explorer of the Syrian churches, the dome had collapsed. He restored it as a hemisphere, but it was more

probably of conoid shape.
In any case, the dome was
supported by flat slabs
across the angles of the
square. The same system
obtained at the Kalybé of
Chaqqa, a pagan sanctuary
which was converted into
a mortuary chapel dedi-
cated to S. George and his
companions in the midde
of the fourth century. The
dome had fallen when de
Vogüé saw it.

12 The Kalybé of Omm-es-Zeitoun,
Syria

Here may be mentioned the important sixth-century Tomb of
Bizzos at Roueiha to the south-east of Antioch. It is important
because it is well preserved and because it is a Christian tomb.
Here the Christians took over the idea of the dome from its use
on pagan tombs. It can well be believed that its symbolic significance would appeal strongly to their mind. In this tomb, however, the dome does not rest on corbels: it is set back beyond the
angles of the square on the top of the walls, which contain four
deep arches, one on each side of the square. It has radiating beds.
In a Roman tomb at Amman, the dome is set on a very thick
wall with only small corbels at the angles. According to Cresswell
the dome has "overhanging voussoirs". This small tomb is dated
by Swift to the Antonine period. The dome
supported by the corbels in a sixth-century
polygonal chapel at Moudyeleia may have
been constructed in timber.

Of greater interest than any of these buildings is the ancient Cathedral of S. George at
Ezra (Zor'ah) in Syria. "In it were placed
the relics of the holy conquering martyr
George" (13, 80). Built in A.D. 515, it is still
used as a Christian church. Its dome, which is
now thought to have originally been of wood,
covered an octagonal space formed by an interior arcade. By means of flat stones laid
across each angle of the octagon the walling
above the arches was ultimately reduced to a

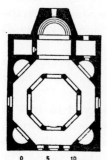

0   5   10
|_._._._|_._._._|METRES
0 5 10 20 50
|ıııılııı|___L___|FEET

13 Plan of S.
George, Ezra,
Syria

45

thirty-two-sided figure (according to de Vogüé) which forms an approximate circle for the base of the dome. The spandrels of the arches as Butler saw them about the end of the century are slightly curved forwards. The church has now got a wooden dome, and extensive repairs were carried out after 1926. Authorities differ as to whether the church had originally a wooden or masonry dome. The dome before the present one was of masonry, as seen by de Vogüé and Butler. There was rebuilding of the walling above the arches between de Vogüé's and Butler's days.

THE SQUINCH

The passage from the square to a suitable base for a dome was effected also by the squinch, which consisted of an arch or a series of arches flung across each angle of the square (14). The squinches caused the square to be transformed into an octagon; a dome might rest, if small, directly on this octagon; otherwise the octagon could be transformed into a circle or an approximate circle by pendentives (*v. infra*) or corbels in its angles. The squinch was of Eastern origin and occurs in the Sassanian architecture of southern Persia at the Palaces of Firouzabad and Sarvistan (15). At the Palace of Firouzabad three square rooms behind what now appears to be the façade were covered with pointed domes on squinches. One of the domes is in half-ruin. They are believed to date to A.D. 226. The domes are partially concealed on the outside. The Palace of Sarvistan, "the cypress-garden", is two centuries later in date. Three squinched domes of different sizes cover irregularly placed rooms. They stand free. A distinct advance is to be discerned in the formation of the squinches in the two palaces: whereas at Firouzabad they are semicircular arches, at Sarvistan they approach to a semi-domical shape.

Squinches are also to be found in Persia in buildings at Ferashabad and Qasr-i-Shier (seventh century).

From Persia the squinch spread to regions in Central Asia. There are grottoes at Banyan, north-west of Kabul in Afghanistan, with domes on squinches of the Firouzabad type. The decoration places these constructions at the end of the third century A.D. Thence the squinch spread to Chinese Turkestan where specimens have been discovered.

14   The squinch

46

The vogue of the squinch extended from Iran also, to the west. In the seventh-century Church of the Virgin at Khakh, in Mesopotamia, described later, the squinches are cylindrical in their lower portions. At Rusafa the basilica of S. Sergius had squinches on colonnettes on the top stories of its two side-chambers.

By the seventh century the squinch had spread widely throughout Armenia in its semi-domical form, where it occurs in such churches as those at Thalin, Mastara and Etschmiadzin.

The Armenian squinches are constructed of stone and have radiating voussoirs. The squinch penetrated early into Asia

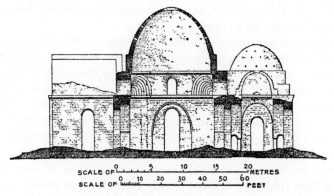

15   Section of the Palace of Sarvistan, South Persia

Minor, where it was found in the domed basilica of Khodja Kalessi in Cilicia, long known as one of the most important examples of earlier Byzantine Architecture and described in a later chapter. The church dates from the first half of the fifth century (63). The squinches in the angles of the slightly rectangular drum rest on colonnettes on brackets and bring the rectangle to an octagon. The dome, as mentioned later, may have been wooden. Fig. 19 illustrates one of the squinches in the ruined church of S. Clement at Ankara, the ancient Ancyra and capital of modern Turkey. The church is described on p. 106.

It occurred also in the domed basilica of Meriamlik, in Cilicia, a building which may date from about A.D. 470.

Only a very few examples of early squinches have been discovered in Syria. Two of them are in a sixth- or seventh-century room at the entrance to the Citadel of Amman, where they support semi-domes.

47

The squinch appears to have been unknown in Egypt at an early date, but it spread to that country about the beginning of the eighth century and is to be found in the reconstructed churches at Sohag, as described in Chapter VIII.

It had, however, reached Italy at a much earlier period. The fifth-century baptistery of Soter beside the Cathedral of Naples is the earliest building in the West in which squinches are to be seen. Of the semi-domical type, they contain mosaics of the symbols of the evangelists on a deep blue background (6).

In the famous sixth-century Church of S. Vitale at Ravenna the passage is from an octagonal base (54). A church at Vicenza and another at Padua have domes on squinches which have been *attributed* to the fifth century.

Briefly summarising the evidence for the spread of the squinch, it took its rise in Iran as early as the third century. By the fifth century it had spread to Asia Minor and by the sixth to Armenia. From Anatolia it was carried across to Italy, whose shores it reached in the latter part of the fifth century. Mention may be made of the use of the squinch in the construction of the actual dome in the Mausoleum of the Palace of Diocletian at Spalato in Dalmatia which is now the cathedral. The dome is of light material set in little squinches mounting upwards. It may be best stated here that the remains of the palace show a strong Eastern influence and it has even been hazarded that the architect came from Syria. Though of pre-Byzantine date many of its decorative features tend towards the Byzantine style.

Although the squinch occupies a position in Byzantine Architecture much inferior to that held by the pendentive, it by no means passed out of fashion. As a result of Armenian influence, which was most powerful in the Empire, it was employed in some eleventh-century churches of Greece, such as Daphni. Architectural writers of an older generation sometimes gave these later squinches the name of "pseudo-pendentives". In a tall niche-like form squinches were also used in Sicilian churches of the twelfth century.

THE PENDENTIVE

The pendentive, the third and by far the most important method of effecting the transition from the square to the circle, is a very logical system of construction which had a widespread and enduring vogue in Byzantine Architecture. A pendentive is

16 S. IRENE, CONSTANTINOPLE

17 SANTA SOPHIA, CONSTANTINOPLE: the Dome

18   ROME: "Temple of Minerva Medica"

19   S. CLEMENT, ANKARA: Squinch

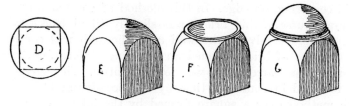

20   The principle of the pendentive

a curved triangle made up of courses of stone or brick wedged into the space between two of the adjoining arches that support a dome. The four arches at the ground-level and at the springing form a square: from the springing of the arches the pendentives curve upwards and inwards, until they reach their apices; thus they form a circle on which the base of the dome can rest. At first pendentives and domes formed one continuous whole (20), all being part of the same hemisphere, a hemisphere which was incomplete, being pierced by the four arches. It was later found that the dome did not need to be part of the same hemisphere as the pendentives: the circle formed by the upper surfaces of the pendentives could form a base on which a higher dome could be substituted for that which was continuous with the pendentives. Thus a break took place in the continuity between dome and pendentives. The latter became independent entities and as such became characteristic features of Byzantine Architecture (17, 21). When pendentives form part of the same hemisphere as the dome it will be convenient to call them "continuous pendentives". When they do not form part of the same hemisphere we may call them "independent pendentives", or simply "pendentives".

The origin of the pendentive has been the subject of a long and exhaustive discussion. There can be few problems in the history of architecture which have evoked such continuous dispute or given rise to such conflicting views. Alfred Choisy assigned its birth-place to Asia Minor. He developed the idea that it arose out of the Eastern practice in building vaults in thin bricks laid, not in beds, but so as to

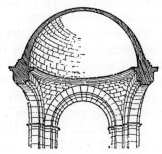

21   A dome on independent pendentives

49

avoid centering, on edge. In this method of constructing vaults the first course of thin bricks was slightly tilted backwards, so as to adhere firmly to the wall until the arch was completed. Each course of bricks formed an adhering surface for the next one until the barrel-vault was formed entire. The barrel-vault was followed in course of time by the cross-vault built by the same method over a square formed by the inter-section of two barrel-vaults. But the cross-vault could be raised in height until it became a domical vault with continuous pendentives. Vault construction with tiles (thin brick) laid on edge arose in Iran and spread to Anatolia: in the course of their experimentation in this vault construction, the Anatolian builders according to Choisy's theory discovered the pendentive.

On the other hand, the developed pendentive may have been the final and logical result of a long series of experiments in filling up the space between two arches at right angles with each other. Excavations at Ur in Mesopotamia seem to show that attempts of this sort were made in the fourth millenium B.C. At Kertch in the Crimea some underground chambers have been discovered which are said to date to the fifth century B.C. By progressively rounding the angles and setting forward the courses, a circular base was formed for a dome. The courses are set, not spherically but horizontally. There are two tombs at Vetulonia in Etruria dating from the seventh century B.C. whose fallen domes seem to have been supported in a somewhat similar fashion. Another example of a much later date was a cruciform chapel at Cassino. A low dome over the crossing is supported on "primitive pendentives" (or rather corbels) between the arches which bound the square. The building was of carefully wrought stone but of uncertain date. Some would assign it to the first century B.C., others to an unfixed date in Imperial times.

Two mausolea stand on the Via Nomentana at Rome, known respectively as the Sedia del Diavolo and the Casale dei Pazzi, both of which date from the latter part of the second century of the Christian era. The former mausoleum is a brick building, square in plan with two stories. Both stories had domes on "continuous pendentives". Those of the lower story are flat in section, of tufa rubble, the upper ones are an agglomeration of brick mortar and tufa. The upper story of the Casale dei Pazzi had a hemispherical dome on pendentives of almost flat section composed of tufa blocks. Swift attaches considerable importance to this building: he claims a date for it which is anterior by fifty years to the Palestinian tomb of Kusr-en-Nueijis of which something will presently be said. He points moreover to a distinct break between the "pendentives" and the dome, giving them an independent character. On the other hand, neither of these "pendentives" is of true spherical form, and they should more rightly be classified as developments of corbels, experimental stages on the way to the true pendentive. Other examples of a similar nature are to be found in an octagonal room in the "House of Augustus" situated among the ruins of the Palatine Hill at Rome. The Domus Augustiana was built by the Emperor Domitian about the year 90 of our era and contains on its lower story three octagonal rooms; the dome of the central one has fallen and the low domes of the other two rest on very primitive and tentative pendentives if they can be called by that name. Cresswell says the spaces are "slurred over".

Then there is the so-called Temple of Minerva Medica whose gaunt ruins beside the railway line seem so melancholy and forlorn in their busy modern setting. It is supposed to have been a nymphaeum in the Licinian gardens, once thought to date from the third century of our era. Here the transition is only from a decagon, the dome resting on a decagonal drum. The building is now dated to A.D. 310 (18).

A tentative effort towards the pendentive was also made in an octagonal hall in the Baths of Caracalla at Rome. Here the lower part is a re-entrant angle, becoming blunter and rounded as it gets farther up.

Another building in the West where an effort at the pendentive was made is in a room in a villa near Amalfi, discovered in 1932 and said to belong to the first century A.D. with a dome on a square and the angles filled in with rubble.

All the small "pendentives" in Italy should be rather classified as kinds of corbels. Their horizontal section is almost flat and their inner surfaces are inclined planes and not portions of a hemisphere. Swift quotes them in favour of his belief in the Roman origin of the pendentive. Even though these be not true pendentives, he stresses their importance in the development of what he calls the "pendentive idea", which was, as it were, in the mind of the Romans. Though Swift has rendered good service in drawing attention to the Roman influence in certain aspects of Byzantine Architecture he appears to make too much of these rudimentary and tentative experiments towards the pendentive. The Romans were certainly trying to solve the problem of effecting the passage from the square to the circle, but none of these efforts were crowned with complete success, whereas on Syrian soil at an early date a logical solution had indubitably been found.

A word may be said in conclusion on the "continuous pendentives" which support the dome over the famous so-called Tomb of Galla Placidia at Ravenna whose date can be assigned to about the year 440(25). To Swift they are "the final step in the evolution of the pendentive idea on Italian soil" and "clearly defined merging pendentives". Cresswell, who points out how difficult their mosaic covering makes it to grasp their form, says the space between the arches is really a re-entrant angle which gets rounder as it rises. Statham said that "the Tomb of Galla Placidia looks at first sight like a kind of rude attempt at a pendentive dome, but in reality it is the opposition of four barrel-vaults on four sides of a square with the roof space between them 'fudged' into a kind of approximate domical form". It seems better not to describe these supports as true pendentives: in any case they are much too late to have any bearing on the question of its origin. Like the dome they are constructed of bricks and of terra-cotta tubes.

So far we have dealt mainly with Italian experiments to bring the square to a circle by filling up the angles between the arches. We must now pass to the Eastern provinces of the Roman Empire and find out how the builders of those regions attempted a solution. Now, it happens that a stone tomb with continuous pendentives still exists in eastern Palestine near Amman beyond the Jordan. It is called Kusr-en-Nueijis and is dated by its carved entablature to the middle of the second century of the Christian era, and described by Conder in his survey of eastern Palestine in 1889. Well constructed of excellent masonry, it has the form of a square forty feet in diameter and is covered with a dome on continuous pendentives between arches which extend to the outer walls. Four little chambers occupy the corners of the square, and the exterior is adorned with Ionic pilasters and a Hellenistic entablature. The pendentives are true spherical triangles and with the dome form a hemisphere pierced by the four arches. There thus exists in the East a building with completely developed continuous pendentives of a much earlier date than any similar spherical pendentives in the West.

There is a pagan tomb at Samaria with a shallow dome over the square on continuous pendentives. They are according to Cresswell "true spherical pendentives". One of its sarcophagi with its heavy garlands on pilasters seems to date from the third century A.D.

Less important is a small room in the Baths at Brad, north-west of Aleppo, where monolithic pendentives over a square carry an octagonal dome. It is of fourth-century date.

Pendentives in the Baths at Jerash (Gerasa) beyond the Jordan have the same technique as those of Kusr-en-Nueijis, composed as they are of fine ashlar masonry and having true radiating beds.

De Vogüé saw traces of pendentives in a little sanctuary at Chaqqa; in a fifth-century gateway at Latakia there is an archway with stone pendentives in radiating voussoirs.

Attention has for long been directed to the continuous pendentives in the Golden Gate at Jerusalem through which in 629 the Emperor Heraclius rode in triumph, bearing the recovered Relics of the Cross. In the Golden Gate pendentives and dome comprise less than a hemisphere. The gate was in a ruinous state at the time of the death of Justinian and was restored by Modestus after 616. It is quite possible, however, that the form of the dome and pendentives may date from the later part of the sixth century. The Double Gate at Jerusalem, a walled-up door in the long corridor beneath the Mosque of El Aksa, has domes and pendentives like those of the Golden Gate. It too may date from the sixth century.

In Egypt we find the dome with continuous pendentives in the Mausoleum of S. Menas. This small chamber lying beneath the altar of the older basilica, a famous place of pilgrimage, dates from the end of the fourth century. It is built of brick. There are also two small fifth- or sixth-century chapels connected with a church at Ptolemais in Cyrenaica excavated in 1935 and with domes on continuous pendentives.

Let us pass to Asia Minor. We have already quoted Choisy's theory that the idea of the pendentive arose in western Anatolia as a result of experimentation in vaulting without centering. His view would seem to have much to commend it on *a priori* grounds, but he is somewhat indefinite in his citation of actual examples. He makes mention of the pendentive in a vault beneath a Roman wall at Magnesia and in churches at Philadelphia, Ephesus and Sardis. It is, however, quite within the bounds of possibility that the Hellenistic builders of the Anatolian coast may have arrived at the use of the pendentive by a double route. They may have been led to some such device as they raised their cross-vaults, and then have given a more scientific form to their device by seeing the pendentives in small mausolea. From Asia Minor the pendentive spread to Armenia on the one side and to Constantinople on the other. Its earliest appearance in the capital is in the great underground cisterns whose multitude of columns carry domes on continuous pendentives. One of these cisterns, Jere-batan Serai, dates from the late fifth and the other, Bin-bir-derek, from the early sixth century.

The next stage in the evolution of the pendentive was its development from the continuous into the independent form. A dome struck from a higher centre and with a shorter radius was substituted for the lower dome. As we have already seen, the higher dome rested on the circle of the pendentives but did not form part of them, so that the pendentives became independent structural elements with a character and significance of their own; it is to such a pendentive that the appellation is most commonly applied. It is quite possible that the independent pendentive first appeared in brick buildings in the cities of the Anatolian littoral. The step from the continuous to the independent pendentive is no very great one and it is easy to conjecture how it could have occurred. An earthquake shock might cause a somewhat shallow dome to collapse and in rebuilding it the restorers decided to make the new one higher. This would bring about a break between the new dome and the old pendentives, which now became independent entities. Wherever the origin of the independent pendentive took place the earliest surviving examples are the enormous spherical triangles which support the dome of Santa Sophia at Constantinople. It has been widely held that those pendentives at Santa Sophia were the first independent ones ever to be constructed. The first dome was a shallow one, almost continuous with the pendentives and an earthquake made it collapse along with part of the eastern semi-dome. A new dome of a higher curvature was erected in 563 by Isidore the Younger. It is suggested that it was the sight of the continuous pendentives of the first dome which, remaining intact on the west, inspired Isidore with the idea of independent pendentives. "Thus," says Swift, "the first independent pendentives were built at Hagia Sophia as the result of an accident intelligently utilised to give greater stability to the second dome." On the other hand, it is quite possible that the invention may have been discovered in Asia Minor when a similar collapse took place of too shallow a dome in a building of a much smaller scale.

THE PLAN

The dome over a square space was used in connection with several plans of which the following are the chief.

(a) *The domed hall-church (or domed oblong).*

(b) *The domed square.* Buttressed with an apse on each side, this became the *quatrefoiled square* of Armenia (see Chapter VII; see also Chapter X for a further development of this plan in Greece). The ordinary domed square can have an ambulatory.

(c) *The domed cruciform.* With a dome over the crossing and, it might be, with a dome over each arm of the cross also.

(d) *The domed basilica* (63). The basilical ground-plan combined with a domical superstructure. The domed basilica has a long nave and aisles. In front of the apse and chancel the barrel-vault of the nave is broken by a dome. To east and west the arches supporting this dome span the nave: to north and south they rise above the nave arcade and are filled in with tympana.

(e) *The cross-domed basilica* (16). This resembled the domed basilica, but the north and south arches of the dome are prolonged as barrel-vaults to the exterior walls of the aisles. The galleries in the aisles are carried right through the north and south arms of the cross. The crossing is separated from the aisles by arcades on the ground-level and sometimes on the gallery level. It should be noted, however, that the name cross-domed basilica is sometimes applied to churches where there are no arcades in the crossing and no galleries, but where the nave is long and the aisles narrow.

In both the domed basilica and the cross-domed basilica the nave was often considerably shortened, forming what has been called a "half-basilical" type.

(f) *The cross-in-square* (8, 22, 96). This is the plan which became the typical and classical expression of Byzantine Architecture, and which achieved a pre-eminence of popularity that has endured to the present day. From the centre of the church rises the dome supported on a high drum cylindrical inside and polygonal outside. The drum rests on the circle formed by four pendentives wedged in between four semicircular arches prolonged as barrel-vaults to the exterior walls. The arches rest on four piers or columns at the corners of the square covered by the dome. All this disposition

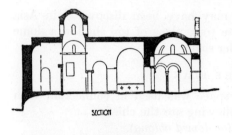

SECTION

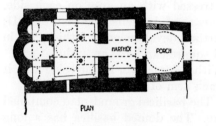

NARTHEX PORCH

PLAN

22   S. Strategos, Boularioi, Mani, Greece

of the various elements creates a cruciform plan. But the angles between the arms of the cross are brought within the interior space by making the ground-plan of the exterior walls a square. The four angle-compartments thus formed are roofed at a lower level than the arms of the cross, and so a cruciform plan prevails above. (A slight prolongation of the western arm may turn the square into a rectangle, but in such event the term "cross-in-square" is still employed.) A central apse and as a rule two side-apses project from the eastern end. In many small churches the side-apses are not projections, but mere niches in the thickness of the wall. The apses are round internally, semicircular or stilted or horseshoe shaped. Externally they usually show several sides of a polygon. The angle-spaces mentioned above are roofed with barrel, cross, or domical vaults. Sometimes each angle-space is covered with a dome on a polygonal drum.

In this church the structural elements, intimately tied together, form a compact unity. The thrust of the dome is carried through the pendentives and arches down the piers and along the barrel-vaults to the outside walls. The vaults of the arms of the cross are in their turn buttressed by those of the angle-spaces. The whole building is therefore sustained by a system of internal buttressing. Each part of the edifice thrusting, counter-thrusting or supporting performs its necessary part in the maintenance of the equilibrium.

There are several varieties of the cross-in-square church.

(I) *The two-column variety* (22). The dome rests on two columns (or piers) to the west, and on the antae (the inner walls) of the apse to the east. The apse thus follows directly on the eastern arm of the cross, which forms part of the bema or sanctuary.

(II) *The four-column variety* (23). The dome rests on four columns or piers.

Of this type there are two varieties.

(A) An additional bay is intercalated between the eastern arm of the cross and the apse (23). There are corresponding bays before the side-apses. The eastern arm thus lies outside the bema. This four-column type with the additional bay may also be divided into two sub-varieties, according as the additional bay is (α) vaulted under the same vault as the eastern arm or (β) under a different vault at a lower level.

(B) In this variety (24) there is no additional bay.

Types I and II A (α) are prevalent in Greece. Type II A (β) prevails in Constantinople. Type II B is to be found in Sicily and Serbia.

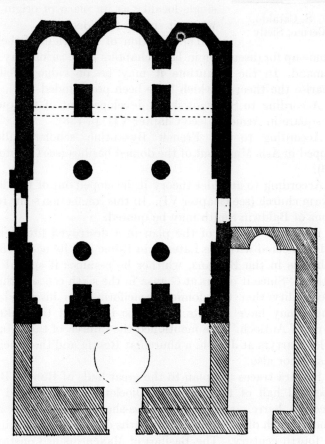

23 Kaisariani, Attica

24 S. Cataldo,
Palermo, Sicily

It is impossible to be certain about the origins of the cross-in-square plan. The problem has given rise to several answers, and scholars have differed widely as to where and how the type originated. The champions of the several theories have had to venture into the realms of conjecture, and the proposed solutions can only remain hypotheses. It should, however, be borne in mind that the type may have developed in different areas in different ways. It is not necessary to fix upon one single locality as its place of origin from which it spread to wider areas.

The question of the origin of the plan will come up for discussion in later chapters as occasion may seem to demand. In the meantime it may be of value briefly to summarise the theories which have been propounded.

(a) According to Strzygowski it developed out of the quatrefoiled square in Armenia (see Chapter VII, p. 138).

(b) According to the French Byzantine scholar Millet it developed in Asia Minor out of the domed basilica (see Chapter VI, p. 115).

(c) According to an older theory it developed out of the domed cruciform church (see Chapter VI). In this connection some recent opinions of Baldwin Smith may be quoted.

He mentions the use of the plan in a destroyed fifth-century chapel connected with the Lateran in Rome and its occurrence in two chapels in the Balkans, whither he assumes it spread from Palestine. "Since it occurs at Gerasa in the sixth century there is the possibility that the domical cruciform plan inscribed in a rectangle may have had its prototype in one of the unknown martyria of Antioch." He mentioned the Church of the Prophets Apostles Martyrs at Jerash, a church at Resafa and the cruciform in Asia Minor also.

(d) Rivoira traces the plan to the great halls of Roman Baths. The central hall of the Baths of Diocletian was covered with intersecting barrel-vaults. This cross-shaped hall had a small chamber in each of its angles. The Baths date from the beginning of the fourth century. The Basilica of Maxentius or Constantine at Rome, dating from the first half of the fourth century, was of

25 RAVENNA:
Mausoleum of
Galla Placidia

26 RAVENNA,
S. APOLLINARE
IN CLASSE:
Nave Capitals

27 Capital, S. Vitale, Ravenna

28 Capital, Parenzo

29 Capital, S. Vitale, Ravenna

much the same type. The substitution of a dome for the cross-vault in the centre would bring about an approximation to the cross-in-square plan.

(e) It has more recently been held that the plan derives from a type of pagan tomb. That of Kusr-en-Nueijis, already mentioned above, has been cited in this connection. It is true that the tiny angles of the cross are here filled in with vaulted chambers, but the walls between them, though pierced by doors, are solid. This is not yet the closely articulated cross-in-square. Recent investigations have related the plan to that of temples and tetrastyle houses in Syria. The Tycharion (formerly called the Praetorium) of Musmiyeh was of this description. Seen by de Vogüé, it was totally destroyed in the latter part of the nineteenth century. It appears to have had a cross-in-square ground-plan, but it is uncertain how it was roofed. It had three apses and was converted into a church, but it is very doubtful if this and similar pagan buildings had any real and widespread influence on the development of the cross-in-square Christian church.

In face of all the different theories which have been put forward, the present writer still feels that an evolution from the cruciform is the most probable and natural line of development. He would only make the proviso that while this is generally the case, other lines of development may have been the rule in certain areas; in Ephesus the plan may have evolved from domed basilicas, in Armenia from quatrefoiled squares. As he wrote in the first edition, "According to a still older theory, it was a development of the cruciform. There is still much to be said for this theory which is certainly based on a simple line of evolution." Elsewhere in Chapter IV in the former edition, the theory was further developed, and is repeated in the sixth chapter of the present volume.

Liturgically the Greek church is divided into three parts (23). The eastern end is occupied by the sanctuary where the Divine Liturgy or Mass is celebrated and which is usually known as the bema or hieron. It is separated from the rest of the building by a solid screen of wood or marble which extends right across the church. This screen is known as the iconostasis or iconostasion, because it serves as a frame for a number of icons or sacred pictures. Other icons are set in prominent places throughout the church, some of them illuminated by the flickering light of the candles with which they are venerated by the faithful.

The solid iconostasis conceals the whole sanctuary from view.

It has been thought by some writers that in Byzantine days the iconostasis was so low that the altar was visible. It is true that the screen was not always the solid one now in vogue. It used to consist of a row of columns supporting an architrave and resting on a parapet. But curtains suspended from the architrave closed off the view of the sanctuary. In fact, an early name for the screen was katapetasma, the veil. The practice of inserting icons in a solid screen and designating it iconostasis was a later development.

There are three doors in the iconostasis, of which the centre folding door (the Holy or Royal Door) plays an important part in the service. Sometimes it is closed and the priest performs his ritual acts in the mysterious recesses of the invisible sanctuary: at other times a curtain across the upper part of the door is drawn aside and those who stand in a favourable position can obtain a glimpse of the Holy Place: at other times it is flung open wide as when the priest passes through it to the altar in making what are called the Great and Little Entrances.

Of the three apses the northern one is called the prothesis. It contains the Table of the Prothesis where the sacred elements are placed for the performance of symbolic acts upon them and where the first part of the service takes place. There the bread is stamped with mystic letters, divided into pieces, and pierced with the lance, even as the body of Christ was pierced upon the Cross. There it is placed in the dish which symbolises the manger at Bethlehem and covered with the asterikos which stands for the Star which guided the Wise Men of the East to the Infant Christ. There other symbolic acts take place. The prothesis has therefore a liturgical function today. Originally it may have been a shrine for relics. The office of the prothesis was a development in the Liturgy which did not take place till the second half of the sixth century, and churches have been found in Syria which possess chapels flanking the apse but which are anterior to that epoch.

The southern chamber, known as the diaconicon or skeuophylakion, served the purpose of a vestry to house the vestments and Eucharistic vessels.

The second part of the church is the naos or nave, west of the iconostasis, where the congregation gathers for worship. The part adjacent to the iconostasis is raised above the level of the rest of the floor and is called the solea. In Byzantine times the name seems to have been applied to a wider area than now. Certain

60

litanies and prayers are chanted by the deacon standing on the solea. The third division of the church is known as the *narthex*, and is a long passage extending as a rule along the whole of the western end. It is separated from the naos by a wall with three doors. Formerly a place for penitents and catechumens, the narthex has now lost its original significance, but is still sometimes used for the celebration of baptisms and certain funeral rites. In monastic churches where the narthex may reach considerably larger dimensions it is employed for various monastic offices. Beyond the narthex might extend another one, which receives the appellation of exo-narthex, and usually takes the form of a portico with an open arcade. It provides shelter from rain. Both narthex and exo-narthex (if any) were often additions made at a later date to the original church. Parecclesia—side-chapels—might be built to run along the north or south sides of the church.

The windows, sometimes recessed in arches of several orders, have semicircular heads. Usually of narrow dimensions, they are often double or triple with their lights separated by shafts or colonnettes supporting sculptured capitals (31, 100). The apses, the gables and the drum are favourite places for windows. Doors are square-headed and are sometimes enriched with sculptured jambs, lintels and relieving-arches. There may be a tympanum above the door.

The building material varied according to the locality. Brick was commonly employed in Greece, the Balkan peninsula, southwest Russia, Egypt and part of Mesopotamia: stone was customarily used in Armenia, Georgia, the interior of Asia Minor, Cyprus, Syria and Aquitaine. Professor Talbot Rice points out how the use of stone instead of brick produced in the early period a different type of dome. "Thus in Hellenistic Syria where stone is universally employed, the hemispherical dome was the rule, while in Sassanian Persia where large bricks were used, the domes were of an ovoid form."

A popular method of constructing the walls of the churches was by means of squared stones laid in courses with a thin brick or tile laid in each vertical and horizontal joint. Admirable examples of it are to be found in Greece.

Exterior decoration in the stone churches of Syria and Anatolia is generally limited to simple mouldings, but in those of Armenia there often exists a richer scalloped or sculptured ornamentation.

61

Later churches in Greece, Constantinople and the Balkans were often elaborately treated with brick patterns, but the adornment is admirably adapted to the structure and fulfils its aesthetic purpose in harmony with the architecture of the edifice (135). The lavish employment of red-brown tiles in decoration produces a charming colour effect, harmonising as these do most beautifully with the rich brown stone. Often they are set in radiating arches above the windows and as saw-tooth bands along the walls.

BYZANTINE CAPITALS

It is in the capital of the column that Byzantine architectural sculpture is to be seen at its best. The chief object represented on the capital was the foliage of the acanthus, so well known in Greek art. During a considerable part of the fifth century it was the *Acanthus spinosa*, the sharp-leaved variety, which was most frequently imitated, but at other times the *Acanthus mollis* or soft-leaved type. The Corinthian and more especially the composite Corinthian capital was taken over from classical art and adapted by the Byzantines (50, 159). In very many instances they retained the two circlets of eight acanthus leaves, but for the egg and dart moulding between the volutes they substituted a band of acanthus. The rosette in the abacus was replaced by a monogram or a cross within a circle. A band of oblique leaves encircled the column above the torus. This type of capital, which prevailed in the fifth century, is known as the "Theodosian", from the Emperor Theodosius. It was early discovered that the arches in a church nave required a broader support than was afforded by the limited space of a normal Corinthian capital. A block of approximately trapezoidal shape called the impost (pulvino, or dosseret) was inserted above the capital (29). It was often carved with a monogram, a cross or some other device and came into use probably as early as the fourth century. Its use caused a change in the shape of the abacus of the Corinthian capital, transforming its edges from curves to straight lines. By the sixth century the two separate members, the impost and the capital, had become welded together into one (27). The united member has been called the impost-capital. A still further development took place, especially in Ravenna, when, not content with an impost-capital, the builders placed an additional impost above it (27). The impost-capital developed into several varieties, which in a general way may be classified in two species. In one of these,

62

30 Capitals, S. Mark, Venice

31 Window, Omorphi Ecclesia, Attica

32　Exterior
from E.S.E.

33　The Interior, looking east

SANTA SOPHIA, CONSTANTINOPLE

"the conical", the shape resembles an inverted and truncated cone, in the other, the "cubical", the form is that of a cube with rounded angles. To a variety of the conical species with grooves or channels running down its sides the name of "melon capital" has been assigned. Another form, intermediate between the cubical and conical, is of a trapezoidal shape.

The sculpture on all these capitals is most varied. The graceful foliage of the acanthus may intertwine around the bowl, or as the "wind-blown acanthus" may represent the motion of the breeze (26). The "basket capital" resembles plaited wickerwork, though some writers apply the name to those of basket *shape*. Sometimes the volutes are replaced by heads of rams or by birds with outstretched wings (28).

The Ionic capital was also combined with the impost to form the Byzantine Ionic impost-capital (30, 37), but as time went on, the volutes became smaller and the whole design somewhat debased.

Byzantine capitals, especially before the sixth century, owe much of their beauty to the deep undercutting which penetrates their surface and makes the white marble stand out in plastic boldness against the black undersurface. In other instances the drill was freely used to pierce the leaves with many small holes and give the effect of light and shade. As a result of Oriental influence a preference came to be evinced for capitals in low relief and reliance for effect was placed not on bold modelling but on sharp contrasts of light and dark.

Capitals of the types which have been described were exported in large quantities from the marble quarries of Proconnesus, on islands near Constantinople and have been found scattered over a wide extent of the Byzantine world.

The high standard of early days was, generally speaking, not maintained: many Byzantine capitals are weak and mediocre in design, for imagination and invention seem to have languished in later centuries. Leaves become flattened out and vigour declines. But beauty and grace of form never disappear, and many examples remain from the finest period which display the most extraordinary skill. At its best, the Byzantine capital is an exquisite work of art. Fashioned from pure white marble, deeply and beautifully undercut, sculptured with standing or twisting foliage or with formal but intricate design, it ranks among the highest achievements of Byzantine sculpture.

CHAPTER V

Early Churches in Constantinople, Salonica and Italy

HISTORICAL SURVEY

O F all the Emperors who occupied the throne of Byzantium there is none, with the single exception of Constantine the Great, who is more justly celebrated than Justinian. An amazing and enigmatic personality, he raised the Empire to the summit of its power. Possessed of a tireless energy—he was described by one of his contemporaries as "the Emperor who never sleeps"—and animated by visionary ideals, he was fortunate in the possession of brilliant generals and statesmen who transformed his dreams into a reality. It is true that his ambitious projects impoverished the state and that much of the noble fabric he erected soon crumbled away. Nevertheless, his actions left an indelible mark upon the world's history, and some of his achievements have survived to the present day. Justinian succeeded his uncle, Justin I, as sole Emperor in 527, and continued the tasks he had undertaken before that date with unflagging zeal. In his ambition to rival the greatness of Imperial Rome, he determined to recover the territories which barbarian invaders from the north had overrun. Africa he wrested from the Vandals, and after twenty years of struggle he captured Italy from the Ostrogoths. A portion of the fortification in Rome of his general still retains the name of the "Wall of Belisarius". He extended the sway of the Empire to distant Spain. He held the Persians at bay, and before the end of his reign had almost doubled his domains. His care for internal affairs was equally active. The legal system was reformed and the laws were codified; commerce was encouraged and administration improved. Literature was patronised and among the writers of his day Procopius, Agathias and Evagrius may be singled out for special mention.

As an incessant builder, Justinian earned the wondering admiration of his contemporaries, and to his numerous constructions the historian Procopius devoted a special book. He built the Chalké or Palace vestibule in the form of a cross surmounted by a dome. Its walls were sheathed with marble, "green as emerald", and "red as flames", while its mosaics represented the victories of Belisarius and the Senate's homage to the sovereign. Of vital importance to the safety of the state was the series of forts and strongholds he built throughout the Empire, some of whose ruins still survive. He strengthened the fortifications of Dara, an outpost on the Persian frontier, and built barracks. He made a new channel for the river at Edessa. At the flourishing city of Antioch he constructed streets and market-places, a water-channel, theatre and baths. In Armenia he restored forts and strongholds, churches and monasteries. On the Danube and in Thrace he built aqueducts, forts and walls. In these places and in many others buildings of all kinds were erected under the direction or patronage of Justinian—forts, walls, bridges, aqueducts, infirmaries, barracks, residences. Everyone was active under his will.

Most important of all his erections were his churches. Says Procopius, "The emperor Justinian built many churches in all parts of the Empire to the Mother of God, churches so magnificent and large and erected with such lavish expenditure of money that if one should see one of them by itself he would suppose that the Emperor had built this one only and had spent the whole time of his reign occupied with this alone."

It must be remembered that the Emperor, as the supreme ruler, was credited with being the source and originator of all buildings in his realm as well as of all actions which tended to the public good. Nevertheless, Justinian had himself a passion for sacred building as the champion of the Orthodox faith and the representative of God. Of his extant churches more will be said later. The most famous of those which no longer exist was that of the Holy Apostles at Constantinople. A five-domed cruciform church, it was furnished with antique columns and sumptuously adorned with marble and mosaic. Replacing the Church of the Holy Apostles built by Constantine, it was, in its turn, destroyed by the Turks, but long before its disappearance it had left its impression on the Venetian Cathedral of S. Mark.

Procopius tells us that his Church of Blachernae was "a stately building of unusual height" but well proportioned, and his description of the Church of the Pege shows us what store was placed on beauty of environment. It stood in a verdant park full of trees and flowers and enlivened with a rivulet "bubbling forth with a gentle stream". Other churches he built in the city. "Seeking to rival the sea in its beauty he set all these shrines around the gulf like an encircling necklace."

Justinian did not overlook the provinces in his provision of churches. In many different towns he built them, like the great church of S. John at Ephesus and the "many churches" in his new city of Mocesus in Cappadocia.

It was not long before the Persian War again broke out, and in 608, when Phocas was Emperor, the foe was at the very gates of the capital. The Persians swept over the Empire and abstracted the Holy Cross from Jerusalem. The valour of the great Emperor Heraclius regained by 630 all the territory which had been lost, but it was a short-lived triumph. A new and more terrible enemy, the Arabs, invaded the Empire and had, before the end of the seventh century brought vast stretches under Moslem rule. The seventh century was in other respects a crucial one for the Byzantine state. The government took on a more military form in the provinces, Greek supplanted Latin as the official language, and the Empire became more and more a country of the Near East. The closing years of the seventh and the opening years of the eighth century were a period of anarchy, until in 717 another great Emperor donned the purple and rehabilitated the fortunes of the distracted state. This was Leo III, the Isaurian. He reigned until 740, when he was succeeded by his son Constantine V, who in his turn held the reins of power until 775. Under these two Emperors, both of whom were able statesmen and generals, the fortunes of the Empire were revived. The Arabs who in 717 were at the gates of the capital were by 780 driven out of Anatolia. In 750 they had transferred their capital from Damascus to Baghdad. The Bulgarians were also checked in their attempts against Byzantium. The Isaurian Emperors improved the finances, carried through administrative reforms and strove to improve the lot of the peasants.

In other ways the eighth century was fraught with destiny for the Empire. It gradually took on a different character, becoming more and more orientalised. Influences from the East permeated its culture to an increasing degree, and many of the Emperors were of Asiatic—some of Armenian—descent. With the loss of former territory it became more compact, and the representatives of the many different races within its borders were welded together in such a way that a new character was given to the population of the Empire. At the same time the breach widened between Constantinople and Rome. The Popes looked not to the Emperor of the East but to the ruler of the Franks as their ally and protector. In 751 the Pope accepted from Pepin the Frankish king the lands which became the Papal States, and on Christmas Day in 800 Charlemagne was crowned by the Pope Emperor of the West. Only Venice and a few towns in the south comprised the Italian possessions of the Eastern Empire. After the death of Constantine VI there again ensued a period of weakness at Constantinople, but the affairs of state were settled on a firmer basis by Leo V, the Armenian (813–820), and the cultured Theophilus (829–842). Under him the University of Constantinople flourished anew. Theophilus was followed by an unworthy successor—Michael the Drunkard, who was assassinated in 867 by a prince who was destined to found an enduring dynasty, which brought the Empire to the apogee of its fame and power.

THE CONTROVERSY ABOUT ICON-WORSHIP

The era of the Isaurian Emperors, Leo III and his successors, has a particular interest for the student of Byzantine Art. It was the period of the great dispute known as the Iconoclastic Controversy which concerned the use of icons or sacred pictures in worship and which convulsed the Church and state for a hundred and fifty years. Representations of divine and holy persons or of sacred scenes had long played an important part in the life of the people. In addition to the frescoes and mosaics the churches contained numerous icons, paintings on wood or canvas, or bas-reliefs in metal or marble. Icons were everywhere. They were displayed in public places, they were cherished in every home, and they were carried about by the traveller on his journeys and the soldier on his campaigns. Representing Christ or the Virgin, an angel, a saint or some sacred episode, they were often covered with precious metal, leaving only the face and hands exposed. Others were encircled with costly gems, while millions of others were simple paintings, the works of obscure monkish artists, but the treasured possessions of humble citizens and peasants. The practice of artistic representation had at first been held in disfavour by the early Christians. When the ecclesiastical authorities began to approve it, they felt it was a means of teaching the truth and helping the faithful to think of Christ, the Virgin and the saints.

67

As time went on the icons assumed another character and were thought by many to possess a strange virtue in themselves. The veneration which was accorded them resulted in a widespread superstition. It was believed that the sacred pictures exercised a miraculous power in healing disease and warding off disaster, while the monks, fanatical believers in the icons, encouraged the willing superstition of the populace. Nevertheless, a prejudice against the representation of sacred personages had always existed in certain quarters especially in inland Asia Minor and farther east. In 488 Xenaias, a Monophysite bishop in Phrygia, had forbidden icons in his diocese, and Syria in the sixth and seventh centuries was much impregnated with Iconoclastic tendencies. Opposition to the icons became widespread in educated circles throughout the Empire as well as among soldiers who had come into contact with Islam. Space forbids more than the briefest mention of the long and complex story and of the varied and changing arguments with which the Iconoclasts, the opponents, and the Iconodules, the supporters of images, defended their respective causes. Both parties placed most reliance on texts from the Bible and the Fathers of the Church, torn arbitrarily from their context to suit their purpose. The Iconoclasts accused the Iconodules of idolatry and the latter distinguished between the veneration due to a sacred picture and the worship given to God alone. At a later stage a philosophic foundation was laid for the arguments. Very significant was the attitude of S. Theodore of Studion, a champion of icon-worship, when he maintained that there is some sort of identity between an icon of Christ and Christ Himself; that the icon cannot be separated from the original, that the relationship between the two is like that between a man and his shadow, that the icon is a channel of divine grace and therefore it is right to prostrate oneself in veneration and burn candles before it.

The Iconoclastic Controversy was initiated by the Emperor Leo III. By descent an Armenian, he had deep ancestral qualities of temperament predisposing him towards his chosen course, but he was honestly desirous to free Christianity from the trammels of superstitious abuse. He openly proclaimed himself an Iconoclast: a number of images were destroyed, but, though riots and insurrection ensued, Leo appears to have acted with much restraint. His son and successor, Constantine V, pursued his policy with greater vehemence and determined to maintain the supremacy of state over Church. A council held in 753 declared "that there shall be rejected and removed and anathematised out of the Christian Church every likeness which is made out of any material and colour whatsoever out of the evil art of painters". The violent opposition shown to Constantine led him to active persecution, while many precious works of religious art perished in his reign.

The Iconodules achieved a temporary victory by a decree of a council which opened in the Church of the Holy Apostles at Constantinople in 786, but the dispute broke out again in 815 under the Emperor Leo V, "the Armenian". He was actuated largely by policy and was less extreme. A council he convened did not condemn icons as such, but only the superstition associated with them. They could be placed high up on church walls, but incense was not to be swung or candles lit before them.

The compromise of Leo did not satisfy the extreme Iconoclasts. On Palm Sunday over a thousand monks walked around the Monastery of the Studion carrying icons and chanting the canticle, "We venerate your images, O blessed saints." Their efforts were of no avail. Theodore of Studion describes the measures taken to enforce the Emperor's will; "the holy vessels are melted down, the sacred vestments cast into the flames with the pictures and the books which contain anything concerning images". But the policy of Iconoclasm was doomed to end in failure, and in 842 under the Empress-Regent Theodora icons were finally restored and permitted.

Though so strongly opposed to the representation of sacred persons, the Iconoclasts were by no means hostile to every form of art. The Emperor Theophilus, a great builder, decorated his palaces magnificently, and impressed by the accounts of the luxurious dwellings of the Caliphs strove to emulate the splendours of Baghdad. Throughout the Iconoclastic period, Constantinople was profoundly affected by Oriental influence, and decorative features of Eastern origin had considerable vogue.

Not only secular but also sacred buildings were adorned, for Stephen the Deacon says that Constantine V, after destroying its sacred pictures, decorated the Church of Blachernae with "trees, birds and beasts of various sorts, leaves of ivy, cranes, jackdaws and peacocks, in festoons". He complains that the Emperor made the church "a fruitshed and aviary". Theophilus built churches and painted landscapes on their walls. Secular art flourished: dealing largely with mythological subjects it was Hellenistic in style and had its influence, along with an Oriental one, on the revived religious art when the Iconoclastic struggle had come to an end.

SANTA SOPHIA, CONSTANTINOPLE

In the first half of the sixth century, Byzantine Architecture, having assembled its components and realised its nature, suddenly attained a level of achievement, which in all the long centuries that followed was destined never to be surpassed. No other Byzantine monument can compare, either in magnitude or splendour or constructive audacity, with the Cathedral of Santa Sophia at Constantinople (33). Poets and historians have lavished their praise upon this incomparable building in the most grandiloquent terms. Sometimes it is the boldness of the construction which has evoked their admiration, as when Procopius the contemporary historian tells of "its golden dome, which seems not to rest on solid masonry but as if suspended from heaven to cover the space". He describes how "all these details, fitted together with incredible ability in mid-air and floating off from each other and resting only on the parts next to them, produce a single and most extraordinary harmony in the work". To the historian Evagrius, Santa Sophia was "a great and incomparable work, hitherto unparalleled in history, the Church's greatest temple, fair and surpassing and beyond the power of words to describe".

At other times it is the magnificence of the marbles adorning its walls and composing its columns which evokes the praise of the ancient writers.

> Who [says Procopius] can reckon up the splendour of pillars and stones with which this fane is adorned? One might imagine oneself to have come upon a lovely meadow of flowers. One might admire, of some the purple, of others the green; and in some the bloom of crimson, and in some white flashes out, while Nature like a painter tricks out the rest in contrasting tints. And when one goes there to pray, he realises immediately that it is not by human power or art but by the influence of God that the work has been fashioned, and his mind lifted Godwards, walks the air, not thinking Him far off, but rather that it pleases Him to walk with His elect.

Or listen to the glowing words of Paul the Silentiary, a dignitary of Justinian's Court and author of a long hexameter poem in honour of the dedication of A.D. 563.

70

Yet who even in the measures of Homer, shall sing the marble pastures gathered on the lofty walls and spreading pavement of the mighty church? These the iron with its metal tooth has gnawed— the fresh green from Carystos and the polychrome marble from the Phrygian range, in which a rosy blush mingles with white or it shines bright with flowers of deep red and silver. There is also a wealth of porphyry powdered with bright stars, that has once laden the river-boat on the broad Nile. You would see an emerald green from Sparta and the glistening marble with wavy veins which the tool has worked in the deep bosom of the Isaurian hills, showing slanting streaks blood-red and livid white. Stone too there is that the Libyan sun, warming with his golden light, has nurtured in the deep-bosomed clefts of the hills of the Moors of crocus colour glittering like gold, and the product of the Celtic crags, a wealth of crystals like milk poured here and there on a flesh of glittering black. There is the precious onyx, as if gold were shining through it and the marble that the land of Atrax yields, not from some upland glen, but from the level plains; in parts fresh green as the sea or emerald stone, or again like blue cornflowers in grass, with here and there a drift of fallen snow—sweet mingled contrast of the dark and shining surface.

No less eloquent is Paul the Silentiary when he comes to describe the rich furnishings of precious metal with which the cathedral was once equipped and whose details are now known only through the written records.

Procopius and Paul the Silentiary lived in the century when the church was built: writers of succeeding generations have never ceased to echo the spirit of their praise. One author may be quoted who visited the church in the fatal year of 1453 and describes it as "the heaven upon earth, the throne of the glory of God, the second firmament and chariot of cherubim, the handiwork of God, a marvellous and worthy work".

Santa Sophia embodies at one and the same time the spirit of the Greek Church, of the Imperial Byzantine Court and of the Emperor who built it. By reflecting the heavenly splendour in the magnificence of earthly art it raises the soul to the contemplation of the celestial. The stupendous dome and soaring vaults hang over the vast extent of nave like the canopy of heaven, and the glories of the unseen realm are adumbrated in the golden mosaics and shimmering marbles which cover vaults and walls. In its sumptuous stateliness it repeats the tradition of a court which clung with insistence to a gorgeous ceremonial and dazzled the stranger and citizen alike by the pageantry of its rites. There could be no more appropriate environment for the reception of the Emperor on some great day of celebration and for his slow procession to the throne, followed by a host of dignitaries in their stiff bejewelled robes or flowing silks. And, finally, Santa Sophia, by its very magnitude and audacity of construction, was the typical expression of the mind of Justinian himself, an Emperor who was consumed with a boundless ambition and whose projects, both in war and peace, were conceived on the grandest scale.

The Church of Santa Sophia (properly "Hagia Sophia"—the Holy Wisdom) was begun to be built by the Emperor Justinian in the year 532: its architect was Anthemius of Tralles in Asia Minor, who was assisted by Isidore of Miletus. It occupied the site of a church which according to the Byzantine historian Socrates was planned by the Emperor Constantine and completed by his son Constantine II in 360. A wooden-roofed basilica, it was burnt and rebuilt in 416. Recent excavations are believed to have brought to light portions of the first church, while in 1935 a portico was discovered which adorned the west end of the second church. In 532 the second church was consumed in the conflagration incited by the famous "Nika Riot" which caused such terrible loss of life and widespread devastation throughout the city. The work proceeded with great rapidity, ten thousand workmen being employed on the construction and adornment. On 27th December, 537, only six years after its commencement, the great church was consecrated in the presence of the Emperor amid scenes of gorgeous ceremony. Justinian, having entered the Royal Gates with the Patriarch, proceeded alone up the nave and mounted the ambo. Standing in this isolated position he gazed around the vast building and, glorifying the Almighty for having granted him the grace to complete so great a project, uttered the oft-quoted words, "O Solomon, I have surpassed thee."

The church was not permitted to remain long in its original state. Twenty-one years later the first of many earthquakes brought down a part of the eastern arch and dome, but Justinian speedily repaired the damage. A higher dome replaced the former flatter one, and was strengthened by external buttresses between its windows.

In 989 a severe earthquake caused part of the west arch and dome to collapse. The architect who completed the restoration was an Armenian, "an illustrious mason and sculptor who was then resident in Constantinople". In 1204 Santa Sophia suffered grievous despoliation at the hands of the predatory soldiers of the Fourth Crusade. An incalculable number of gold and silver ornaments were looted and carried away to the West, although the greater part, as Gibbon mournfully reflects, must have been lost or destroyed in the camps.

It is therefore with a certain satisfaction that one learns that the Latin clergy who secured possession of the church took precautions to preserve the structure. Swift has shown that some flying buttresses, now mostly embedded in later masonry, are of Western type and were built during the period of the Latin occupation (1205–61). But it needed to be still further strengthened, and in the year 1317, during the reign of the Emperor Andronicus Palaeologus, Santa Sophia received its most obvious additions, the massive and ungainly buttresses which back the walls to north, south and east, and are such a prominent external feature today. Unnecessarily cumbrous though they be, they served their purpose. Yet they could not prevent a further collapse due to a subsequent earthquake. Nicephorus Gregoras narrates the disaster of 1347. "It was now evening and not far from midnight when with the sky calm and clear, one of the four lofty circles— that which faces the rising sun—fell to the ground, dragging with it the adjacent vault." Great was the distress among the populace until the venerable sanctuary of which they were so proud was repaired by John Cantacuzenus and John Palaeologus I.

When the Turks conquered Constantinople in 1453, the Sultan took possession of the church and ordained its use as a mosque. The necessary arrangements were made for its adaptation to Moslem worship and four tall minarets were eventually erected outside. The great green plaques with Arabic inscriptions which were so familiar to visitors were removed soon after 1929 when the famous building, a church for a thousand and a mosque for five hundred years, was converted into a Byzantine museum; they have now been replaced. During its occupancy as a mosque it was well cared for by the Turks who erected the massive buttress at the south-east angle and did certain other repairs. A notable restoration was that undertaken under the skilful guidance of the Swiss architect Fossati about the middle of the nineteenth century. His drawings which were published in 1852 admirably express the sublimity and spaciousness of the vast interior.

Santa Sophia is an example of the domed basilica (34), but has its dome set against semi-domes on east and west instead of

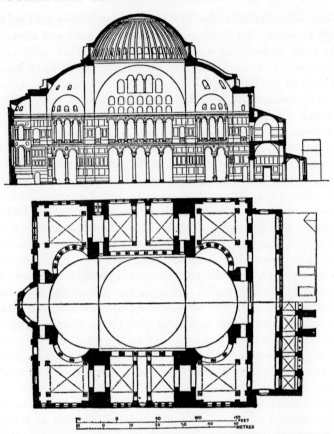

34　S. Sophia, Constantinople: longitudinal section and plan

barrel-vaults. Short barrel-vaults extend from these semi-domes to the conch of the apse and to the western wall. On north and south the dome is buttressed by broad arches filled in with walling on the interior and pierced with many windows; some of these windows are later in date, and the upper part of the tympana originally had columns rising to the intrados of the arches.

The tremendous dome of the church(17) is ribbed, encircled with a ring of forty-two windows and covered like the vaults with lead. It rests on four huge pendentives springing from piers that are prolonged to form massive interior buttresses or responds. It is at these points that in 1317 Andronicus added four of the external

74

buttresses. The walls which form the piers and interior buttresses are pierced by arches in aisles and galleries.

The semi-domes are buttressed by secondary semi-domes resting on two-storied arcades. The upper columns are of green marble, while the lower are magnificent porphyry monoliths. By a singularly happy arrangement, the upper story has six columns (37), but the lower only two. Compared by Procopius in their formation to "dancers in a chorus", and by Paul the Silentiary in their appearance to "well-graved warriors from Thebes", they form exedrae, which, rounding off the nave with their sweeping curves, complete the design with a perfect harmony.

The nave is flanked on either side by four magnificent columns of green Thessalian marble, with six green marble columns above (35). The vaults of each aisle have eight green circular and four white rectangular columns. There are beautiful coupled columns in the arcade of the west gallery.

The aisles are roofed in a complex and intricate fashion with cross-vaults and barrel-vaults. There is a striking contrast between the complexity of the aisles and the simplicity of the nave, and Zaloziecky, followed by Swift, sees in this contrast a deliberate aesthetic purpose on the part of the architect Anthemius. He has designed from two different architectural conceptions of space. The aisles afford intricate fragmentary views, with illusive vistas and receding planes, with shadowy recesses and picturesque effects: the nave is clear and open and easily grasped, with its impression of closed and substantial space. Yet the two are not disparate, for by means of the nave arcades there is a spatial relationship between nave and aisles.

The exterior of Santa Sophia forms a rectangle, broken by an apse at the eastern end (32). There has been controversy as to whether or not Santa Sophia ever had a prothesis projecting from its eastern end. Be that as it may, it seems clear that the space between the outer walls and the north-eastern exedra was used for many centuries—or perhaps always—as the prothesis.

The diaconicon occupied part of the corresponding space on the south, the rest being reserved for the Emperor and his attendants. A detached circular building to the north was once the skeuophylakion where the sacred treasures were housed. Of the many independent buildings which occupied the courts of Santa Sophia the only other one which has been preserved is the domed baptistery on the south. Close to it are several Turkish tombs, or *turbehs*. The most important building in Byzantine days beside Santa Sophia was the Palace of the Patriarch with its library.

. A narthex in two stories extends along the west front of the church, and beyond it an exo-narthex in one story. The exo-narthex was once preceded by a vast atrium with colonnades on three sides. It was once believed that the exo-narthex (which formed the east side of the atrium) originally had the form of an open portico also, but Antoniadi has shown that the western wall of the exo-narthex is contemporary with the church. A belfry, which once stood in the centre of the exo-narthex was of a Western design and belongs to the period of the Latin occupation. Of the same period are the flying buttresses against the exo-narthex, most of which are now built up. The belfry occupied the site of the great entrance to the church, the "Beautiful Gates". The magnificent bronze doors—the finest specimen of Byzantine bronze-work extant—now hang in a vestibule south of the narthex. They were reassembled in 841 from older pieces, some of which may belong to the first church on the site(36).

In the construction of Santa Sophia thin square bricks were used for the vaults, arches and walls. "He built it," says the contemporary historian Agathias, "of burnt brick, binding it everywhere with iron and avoiding the use of wood, in order that it might not be burned easily." These tiles or bricks are laid in beds of mortar almost as thick as themselves. They were often stamped with letters signifying their destination, e.g. "Of the great church." The letters are preceded by a cross. The piers and their responds were composed of stone, and there are stone courses interspersed throughout the brick courses of the walls.

Various theories have been adduced to explain the origin of the plan of Santa Sophia. Influence has been assigned to the great bath-halls and to the Basilica of Constantine in Rome, to the foiled plans of Armenia, to the domed basilicas of Asia Minor, to the destroyed Church of the Holy Apostles in Constantinople and to that of SS. Sergius and Bacchus in the same city. It is best considered to be in the direct line from the domed basilica modified by factors emanating from other sources. There is something of a similarity in the layout of the Roman bath-halls and that of Santa Sophia, though the differences are also very marked. The idea of the exedrae may have been derived from their use in such a church as SS. Sergius and Bacchus, but the brilliance with which

35　Santa Sophia, Constantinople:
North Side

36　Santa Sophia, Constantinople:
Bronze Doors

37, 38   SANTA SOPHIA, CONSTANTINOPLE: The Gallery of Exedra

the exedrae in Santa Sophia are fashioned and placed is an indication of original genius. Anthemius of Tralles was an architect of outstanding merit, claimed by Procopius to be not only the ablest of his own time but of former ages. In the course of his studies and travels he may have gathered ideas from many sources, but their adaptation and employment, when the need arose, must have been due to his own surpassing talents. He may have achieved his master-stroke, the adoption of the two great semi-domes, simply by considering the familiar semi-dome of an apse and thinking how it could be substituted for a barrel-vault springing from a central dome.

The exterior of Santa Sophia reveals no rich display of ornament. It has often been most adversely criticised and compared in unflattering terms with the splendid interior. It must, however, be said in justice that the present aspect of the outside is very different from that of the church which Anthemius built. If the minarets, the later unsightly buttresses and the massive cube beneath the dome (due to the rebuilding by Justinian), be eliminated from the mind, one can envisage a building far more compact and unified. In its original state there would also be an effective contrast between the rounded and defined superstructure and the high vertical walls, unbroken by projections and with all the articulation of structure concealed in internal buttresses.

But the interior of Santa Sophia ranks as one of the greatest architectural achievements of all time. The great semi-domes swelling majestically upwards carry the eye at once to the very culminating point of the edifice, and, with the huge spreading pendentives and the enormous dome, poised in shadow above the light which streams through its forty windows, form a superb canopy over the vast extent of unimpeded nave. From the nave the apse and exedrae sweep out in graceful curves, and the high round arches echo each other in a majestic harmony. Contrasted with these curving lines are the high vertical walls to north and south, broken by their precious marble columns, while the aisles and galleries form mysterious vistas beyond.

The decoration of the interior is a superb enrichment of the fabric, a sumptuous manifestation of the Byzantine spirit. A great part of the walls is sheathed with marble of many different kinds, prominent among which are the green verd-antique from Thessaly, the grey-white from Proconnesus and the rose from Phrygia. Veined slabs were opened out and set side by side to form patterns, in which imagination traced the figures of sacred persons and accorded them a special veneration. Some marbles are set out in panels surrounded by notched fillets, some are sculptured with lozenges and other devices and some are inlaid with marble of a different colour. The capitals which crown the columns, exquisitely designed and fashioned, are masterpieces of Byzantine sculpture. Among them are to be found the Melon, the Byzantine Corinthian and the Wind-blown Acanthus types, while Byzantine Ionic capitals appear in the galleries (37, 38). The impost-capitals on the columns of the nave and gallery arcades, richly adorned with acanthus foliage and deeply undercut, have the monograms of Justinian and Theodora on a central boss and Ionic volutes at the angles. All the capitals are of white marble, but it must be remembered that their foliage was once gilded and their backgrounds coloured blue.

The dome, vaults and part of the walls were embellished with mosaics, partially covered by the Turks, but recently uncovered by the Byzantine Institute. A large cross (later, a figure of Christ) occupied the centre of the dome, seraphim filled the pendentives, the Virgin and Child adorned the conch of the apse, and saints and prophets stood upon the walls. A mosaic in the lunette in the narthex, long known from a drawing made by Salzenberg, has again been uncovered. It shows Christ, richly clad and seated on a throne with his feet on a golden cushion. Busts of the Virgin and an archangel flank the Christ, before whom an Emperor, probably Leo the Wise, prostrates himself, wearing the imperial robes. In the room south of the narthex there can now be seen the Virgin flanked on one side by the Emperor Constantine holding a model of the city and on the other by Justinian with a model of the church (5). In the galleries valuable contemporary portraits of Byzantine sovereigns have been brought to light, dating from the eleventh and twelfth centuries. In the south gallery there is a magnificent representation of the "Deisis" Christ enthroned between the interceding Virgin and Baptist.

Many of the mosaics were of a non-representational character and of great charm in their design and colour. The gleaming golden surfaces of the aisle-vaults were adorned with rosettes, stars, geometric bands and crosses. In the soffits of the gallery arches foliage is enwreathed, green against the gold, and the blue vaults are spangled with stars.

In Christian days the church was filled with magnificent objects of incalculable worth. Between the most easterly piers there stood the Iconostasis with its silver columns and reliefs of angels and prophets. The Holy Table, of gold inlaid with precious stones, gleamed beneath a silver ciborium. The *Novgorod Chronicle*, recounting the irreparable destruction wrought by the Fourth Crusade, descants on the furniture of surpassing beauty, the silver screen around the bema, the many ornaments in which gold was used, the wonderful table with gems and a great pearl, the silver candelabra, the forty censers made of pure gold, and the priceless vessels without number which the church contained. One of the most notable objects was the ambo, which stood in the nave between the great east piers, and which was used, among other purposes, for reading the Gospel. Santa Sophia possessed four ambones in succession, of which the second is described by Paul the Silentiary in his poem. Circular in shape with semicircular projections and constructed of marble inlaid with silver and ivory, it rested on columns and was approached by two separate flights of steps.

The church employed a multitude of clergy who conducted the long and elaborate services with gorgeous ceremony and meticulous ritual. Of particular splendour were the services for the commemoration of the Great Festivals of the Faith or the veneration of the miraculous relics which the church enshrined. On such occasions the Emperor might attend in state. As the light from thousands of candles gleamed on the polished surface of green marble and purple porphyry, as the figures of austere saints and bejewelled emperors looked down from the incrusted walls, as the wings of the seraphs lay outstretched in the pendentives far above, as the clouds of incense floated through the expanse, as the priests in their coloured silken vestments moved slowly in procession, as the celebrant passed through the iconostasis into the presence of the altar, as a great multitude stood in rapt devotion and as the solemn chant echoed through the nave, it is no wonder that the visitors from the Russian plains felt the throb of an unprecedented emotion in their souls, and beheld mingling with the worshippers angelic visitants from heaven.

In the days when Santa Sophia was a temple for Christian worship its aspect must have been superb beyond all measure. It has undergone many vicissitudes throughout the long passage of the centuries. Earthquake and despoliation, transformation and repair, have left their impress upon its character and structure.

Now it is a museum, a silent memorial of the past. Yet to a remarkable degree the venerable building preserves those features which evoked such admiration from the lips of the men who saw it in the distant century of its erection, and after the lapse of fourteen hundred years it is still the greatest achievement of its style. With its vast area of serene and spacious nave, with the noble curve of its audacious arches, with its sublime proportions and its articulated unity, with its exquisite exedrae rounding off the angles of its nave in perfect elegance, with its green and purple columns and their lovely capitals, with its mighty dome and semi-domes majestic as the canopy of heaven, Santa Sophia is the crowning glory of Byzantine Art.

OTHER EARLY CHURCHES IN CONSTANTINOPLE

The oldest surviving church in Constantinople is S. John of the Studion, which was built in A.D. 463 and was attached to a famous and powerful monastery. It eventually became a mosque under the name of Emir Ahor Jamissi. Though basilical in plan it is almost square, measuring 89 feet in length by 83 in breadth. The contrast between the long basilica of the West and this squarish type in the East is significant of the difference in attitude adopted with regard to the liturgy. The Western worshipper focused his attention on the altar, the Eastern worshipper was more conscious of the all-enveloping presence. The squarish plan, as we have seen, prevailed in the later domed churches, but, as here, it is to be found even in a basilica.

This ancient and famous sanctuary was severely damaged by an earthquake in 1894 and by a heavy fall of snow early this century. It is in a sadly ruined state, but part of the north colonnade still stands. The Studion has beautiful decoration on the outside of its narthex where four Corinthian columns support an entablature sculptured with birds, animals and crosses.

The Church of S. Andrew in Krisei (*Hodja Moustafa Pasha Mesjedi*), which may be dated as early as the sixth century, still preserves some fine Byzantine capitals of cubical form sculptured with acanthus leaves deeply undercut. Much altered in appearance by the Turks, it consisted of a domed central space separated by intervening columns from an ambulatory.

To the reign of Justinian belongs the important Church of S. Irene (40, 43). It stands quite near Santa Sophia, which alone of Constantinopolitan churches surpasses it in size. S. Irene is a

39 SALONICA: S. George

40 CONSTANTINOPLE: S. Irene

41   The Exterior

42   The Interior

SS. SERGIUS AND BACCHUS, CONSTANTINOPLE

building of much historical interest and its site is associated with the days before Constantine transformed the ancient Byzantium into the imperial capital. Constantine rebuilt the old church and dedicated it to Peace (Eirene). For a time—until 360—it was the Cathedral of the City, and in A.D. 381 it was the meeting-place of one of those General Councils whose credal decisions are still accepted by Christian Churches throughout the world. This

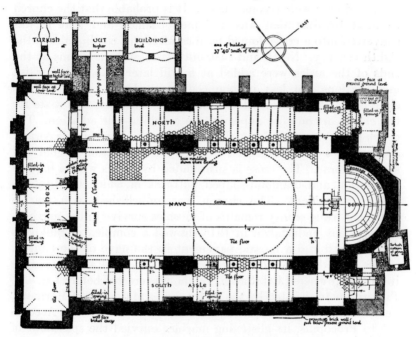

43　Plan of S. Irene, Constantinople

church was consumed by fire in the terrible "Nika" insurrection in the reign of Justinian. Rebuilt by that Emperor, it was finally made a military museum by the Turks. It was strange to behold within this temple of peace, the many trophies of Moslem prowess in war. Weapons were ranged in serried ranks around its apse and lurid pictures of Turkish victories hung upon its walls. The building is now empty and scheduled as an ancient monument.

S. Irene is a cross-domed basilica, though its western portion is covered, not by its original barrel-vault but by a domical vault with elliptical arches to north and south(16). Arcades separate the two parts of the nave from narrow galleried aisles. A spacious apse terminates the eastern end, and the aisles are finished off in square chambers with rooms of a later date beyond. Along the western end extends a five-bayed narthex, preceded by an exo-narthex much modified by Turkish hands. The Church of Justinian was severely damaged in 740 by an earthquake which caused widespread havoc among churches, hospitals and other edifices in the city; the vaults, dome and upper portions of the walls and apse were reconstructed. It is probable that the church as built by Justinian was a domed basilica and that it was converted into a cross-domed basilica after this earthquake in the eighth century. North and east buttresses and the rooms at the ends of the aisles were added at a still later date, but Turkish modifications are less pronounced in S. Irene than in those churches that were turned into mosques. The ranges of seats for the clergy in the apse appear to be a subsequent addition. The conch has a mosaic which was produced in the Iconoclastic period: it consists of a cross in black outline on a foundation of gold and silver tesserae. The cross is surrounded by bands with a biblical inscription and diamond-shaped patterns in which Oriental influence is evident. The church was embellished with marble panelling while scanty remains of mosaics survive in the narthex. Excavations undertaken in 1946 showed a complex of buildings to the south and a mosaic pavement in the nave of the church.

The domed Church of SS. Sergius and Bacchus (41), named by its Moslem owners Little Santa Sophia, was erected before A.D. 527. Picturesquely situated by the rocky shores of the Sea of Marmora, near the maritime walls, it adjoined the Imperial Palace. According to Procopius, its glistening marbles outvied the splendour of the sun, its walls were resplendent with gold and its treasuries were filled with a multitude of costly gifts. Disfigured though it was on its conversion to a mosque, the grace of its lines and the richness of its capitals still distinguish a beautiful example of Byzantine Art. The two saints to whom the church was dedicated, Sergius and Bacchus, were Roman officers who were martyred as Christians in the persecutions of Maximian. They were held in special honour by Justinian who is supposed to have owed his life to their intervention. The future monarch had been involved in a plot against the Emperor Anastasius. As he lay under sentence of death the two saints appeared to Anastasius in a dream, pleading on Justinian's behalf, and in later years Justinian built this church in gratitude to his supernatural benefactors.

The emperors attended the church in state once a year, and on the north wall there are remains which are believed to be those of the hall where they rested after the ceremony.

In plan the Church of SS. Sergius and Bacchus is roughly a square with an eastern apse and a western narthex (42, 44). Eight piers inside this square support a dome, which is composed of sixteen compartments alternately flat and concave, the concave compartments being set back at the angles of the octagonal wall. The dome is encased in walling and has small buttresses outside. It is doubtless such walling, used for abutment, which led to the idea of the drum which was a constant feature in later churches.

Between the piers inside the church pairs of columns are set in two tiers, so arranged that those on the sides are in line with the piers and that those on the diagonals form semicircular exedrae. The plan has such affinities with that of S. Vitale in Ravenna that G. T. Rivoira has derived it from the Italian building, but it is improbable that the one was derived from the other. They are almost contemporary. S. Vitale was planned in 526 but not completed till much later, and according to Cedrinus, SS. Sergius and Bacchus was commenced in 527. Both churches connect themselves with an Eastern octagonal plan exemplified in the Church of Ezra (Zorah) in Palestine, and they may have been developed independently from a common Oriental source.

The carved ornament which still adorns the Church of SS. Sergius and Bacchus is rich and beautiful. The impost-capitals of the lower story are of the so-called "Melon type": those of the upper story are Byzantine Ionic. The lower story supports an entablature with a

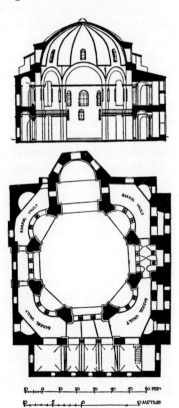

44 Plan and section of SS. Sergius and Bacchus, Constantinople

83

frieze in two parts, the first sculptured with acanthus, the second displaying an inscription in honour of Justinian, Theodora and S. Sergius, "who endured for the sake of Christ, obtaining heaven as his reward". In distinction the columns of the upper story are tied together by an arcade. Marble encrustation still adorns part of the walls and the columns themselves are of green and whitish marble stained with other hues. The interior of the church still impresses by the harmony of its design, its effective contrast of horizontal and nobly curving lines, its elegant arcades, its rounded niches and its crowning dome.

SALONICA

Salonica has been described by Finlay as being in the tenth century, "the second city of the Empire in population and wealth". Its favourable situation for commerce early elevated it to a position of eminence, and in spite of disasters and vicissitudes it maintained its place throughout the course of imperial history. The Via Egnatia, the old Roman road which led from Byzantium to the West, passed through the centre of the city. The furs and amber of the Baltic found their way through Hungary to its markets and the products of a fertile hinterland were loaded on the vessels which anchored at its busy wharves. To its great fair of S. Demetrius, which lasted for a week each year, traders flocked from every part of the Mediterranean world. The importance of Thessalonica was further enhanced by the powerful traditions of religion. For its Church could claim an apostolic foundation and its inhabitants could read in the Book of Acts about the visit of S. Paul and study his Epistles to the Thessalonians. It is not surprising that culture should have flourished in such a city and Salonica contains some notable monuments of Byzantine Art. Unhappily, the most famous of them all, its great and popular Church of S. Demetrius was disastrously damaged by a fire which in 1917 swept over that quarter of the town. It was a wooden-roofed basilica, built in the fifth and restored in the seventh century. The capitals which crown the splendid marble columns of the lower arcade had great beauty of design and exquisite delicacy of execution. Most of the marble panelling perished in the devouring flames of the conflagration, and the same fate overtook the mosaics of the nave which, hidden for many centuries, displayed their splendour to the world for only ten brief years. They included episodes from the life of S. Demetrius. Others,

84

however, escaped destruction, and one or two new panels were discovered after the fire. Among the former is one which shows the saint standing between the prefect Leontius and a bishop. Distinguished by its monumental aspect, its expressive realism and its brilliancy of colour, this mosaic appears to be a work of the late sixth century. After the fire interesting discoveries were made of frescoes and a crypt.

The spacious fifth-century Church of the Virgin Acheropoietos (formerly called S. Paraskevi), now cleared of its Turkish additions, has affinities with Syrian churches. The remains of its fine mosaics, which survive only under the arches of the nave arcade, show an Alexandrian influence; they depict birds, vases, fruit and flowers in addition to the Cross.

The Church of S. George is a rotunda (39). Investigations have proved it to be a Roman building, erected towards the end of the third century A.D. It was transformed into a church in the fifth century when an ambulatory (now destroyed) was built around it and a choir was added at the east. The upper part of the choir was rebuilt in better material and other alterations were made some time after the tenth century. The interior of the dome was adorned with fifth-century mosaics of which the lowest zone survives. They depict Eastern martyr-saints standing with outstretched arms in front of varied architectural compositions. These backgrounds with their domes, gables, arches, vaults, canopies and columns are of much interest, and the total result has been described as "one of the most beautiful decorative ensembles of the Christian Art of the fifth century". Many of the compartments have been repaired, and one was completely restored in 1885. Along with some other mosaics in the niches showing fruit and birds, these works are Hellenistic in design and treatment.

The Church of S. Sophia at Salonica has been the subject of much discussion and of widely divergent points of view (45–7). In plan it is a domed basilica with short western arm (cf. p. 55). The dome, springing from imperfectly formed pendentives on massive piers, is buttressed by short barrel-vaults which are closed below by two-storied arcades on the longitudinal axis: a nave is thus formed flanked by galleried aisles. An additional bay extends beyond the eastern cross-arm to the apse, and a narthex runs along the western end. The side-apses have square chambers in front of them, walled-off from the rest of the church and entered by low doors.

Rivoira, the Italian scholar and champion of Western origins, considered this church to be the most important link in a chain connecting the Byzantine with the Roman basilical system. He thought that it was designed by Julius Argentarius, the architect of S. Vitale at Ravenna, but he overstressed points of resemblance between the two churches. The precise date of Santa Sophia has been the subject of much controversy; some authorities would derive its plan from that of Santa Sophia at Constantinople and

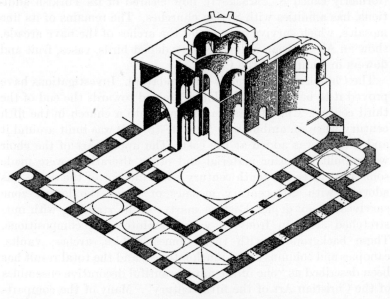

45   Isometric plan of S. Sophia, Salonica

would see in it a feeble adaptation of the great church in the capital. On the other hand the masonry has been adduced as evidence for a fifth-century date for the Salonica church. The plan, too, has affinities with Oriental churches: comparison has been made between its plan and those of the churches of Kasr-ibn-Wardan in Syria, of the Koimesis at Nicea and of churches in Mesopotamia. It is best to give Santa Sophia the earlier date and to connect it with Eastern sources.

The beautiful mosaics in the dome, according to the latest and most probable view, belong to the ninth century. They represent the Ascension by depicting Christ Pantocrator supported by two angels and surrounded by the Virgin, two angels and the twelve

46   SALONICA: S. Sophia

47   The Interior,
S. Sophia,
Salonica

48 RAVENNA: Chair of Maximian

apostles between trees. In 1907 two superimposed mosaics were discovered in the apse—one of the Cross and the other of the Virgin and Child. The figure of the Virgin was inserted towards the close of the eighth century and celebrated the victory over the Iconoclasts by displacing a cross, the outline of which is traceable in the background. The Madonna and Child stand out from a gold background, while on a vault before the apse a great cross within a golden circle shines on a surface of silver.

Santa Sophia has much of the sublime grandeur and deep religious feeling which are associated with Byzantine churches of the early period. Its noble vaults, its massive piers, its sweeping arches, its great curving apse, its sense of space, its stately Madonna and gleaming marble combine to invest it with a solemn grandeur worthy of the best tradition of Byzantine Art.

RAVENNA

At no place in the world is Christian Art of the fifth and sixth centuries more brilliantly illustrated than at Ravenna. It lies on the edge of the wide Italian plain where the waters of the River Po sluggishly debouch through their delta into the Adriatic Sea. A quiet and remote provincial town today, it once occupied a position of unique importance in the West. There the Western Emperor Honorius took refuge about 402 when Italy was invaded by Alaric and his Goths, and there the court and administration were settled for close on seventy years. Honorius was succeeded by his illustrious sister, Galla Placidia, who acted as Regent for her son, Valentinian III, but in 476 the barbarian Odoacer deposed Romulus Augustulus, the last of the Western emperors, and with the consent of the senate became King or Prefect of Italy. In 493 Ravenna fell into the hands of Theodoric, the famous king of the Ostrogoths, who reigned within its walls for over thirty years under the nominal suzerainty of Byzantium. The chroniclers are loud in their praise of the character and enlightened rule of Theodoric, who enriched his capital with stately buildings, both religious and secular.

Some time after the death of Theodoric, the Emperor Justinian sent his Generals Belisarius and, later, Narses to recover Italy, which was conquered by about the middle of the sixth century. But the completeness of victory did not long endure. In 568 Alboin and his Lombards invaded the peninsula which became split up into parts, some belonging to the Eastern Empire, some being permanently occupied by Lombard dukes. A new office was created for the supreme administration of the Byzantine dominions in Italy, the occupant of which was called the Exarch and resided in the Palace of Ravenna. There he ruled as the representative of the Emperor, until the middle of the eighth century when the Lombards captured the town.

It will therefore be seen that for the greater part of three and a half centuries Ravenna occupied the important position of capital of the Byzantine possessions in Italy, and even during the virtual independence under Theodoric it was the residence of a monarch who, though an Arian, sought to imitate the Byzantine spirit. During most of this long period communication was generally possible with Rome along the Flaminian way, while barques from Constantinople and Syria constantly landed their merchandise at Classis, the adjacent port. The exarchs emulated the luxury of their imperial masters, and the long list of archbishops contains the names of prelates like Ursus and Maximian, who were famous in the history of the city and potent in its councils. Secure behind its marshes and canals, it enjoyed a rare tranquillity when the rest of Italy was embroiled in chaotic strife. Incentive urged and opportunity permitted her rulers to embellish Ravenna with splendid monuments, and its relative peace and isolation throughout all succeeding generations have preserved for us the most precious memorials of the Dark Ages which we possess.

The Orthodox Baptistery, originally a room in some Roman baths, was adapted to its present purpose by Archbishop Neon in the middle of the fifth century. A domed octagon with four low apses, it has its dome constructed of small terra-cotta amphorae or jars fitted into each other and arranged in a spiral manner. This type of dome, which is exceptionally light, also occurs in the Tomb of Galla Placidia and the Church of S. Vitale, later to be described. Of an extreme simplicity on the exterior, the baptistery is resplendent with fifth-century mosaics inside. The centre of the dome contains the Baptism of Christ (49); like many other representations of the same subject, it has a reminiscence of pagan mythology in the Jordan portrayed as an aged man—the river-god, as it were—resting upon an urn. Around the Baptism there marches on a blue background a procession of apostles, noble in its rhythmic dignity and vigour of movement.

Farther down still there are mosaics of thrones and altars with the open books of the Gospels. The walls of the octagon are enlivened by two tiers of arches on columns in the angles. The mosaics of the baptistery in general follow the classical tradition, but Eastern elements are also present, as in the facing posture of the heads of the Apostles. A word of caution must, however, be added which applies to the mosaics both of the baptistery and of all the other buildings in Ravenna. They have been restored a great number of times since their original cubes were placed in position. These restorations have often covered considerable areas of the pictures and have entailed the use of new cubes. The restorations executed in previous centuries were sometimes crude and in poor material, but the modern have been carefully carried out. An excellent idea of the amount of restoration to some of the individual pictures can be gathered from the illustrations in van Berchem and Clouzot's *Mosaïques chrétiennes du IVme au Xme siècle*. Nevertheless, the mosaics of Ravenna, restored though they be, are sumptuous and glowing works of art, and in their design and colour, if not in the totality of their material, are true and glorious examples of Early Christian and Byzantine decoration.

The cathedral, known as the Ecclesia Ursiana from its foundation by Bishop Ursus, stands close to the baptistery but was totally transformed in the eighteenth century. It need be mentioned only to illustrate the splendour of Ravenna in its imperial days. Among its treasures was a magnificent silver altar and ciborium while the walls were richly clad with mosaics.

The so-called Mausoleum of Galla Placidia (*c.* 450) is a small cruciform building in brick, with a dome on a species of tentative pendentives over the crossing. Blind arcades decorate the exterior of the building and a low pointed roof covers the dome. The Mausoleum, which Galla Placidia is said to have built beside her splendid Church of the Holy Cross, is also known as SS. Nazario e Celso. The upper part of the interior is clad with mosaics of great loveliness. In the centre of the dome a cross gleams out from a rich blue sky studded with eight hundred golden stars, and apostles are set in pairs on the walls below it. The mosaic of Christ as the Good Shepherd is one of the most exquisite examples of Early Christian Art(51). Young, beardless and holding a cross, He is seated amidst a rocky, tree-clad landscape with His sheep gathered round about Him. One of them He strokes with His hand. The picture is alive with gracious sentiment, and the Christ is at the same time gentle and majestic. On the opposite arm of the cross there is a somewhat mysterious picture about which different theories have been held (25). It most probably represents S. Lawrence advancing to martyrdom. The historical and realistic style of this mosaic is in marked contrast to the idealistic and allegorical style of that of the Good Shepherd. Other mosaics and marble panelling cover the walls of the little oratory and make it a gem of varied and glowing colour. One notable feature is the repetition of the cross, which appears not only in the plan and dome but in the details of the mosaics. The emphasis on the symbolism of the cross at this early period is not without significance for the history of Christian architecture.

As has been already stated, Ravenna was occupied in 493 by Theodoric, who ruled there until his death in 526. His famous tomb, a massive rotunda in two stories, covered by a cupola made up of an enormous block of Istrian marble, stands at the end of a long avenue of trees in a peaceful garden outside the city walls.

With the advent of Theodoric Byzantine elements entered more thoroughly into Ravennate Art. The king had spent some of his early years at Constantinople, and, deeply impressed with the splendour of the imperial city, determined to make his own capital a treasure-house of art. "It will be your duty," he wrote to his architect, "to fulfil the lively desire which I feel to illustrate my reign with many new edifices. . . . And this is a service highly honourable and worthy of any man's ambition, to leave to future ages the monuments which shall be the admiration of new generations of men." He tells of a town where blocks and marble are said to be lying about unused. "Send these slabs of marble and columns by all means to Ravenna that they may be again made beautiful and take their place in a building there." Theodoric built a magnificent palace which was richly adorned with mosaics and set in a park with porticoes. It afterwards became the residence of the Exarchs. There is a brick building in one of the streets with niches—a mere façade—which used to be called "The Palace of Theodoric", but is now believed to be the remains of a guard-house built in the period of the Exarchate and connected with the Palace. It may be classified as a specimen of Byzantine secular architecture. Projecting pilasters emphasise the ends. In the upper story are arches on columns resting on a ledge with corbels. It has been suggested that this is a prototype of the arcades on corbel-tables which are so familiar a feature of Lombard architecture in later days.

50   RAVENNA, S. APOLLINARE NUOVO.
Mosaic: the Magi

51   RAVENNA, MAUSOLEUM OF GALLA PLACIDIA.
Mosaic: the Good Shepherd

52 RAVENNA, S. APOLLINARE NUOVO. Mosaic: Port of Classis

53 RAVENNA,
S. APOLLINARE
IN CLASSE:
Sarcophagus of
Archbishop
Theodore

Beside the scattered foundations of the Palace buildings stands the beautiful Church of S. Apollinare Nuovo, with its tall round tower. Of basilical plan, it was begun by Theodoric in 526 and has an apse altered in the Baroque period and a sixteenth-century portico, repaired after damage by a bomb in the First World War. It was originally the Arian Cathedral, the Goths adhering to the Arian heresy, which rejected the decision of the Council of Nicea on the nature of the Trinity. It was later dedicated to S. Martin and finally to S. Apollinaris, who is said to have been a Syrian from Antioch and a friend of S. Peter and who became the first bishop of Ravenna.

This beautiful church, with its precious marble columns and rich Byzantine capitals, is distinguished for its mosaics. Above the nave windows are twenty-six scenes from the life of Christ, many of which show strong Byzantine traits and bear comparison with the illuminations in Syrian manuscripts of the sixth century. Between the windows are figures of apostles, prophets and saints. Below them run friezes of a later date, thoroughly Byzantine in style and sentiment(50). On the one side a procession of saints issuing from the town of Ravenna advances with rhythmic movement towards Christ. On the other side virgin-saints, led by the Three Magi, move similarly towards the Virgin from Classis, the ancient seaport of Ravenna. The saints, clad mainly in white, are set against a golden background with palm-trees between them. The views of Ravenna and Classis are of great historical interest; that of the town is dominated in front by a view of the Palace of Theodoric, with four columns tied by arches supporting a pediment. The word Palatium appears on the entablature. The central portion is flanked by other arcades, hung with curtains which are a later addition. The domes and roofs of the edifices of Ravenna rise up behind. The picture of Classis, on the opposite wall, shows three ships in the harbour between two towers and the buildings of Classis are visible above a high wall to the right(52).

It may be worth while to mention an interesting detail of restoration. As has been said, the virgins are led by the Magi, who advance towards the Virgin and Child seated on a throne flanked by angels. The heads of the Magi were given crowns in a restoration by Kibel in 1853, but in 1899 Ricci replaced the crowns by the original Phrygian caps(50). Other parts of the mosaics have also undergone restoration. The church contains a marble ambo carved with geometrical designs of a typical Byzantine pattern.

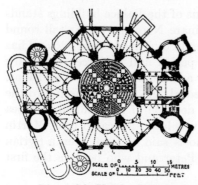

The Arian Baptistery (S. Maria in Cosmedin) is an octagon of the Ostrogothic period. The mosaics are an inferior reproduction of those in the Orthodox Baptistery and more hieratic in style.

The famous and beautiful Church of S. Vitale (56), begun about 526, is an octagon consisting of a domed central space surrounded by a galleried ambulatory (55). According to the chronicler Agnellus, it was founded by the Archbishop Ecclesius, who was so impressed by the splendour of the churches in Constantinople that he determined to rival them in Ravenna as far as he might. So he brought from the East Julianus Argentarius, Julian the silversmith, to aid him in his ambition. The church was consecrated by Archbishop Maximian in 547. It has a projecting apse and choir and a narthex set obliquely across one of the angles of the octagon. Some authorities maintain that this narthex is not original and that the original narthex faced the apse, as set out in Fig. 54. The dome is supported by means of squinches on eight piers between which, except on the east, arched columns form semicircular exedrae. The plan of the church is admirable. The wide central space opens out serenely into the exedrae with their double range of arcades; from the ambulatory beautiful vistas extend into the deep choir, revealing the irregular perspective of the columns and the interplay of the curving arches: the slender columns of the exedrae contrast with the massive piers, while the open arches of the church below contrast with the solid appearance of the dome, lightly constructed though that be.

But if the plan of S. Vitale be admirably wrought out, how much is its glory enhanced by the sumptuous beauty of its columns and its walls! The gleaming marble columns are crowned with capitals which stand in the highest rank of Byzantine sculptured ornament. Deeply undercut and surmounted by the typical Byzantine pulvinos they include the Corinthian and grooved types as well as a trapezoidal form, with borders of plaited bands enclosing a lotus design.

The choir and apse are superbly enriched with mosaics supposed

54 Plan of S. Vitale, Ravenna

55 RAVENNA, S. VITALE:
Facing the Choir

56 RAVENNA: S. Vitale

57   ROME, S. AGNES: Apse Mosaic

58   RAVENNA, S. VITALE: Abraham Mosaic

to date in the choir from about 530 and in the apse from twenty years later. In the vault of the choir four angels sustain a medallion containing the Lamb. The walls portray Old Testament incidents allegorising the sacrifice of Christ and the Sacrament of Communion, appropriately set in the area where the altar stands. In the lunette on the left wall two incidents from Genesis are portrayed. The first is that narrated in the eighteenth chapter when three angels are described as visiting Abraham in Mamre (58). They are seated behind a table upon which are set the cakes representing those made by Sarah of three measures of fine meal. The repast, as Scripture narrates, takes place under a tree; Sarah stands at the door of the "tent" and Abraham advances towards the table with a plate of veal, "the calf tender and good". The second scene (58) is the Sacrifice of Isaac (Genesis, Chapter XXII). Abraham stands on "one of the mountains of Morah" brandishing the knife; Isaac is bound on the altar and below Abraham is to be seen the ram.

Above the lunette float two angels bearing a medallion with the cross. At the sides are Jeremiah holding a scroll, and Moses receiving the roll of the Law from the hand of God, with a group of Israelites at the foot of the rocky mountain.

It is unnecessary to enter into a similarly detailed description of the lunette on the opposite wall, which contains the sacrifices of Abel and Melchizedek, while in the spandrels are to be seen Isaiah and scenes from the life of Moses.

It may be mentioned that the mosaics in concentrating on the Eucharist anticipate the purpose of Byzantine decoration in the tenth century (see Chapter IV). By their rich colour and sumptuous spirit they are in line with Byzantine sentiment, but in some respects they carry on the classical tradition. Purely Byzantine are the two famous mosaics of Justinian and Theodora and their attendants on the apse walls. One panel displays Justinian clad in a purple robe with Archbishop Maximian, two attendants and a guard of soldiers (4). On the opposite panel Theodora, the Empress of Justinian, is represented with two courtiers and seven ladies of her suite. She holds a vase and is richly clad in bejewelled robes. A fountain is represented on the left, the fountain where the faithful purify themselves by washing their hands before entering the church.

In these two mosaics the frontal pose is adopted for the personages, who gaze out of the picture with solemn expressionless faces;

their robes fall from their shoulders in stiff folds covering their bodies without revealing their shape. Yet with their sumptuous ornament and glowing colour they form a pattern of rich beauty and express in their solemn dignity the hieratic grandeur of the Byzantine Court. Their characteristics are typical of the imperial art of the capital.

In the conch of the apse, the youthful and serene Christ is seated on a globe. He is flanked by two angels, beyond whom are S. Vitalis, who receives the wreath of glory from Christ, and Archbishop Ecclesius, who gives Him the domed and octagonal model of the church. Below them all, flowers and peacocks and the four rivers signify the location as Paradise. The mosaic, especially in the figure of Christ, retains much of the classical spirit.

The lonely Basilica of S. Apollinare in Classe (c. 536–550) is the only remaining monument of a town which once was a busy and flourishing port (59). Classis had long before been established by the Emperor Augustus as headquarters of his Adriatic fleet. When Ravenna was the capital many ships unloaded their cargoes on the quays of Classis and many merchants from Syria and Byzantium thronged its streets. After its destruction by the Lombards it was never rebuilt, and, as the silt from the River Po accumulated with the passage of the years, the sea receded and gave place to a long and marshy plain. As the traveller drives across the great solitude all that reminds him of Classis is the abandoned church and its tall round tower, prominent from afar in the vast expanse of level land.

S. Apollinare in Classe, despoiled though it was of its marble to enrich the Cathedral of Rimini in the fifteenth century, remains one of the most strangely fascinating churches in Europe (60). Old and vast and solitary, with its round tower rising isolated beside its apse it is the noblest Early Christian basilica in the world. Byzantine influence is manifest in the polygonal form of the apse exterior, in the mosaics of the apse and of the triumphal arch, in the exterior arcades and in the wind-blown acanthus capitals of the nave with their imposts. The round tower and side-apses are later additions. The great mosaic in the conch of the apse is a remarkable composition, springing from theological symbolic thought rather than from artistic impulse (60). A great cross within a circle stands out from a background of stars. It is flanked by figures of Moses and Elijah, while three sheep gaze upwards from below. This is obviously a semi-symbolic representation of

94

the Transfiguration. S. Apollinaris with outstretched arms stands below with twelve sheep in a landscape of trees and flowers representing Paradise. There seems to be a mystical connection between the two scenes, the idea of the supramundane permeating them both. On the triumphal arch sheep move from Bethlehem and Jerusalem towards a medallion of Christ.

Some fine marble sarcophagi, dating from the sixth to the eighth centuries, line the walls of the deserted aisles. They include that of the Archbishop Theodore, with its affronted peacocks, its gracefully enwreathed branches of the vine and its birds pecking at bunches of grapes(53). The design is of a nature which infiltrated Ravennate Art from the East. Some of the exarchs who ruled in the name of the Emperor at Ravenna from the sixth to the eighth century were of Syrian origin, and an Armenian regiment was stationed in the city.

Oriental style and sentiment are nowhere more clearly visible than in the so-called Chair of Maximian in the sacristy of the cathedral; the most notable example in existence of Byzantine carving in ivory (48). Its sculptured plaques are enclosed in bands of foliage where lions, deer and peacocks play. The chair is made of wood covered with ivory panels, and the figures in front represent John the Baptist and four Apostles. It is now believed that the chair did not come to Ravenna until the year 1001, when it was presented by the Doge of Venice to the Emperor Otto III.

The Church of S. Agnes also reveals Eastern influence in its architecture, the galleries over the aisles copying those of the Hellenistic basilica, where the Roman type had a clerestory. Ravenna is full of Byzantine work, but it is not possible to do more than mention the capitals of S. John the Evangelist, the museum and the mosaics in the Archiepiscopal Chapel.

MILAN

Milan, always a centre of great importance in northern Italy, possesses in S. Lorenzo a church whose "framework" is said by Dr. Corrado Ricci to be Byzantine. A church was consecrated on the site by the celebrated S. Ambrose in the latter part of the fourth century, but it has been damaged and renovated many times, and there are various conflicting theories about the nature of the original plan and the extent of the alterations. Recent researches by Italian scholars suggest that the building was a very early example of the domed square type. In 1573 the dome

95

collapsed with a portion of the walls and the interior was then remodelled by the Renaissance architect Martino Bassi. The outside shows a square with an apse on each side, while the dome is supported on an octagon of eight piers inside. From the main sides of this octagon two-storied exedrae project into the ambulatory. Strzygowski, who dates S. Lorenzo to the ninth century, derives its plan from the Armenian quartrefoiled square, but others give the existing ground-plan with its exedrae a sixth-century date and connect it with S. Vitale, Ravenna. A chapel of the church contains a fine mosaic of the young and beardless Christ in the midst of His Apostles, which has been dated to the fourth century.

NAPLES

By reason of its antiquity, its system of construction and the beauty of its mosaics the Baptistery of Naples occupies an important place among the Early Christian monuments of Italy. It is entered from the ancient but restored Church of S. Restituta, which in its turn is contiguous to the medieval Cathedral of S. Januarius. It dates from the second half of the fifth century and consists of a square covered by a dome on broad squinches (6). Even in their fragmentary state the mosaics of the roof make a profound appeal by their quiet richness and charm.

The prevailing colour of the background is a deep soft blue, whence amid a galaxy of stars shines out the monogrammatic cross. A border of palm leaves, fruit and foliage with peacocks, pheasants and other birds encircles this central space. Farther down the dome there were pictures in mosaic from the life of Christ, separated by strips which contained fruits, flowers and birds springing from a vase. One of these pictures shows Christ, bearded and haloed, standing on a globe, giving the roll of the Law to S. Peter. The figure of S. Paul on the other side of the same compartment has now almost disappeared. In the squinches the winged symbols of the evangelists are represented and it is of especial interest to find the evangelists in the squinches at this early date. As has already been pointed out, the pendentives (or squinches) became the normal location for pictures of the evangelists in a Byzantine church. The ox of S. Luke and the eagle of S. John have disappeared, but the lion of S. Mark (6) and the angel of S. Matthew are well preserved. Above the last a shepherd stands to receive two stags who drink at the river of life. "As the hart panteth after the water books, so panteth my soul after Thee, O God" (Psalm XLII, 1).

Syrian influences have affected these mosaics, which have also pronounced classical traits, while there are striking analogies to be found between them and the mosaics of Ravenna. They are also a particularly interesting combination of representational and non-representational art.

ROME

In concluding this chapter it may be well to mention briefly some of the Byzantine mosaics and frescoes which adorn churches in Rome. It serves to show how profoundly, during the seventh century, Rome was permeated with Oriental influence, when numerous Greeks, Syrians and Armenians dwelt in the Eternal City. The representative of the Emperor ruled from his palace on the Palatine hill, and many of his numerous officials were immigrants from the shores of the Bosphorus. Monasteries were founded in Rome by refugees from those parts of the Eastern Empire which had succumbed to Moslem domination and merchants from Asia supplied the papal court with the precious products of the East. Between the years 606 and 741 no less than thirteen of the popes themselves were of Greek or Syrian origin. A large colony of Greeks dwelt in the neighbourhood of the ancient Basilica of S. Maria in Cosmedin beside the little circular temple on the bank of the Tiber. It gave the name of Ripa Graeca, the Greek bank, to the area, and the basilica itself, reconstructed by Pope Adrian I in the eighth century, was known until a further reconstruction in the twelfth century as S. Maria in Schola Graeca. All these factors contributed to the popularity of Greek customs, manners and language, and a further impetus was given to the movement in the eighth century when numerous priests and monks fled to Rome from the Iconoclastic persecution in Constantinople.

In these circumstances Byzantine and Oriental elements found an easy entrance into the art of Rome, as the mosaics of the churches at once attest. The figure of S. Agnes (seventh century) in the church of the same name is clad in the robes of a Byzantine empress (57). Strings of pearls hang down from her crown on either side, and her imperial stole falling from her shoulders is ornamented in gold and green.

In the Oratory of S. Venanzio, which is attached to the Baptistery of the Lateran and which was decorated by Pope John IV

(640–642), there is to be seen the bust of Christ Pantocrator set amid blue and red clouds and bestowing His benediction in the Greek manner. The Virgin in the same oratory wears a Syrian veil and is accompanied by saints wearing the costumes of Byzantine dignitaries. In the Church of S. Maria in Domnica, pleasantly situated beside the gardens of the Coelian Hill and overlooking the massive rotunda of S. Stephen, the Madonna occupies the central place. With solemn mien she is seated on a typical Byzantine throne and is attended by angels, great numbers of whom are suggested by a crowd of receding haloes. The Christ-child on her lap gives the Greek benediction. This mosaic was the work of Pope Pascal I (817), who is seen kneeling before the Virgin.

The mosaic in the Church of SS. Nereus and Achilles on the broad highway near the gaunt ruins of the Baths of Caracalla is the work of Pope Leo III (795–816). Poor in quality, it depicts the Transfiguration, a subject commoner in Eastern than in Western art. The attitudes of the prostrate disciples are quite Byzantine.

In the important Church of S. Praxede, Pope Pascal I built an Oratory of S. Zeno, which, like the church itself, he decorated with mosaics. The oratory, square in plan, is covered with a dome the decoration of which bears a striking resemblance to that on the roof of the Archiepiscopal Chapel at Ravenna. Four angels support a central medallion with the bust of Christ.

Most noteworthy of all were the mosaics of the Oratory erected by Pope John VII at Old S. Peter's in the spot where the Holy Door now stands. Built in 705, it was destroyed in 1606, seven fragments of its mosaics being dispersed throughout Italy. The imposing Virgin, clad in the bejewelled raiment of a Byzantine empress, is in S. Mark, Florence. Her shoes are red, and a clasp of rubies is fastened on each shoulder. Most beautiful is the lovely fragment from the Adoration of the Magi—which now rests in the sacristy of S. Maria in Cosmedin at Rome: like some other scenes, it may be of later date than the earliest mosaics of the Oratory of Pope John.

The little round Church of S. Theodore (seventh century) which nestles forlorn beneath the slopes of the Palatine has a mosaic of Christ between saints, one of whom is Theodore, very popular in the East.

No less significant than the mosaics are the frescoes of the ruined Basilica of S. Maria Antica in the Roman Forum. Among the frescoes of the atrium are two of S. Agnese and S. Cecilia clad in Eastern garb. Among those on the lower part of the aisle walls are Eastern saints with their designations in Greek characters. A crucifixion in the left apse belongs to the sixth century and recalls the type in a Syriac Gospel now in Florence. The central apse, twice decorated already, was covered by Pope John VII in the eighth century with a third layer of paintings completely in accord with the Byzantine tradition. Thus the faded images of these saints who gaze down so strangely upon the centre of life in ancient Rome, where the fluted columns of pagan temples soar among the ruins, recall the triumph of the new Rome on the Bosphorus, and the potency of its dominion. Along with the mosaics they indicate how great an influence the art and culture of the East exercised upon Rome from the late sixth to the early ninth century, an influence so profound that for a considerable period of time the art of the Eastern city was to a very great extent transplanted to Italian soil.

Finally, there must be mentioned the famous wooden doors in the Church of S. Sabina, carved in the sixth century and depicting scenes from the life of Christ and the Old Testament. Dalton brings forward strong evidence for their Byzantine origin.

CHAPTER VI

Asia Minor

GEOGRAPHICAL BACKGROUND

THE peninsula of Asia Minor or Anatolia consists of a central plateau separated by a series of lofty mountain ranges from the coast lands which fringe the Mediterranean and Euxine Seas. The ranges on the north and south of the plateau are difficult to cross, but those which face the west are penetrated by spacious valleys up whose inclinations the traveller could penetrate with comparative ease to the interior. It has therefore been from east to west that the channel lay along which the stream of commerce and migration flowed. Anatolia was an arena where East and West contended, and a meeting-place of influence from both directions. It is therefore not surprising that it occupies a highly important position in the history of Byzantine Architecture and Art. The stream of influence scarcely ever ceased to flow. Even when, with terrible regularity the Arabs raided the fields of the province year by year, intercourse between Constantinople and Baghdad continued to subsist. The Orient was always bringing the force of its art and thought to bear upon Byzantium: when the Seljouk Turks had conquered a part of Anatolia they fostered culture and built universities in their realm, and the intellectual contact between East and West endured.

The configuration of Asia Minor caused the civilisation of the coast-lands to differ widely from that of the lofty interior. The climate and vegetation of the plateau were related to those of districts which lay farther to the east, and during long periods of its history from early days it had been a ready receptacle for Oriental modes of thought and expression. It consists of long stretches of rolling plains, intersected by slowly moving streams, some of which evaporate in the salt lakes of the marshlands. Desolate as much of it may be, there is evidence to show that it once was fertile and populous. Rich cities occupied places which now are barren. Great engineering works had been constructed and artificial streams irrigated the soil. For many centuries the interior of Anatolia provided the capital with a large measure of

59, 60 Ravenna: S. Apollinare in Classe

61 CYPRUS: Peristerona

62 CYPRUS: S. Barnabas, Salamis

its subsistence and was a vital part of the Byzantine Empire. Yet there was a great difference between the lofty uplands and the lower regions of the coast from which they were divided by their mountain-walls. The coastal districts partake more of the nature of southern Europe, and the seaports on the indented bays of the Aegean coast looked towards the West. In the immediate hinterland a number of broad and luxuriant valleys provided with a rich abundance the finest products of the soil.

In the Hellenistic age and in the early centuries of the Roman Empire the coast-lands of Asia Minor were famed for their grand and prosperous cities—Pergamum, Philadelphia, Sardes, Magnesia and the rest, Ephesus supreme among them all. With their long regular streets, their marble temples, their stadia, their schools of learning, their busy markets, they attracted a multitude of inhabitants and within them Western and Eastern influences had every opportunity to mingle.

HISTORICAL SKETCH

Until the middle of the seventh century the province enjoyed much peace and prosperity. Nevertheless a certain amount of decay had set in and Finlay says that "the Greek cities" in the coast-lands "were still numerous and wealthy", but that "oppression and neglect had already destroyed the trade of the internal provinces". In 651 there began a series of Arab invasions which continued for close upon four hundred years and brought misfortune and devastation to the land. But the Arabs came and passed away, and while the miseries they inflicted were terrible, the compact Byzantine society proved capable of maintaining its position. One result of these raids was the construction of strongholds upon mountain summits which formed a safe retreat for the threatened population. The Arabs were succeeded by a more formidable enemy, the Seljouk Turks, who actually established their authority over almost the entire land in the short space of a decade. Nicea, the city of the Christian Councils, and Konia, the ancient Iconium, became the successive capitals of the Seljouk Sultanate of Roum. The Seljouks fell into a state of disunion, but the Ottomans, consolidating the Turkish position, finally achieved the conquest of Anatolia.

As a result of the missionary activities of S. Paul, Christianity had taken root in Asia Minor at an early date. As time went on the visible evidences of religion began to abound. Churches were erected in the towns and villages. Monasticism struck deep into the soil, and the innumerable monasteries which were scattered throughout the whole peninsula attracted thousands of devotees to their precincts. The monks wielded a great influence among the populace, and, as has already been stated, played no little part in the Iconoclastic controversy as the fervent defenders of images. Sometimes the monasteries and churches were erected on the summits of the fortified hill-tops and were dedicated to the saints who had lent their supernatural aid to keep the Empire's enemies at bay.

ARCHITECTURAL SITES AND PLANS

The largest group of churches in Anatolia is to be found at Bin-bir-Kilissé, "the remains of a typical provincial town of the early Byzantine age", situated high on the Kara Dagh, "the Black Mountain" in Lycaonia. Its Turkish name of Bin-bir-Kilissé, the "Thousand and One Churches", indicates how numerous the churches were whose ruins occupy the site. For long abandoned and visited by few Western travellers, they were exhaustively studied and described by Sir William Ramsay and Miss Gertrude Lowthian Bell. The churches were set in the middle of enclosures which contained subsidiary buildings and were the centres of social life. Well over thirty of them were found in a more or less ruined condition, though some of them were in a remarkable state of preservation. Their date is uncertain but they belong to two periods, one dating from the sixth century till the Arab invasions, and the other from the middle of the ninth to the eleventh centuries, when the Arab invasions were not so harassing. It seems likely that the churches of the later period followed the plan and design of those of earlier date.

The whole of the Black Mountain had a sacred character and its peaks and declivities abounded in sanctuaries and monastic habitations, while other hilly regions of Lycaonia possessed a like abundance of religious buildings. The churches were built of stone and show a great variety of plan, and while each area had certain peculiarities it may be noted that the horseshoe form of arch prevailed in the doors, arcades and the ground-plan of the apse: the apses show several sides of a polygon externally; windows are round-headed; the outside walls are plain but projecting mouldings of a simple nature run along them. A remarkable series of churches exists in Cappadocia hewn out of the solid rock and adorned with

102

frescoes of crude design but compelling interest. At the other extreme from these remote and rock-cut chapels are the excavated foundations of large and splendid churches which stood in the wealthy city of Ephesus from an early period in the Byzantine Empire. From the opulent cities of the luxuriant coasts to the remote fastnesses of the interior plateau, from the early centuries of the Christian faith to the final Mohammedan invasion, Christian architecture flourished with remarkable vigour within the whole of that wide Anatolian peninsula, which for generations was so essential and important a possession of the Byzantine Empire. The churches exhibit a wide variety of plan. Among the dispersed sites there are to be found the simple oblong type with the apsed eastern end, the basilica, the "three-naved hall church", the domed basilica and the cross-domed basilica. There are octagons, like one at Soasa, and other varieties of polygon. There were round churches, like one which was seen at Nicea as early as the fourth century. Probably it was derived from Constantine's Church of the Holy Sepulchre at Jerusalem whose fame and sanctity led to the widespread popularity of the rotunda. Two circular martyria at Pergamum may be mentioned which are at least as early as the fourth century. The plan of one of them strongly resembles the Pantheon at Rome, and the rotunda discovered at the Myrelaion, Constantinople. Many of these central-planned churches were "martyria" hallowed by the relics of the saints, for the cult of the martyrs took early possession of Christian thought. Some of them in earlier days were crowned with domes of timber, and the domes, as has been pointed out in a previous chapter, had a cosmic and symbolical significance. The union of the square-planned domed martyrion church and the basilical congregational church would lead to the domed basilica.

THE CHURCHES OF ASIA MINOR

In a summary of the ecclesiastical remains of Anatolia it is well to commence with a church which, for the combined reasons of construction and date, has long been considered one of the most important monuments in the history of Byzantine Architecture. It is the Church of Khodja Kalessi, built before A.D. 451, which stands high on the slopes of the Colycadnus Valley in Cilicia beside a ruined monastery (63). Well built of squared stone, it consists of a nave terminating in an apse and of two aisles with

galleries. The apse is enclosed on the outside by a straight wall
and is flanked by two chambers. Between the second bay of the
nave from the west and the space before the apse there is an area
surmounted by a tower. It is disputed whether this tower was
covered by a dome—in which case the church was a domed

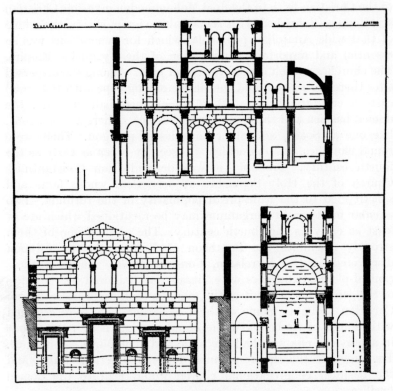

63   Khodja Kalessi: longitudinal and horizontal sections
and western elevation

basilica—or by a wooden roof. The intention seems to have been
to construct a dome as there were squinches in the angles of the
tower. These squinches, which have little colonnettes on brackets,
bring the oblong plan of the tower to an octagon, suitable for a
dome. In any case Khodja Kalessi marks an advance on the
basilica, with the latter's regular line of columns and nave vaulted
at the same level throughout its length. The same type is exemplified in the fragmentary ruins of a fifth-century church at

Yürmé in Galatia. The domed basilica of S. Nicholas at Myra originally had a dome upon pendentives, but in 1862 it was replaced with a cross-vault by the Russians under Salzmann. A considerable amount of restoration was then carried out, though the intended work was never completed. The church is of uncertain date but was probably completely restored after 1042, Myra having been destroyed by the Moslems a few years before that date. The plan is somewhat complicated and irregular. The aisles, which had galleries, are raised higher than those at Khodja Kalessi, so as better to counteract the thrust of the dome. The basilical plan is much shortened towards the west, as the central space is almost immediately preceded by the narthex: the exonarthex is modern. Along the south side there runs an external aisle which contains the reputed tomb of S. Nicholas.

There was also a domed basilica at Meriamlik some miles to the south of Seleukia in Cilicia. Meriamlik was a famous place of pilgrimage for its magnificent fifth-century basilica of S. Thekla. The domed basilica, though smaller in dimensions, is of greater architectural interest. The atrium, which is as large as the church itself, has a western apse, while the church has a narrow narthex. The church was in two bays separated by columns and piers from aisles furnished with galleries. The eastern bay was covered with a dome, and an apse, polygonal in plan outside, terminated the building. This domed basilica of Meriamlik seems to be of fifth-century date and may have been the church built by the Emperor Zeno in A.D. 470. The fragments of mosaic pavements, richly carved friezes and Byzantine Corinthian capitals show it to have been a beautifully adorned sanctuary.

In the midst of the ruins of Ephesus there have been discovered the scanty fragments and foundations of some ancient Christian edifices, of which the most notable is the famous "Double Church"(64). Four building periods have been distinguished in its history. There was first an antique structure of great length with pillars. Secondly, a basilical church of much shorter plan was substituted for the eastern part of this ancient building, the western part being transformed into an atrium; it was within this basilica that the famous Oecumenical Council met in A.D. 431, the "Council of Ephesus". Thirdly, a brick cross-domed basilica of still shorter dimensions took the place of this basilica. Fourthly, after the decay of the cross-domed basilica, a small basilica was built to the east of it, the apse of the basilica of the second period being used as the apse of this basilica of the fourth period. To the north of the atrium there was a domed polygonal baptistery.

It is quite possible that Ephesus may have been the birthplace of the domed and cross-domed basilical plan and that it may have been carried thence to Constantinople. Tralles and Miletus, the cities to which the architects of Santa Sophia belonged, lay at no great distance from Ephesus. As far as the origin of the ground-plan of the cross-domed basilica is concerned, it is possible that some influence may have been exercised upon it by the plans of the halls in the great baths which were so prominent a feature of Ephesus and the other cities of the Anatolian littoral (cf. p. 76).

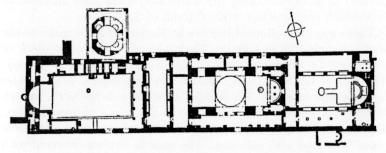

64   Plan of the so-called "Double Church" at Ephesus

So rich and populous a city as Ephesus must have contained many splendid churches after the recognition of Christianity by the state and its firm establishment in the Empire. Among them there was one which was dedicated to S. John and which is mentioned by Procopius. It replaced a former church which had contained the relics of S. John and which was "small and ruinous with age". The new church was of such magnitude and beauty that it rivalled the imperial Church of the Apostles at Constantinople. In succeeding generations it was venerated as a shrine of great sanctity, and achieved a fame which was comparable to that of the Temple of Diana in antiquity. Another church was dedicated to the "Seven Sleepers of Ephesus".

The cross-domed basilica developed out of the domed basilica in order to provide a better abutment for the dome. In the cross-domed basilica of S. Clement at Ancyra—the modern Ankara, the capital of Turkey—short barrel-vaults are employed in place of arches on the north and south of the dome. The church, which

106

has suffered considerable damage since it was seen by the French architect Texier in the middle of the nineteenth century, had barrel-vaulted aisles and was built of brick. The dome is supported by squinches(19). Its date is between the fifth and seventh centuries.

The eighth-century Church of the Koimesis (Dormition of the Virgin) at Nicea corresponded closely with that of S. Clement at Ancyra. The dome rested on four great piers tied to the walls of the nave and bema. The narthex was adorned by a series of flat blind niches. The church had undergone considerable restoration in the course of its long life before it was completely destroyed by the Turks after the Greco-Turkish War of 1922. It contained some mosaics of great beauty, those of the narthex being of eleventh-century date and those in the apse of an earlier period. Worthy of special note was a half-length figure of the Virgin in the tympanum of the narthex door. Wearing a violet mantle edged with gold, and stretching out her arms as an orans, she wore an expression of tender and simple gravity.

The cross-domed basilica of Cassaba or Dere-Ahsy(65), which may belong to the eighth century, was described by the travellers Spratt and Forbes in 1847 as "a large Christian Cathedral of early Byzantine Architecture, one of the most interesting and picturesque as well as best-preserved ruins in Lycia". The dome, now completely destroyed, rested on pendentives. The aisles had two stories and are separated from the nave by arcades which run right along the sides of the central space. Here again the basilical plan is shortened between central area and narthex. The narthex is flanked by towers with staircases, a feature which betokens Syrian influence. On the other hand, niches in the chambers before the side-apses, and cross-vaults in the aisles, point to a connection with Constantinople.

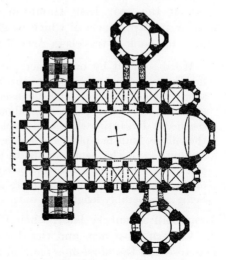

65   Dere-Ahsy, Asia Minor

107

There are still a number of *cruciform* churches to be found on the soil of Asia Minor. The cruciform plan early became popular throughout the Christian world owing to the symbolism which its shape afforded. An inscription of the year 382 on the Church of the Apostles at Milan in Italy states, in reference to the cruciform shape of the building how "the sacred triumphal emblem marks the place". If these sentiments occurred in the West, they would appeal with even stronger intensity to the mind of the Oriental Christian who was always ready to grasp every opportunity of symbolising the truths of religion. The domed cruciform plan was a simple development of the domed square and was a suitable form for memorial chapels. Once employed, its symbolical significance assured its widespread and enduring popularity in the East. There is a witness to its prevalence in a letter from S. Gregory of Nyssa to S. Amphilochius, Bishop of Iconium, in which the writer assumes the familiarity of Amphilochius with the cruciform church. He is writing about a church which is to be a combination of the octagonal and cruciform plans. The whole building was to be vaulted in stone because the place supplied no timber for roofing, and masons were to be sent who were skilled in making vaults without supports. Some people in his place contract "to furnish thirty workmen for a stater for the dressed stonework with a specified ration along with the stater". The letter dates from the fourth century.

About the year 1840 Hamilton saw a cruciform church at Göreme in Cappadocia of which he gave this picturesque description in his book of travels in Asia Minor.

> We descended by our former path to near the "gaila" above-mentioned, when striking off to the west, we descended a steep and sandy ravine of pumice stone and ashes to visit some ancient remains at Gerameh. After proceeding about a mile in this direction we reached a Byzantine church in ruins standing by itself away from the village, built in a plain and severe style and constructed of brown trachyte. . . . The bema was quite perfect, as well as parts of the sides, and the arches which supported the central dome. The length of the whole building was not more than forty feet, the Greek cross being considerably lengthened out.

About half a century later, when Rott visited the church, only the western cross arm and the dome-arches remained standing. The apse had the horseshoe plan on the inside and was five-sided externally. The windows were round-headed and a strongly projecting moulding ran along the walls. Rott considered the church to have been originally a basilica.

Considerable alterations have taken place in the Church of the Forty Martyrs at Skupi, east of Kaisarieh, which has the plan of a Latin cross. In this church and also in that of the Virgin at Tomarza shallow pilasters are attached to the exterior of the side-walls and to the angles of the apse. Both churches have been assigned to the fifth century, and had domes supported on corbels. Ramsay and Bell thought that the pendentive does not appear to have been employed on the Anatolian plateau until the eighth or ninth century, before that date the corbel or the squinch being employed. Mr. Gough, however, has recently discovered what appears to be a fourth-century pendentive at Augusta in Cilicia. At Busluk-Ferek there is also a church of cruciform plan. All these three cruciforms are in Cappadocia, are built of stone and were adorned with frescoes of which some traces still survive. There were some cruciform chapels at Bin-bir-Kilissé, the ruined city in Lycaonia mentioned in a previous paragraph. One of them, called No. 37 by Ramsay and Bell, is attested by an inscription to have been a memorial chapel, the sepulchre of one Paul, whose house adjoined it. It is a small Latin cross, the eastern arm consisting of a round stilted apse. The centre was covered with a small dome and the arms, like those of other churches in Bin-bir-Kilissé, with barrel-vaults. Then there is the church known as No. 44, a little once-domed chapel in the form of a Greek cross attached to a monastery at Deghile, the place high on the mountain whither the inhabitants of Bin-bir-Kilissé retreated during the worst period of Arab invasion. There are also the ruins of a domed cruciform church and chapel attached to a monastery on the very summit of Mahaletch, the highest peak of the "Black Mountain", on whose lower slopes the ruins of Bin-bir-Kilissé lie scattered. They follow the familiar plan where the eastern arm of the cross is equivalent to the stilted round apse.

Of more remarkable plan is the so-called Octagon at Bin-bir-Kilissé, which is a cross, as it were, superimposed upon an octagon, the eastern arm of the cross terminating in a polygonal apse. It was a small building, each arm of the cross being only about ten feet long, but was well built of squared stone with a dome and frescoed interior. The plan may be compared with that of the church described in the letter of S. Gregory of Nyssa to S. Amphilochius cited above.

In some cruciforms the barrel-vaults which spring from the central dome are curtailed to the breadth of arches, as in the Church of the Archangels at Syge in Bithynia and that of S. Stephen on the island of Nis. Choisy cited specimens at Philadelphia and Sardis which were of early date and appear to have been of the same type. The curious Church of Utschajak in Galatia, which is built of brick, consists of two square rooms, each covered by a dome on a high drum resting on massive arches engaged in the walls. All these may be classified as "domed squares".

In some of the cruciform churches of Asia Minor, one or more of the angle-spaces is filled up to form a part of the interior: in other words, the terminating walls of two adjacent cross-arms are prolonged until they meet, to enclose an additional space. When, however, in such a type of plan, all the four angle-spaces are filled up, it must be distinguished from that which is known as the cross-in-square. In the cross-in-square type, the vaults and outside walls of the angle-chambers are a constructive necessity for the support of the edifice as a whole: in the simple cruciform plan, any angle-chambers are an addition which could have been dispensed with. The cruciform plan with completed angle-spaces is, however, of great significance because, if the theory that the cross-in-square developed out of the cruciform be correct, it forms a transition stage between these two. The matter has already been dealt with in the fourth chapter of this book, but, as Anatolia shows important indications of the development, it is well to mention it again even at the cost of repetition.

First, one angle-space would be completed: then the openings between this angle-compartment and the rest of the church would be so widened and heightened that it became constructively an essential part of the edifice: a similar development would take place with regard to the other angle-spaces; finally the portions of walling at the angles of the dome-area are reduced to the dimensions of piers or columns, and the cross-in-square plan is definitely achieved. It is of course impossible to trace a development chronologically from extant buildings, as they are of late or uncertain date, but they at least show how the development could easily have proceeded at an earlier time.

At Sivri Hissar, near Gelvere, there stands a church called Kizil Kilisse or the "Red Church" (66) which has its north-west angle-space completed. Though ruined, it is in a remarkably good state of preservation and its squared masonry is of excellent quality. The vaulted angle-compartment, which was contemporary with the remainder of the church, opens widely into the north arm of the cross, and is separated from the western arm by an arcade of three horseshoe arches. The horseshoe shape appears also in the apse and in the windows. The dome is supported by means of corbels upon an octagonal drum, the masonry being set back over the sides: and the drum was carried on the central arches by means of squinches. Ainsworth, about 1840, described his visit to the church:

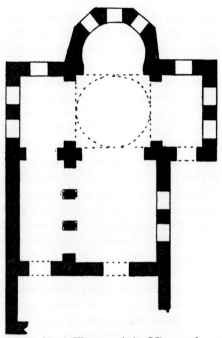

66　Sivri Hissar, Asia Minor: the "Red Church"

The ascent over the next low range of hills brought us to another of these secluded and rocky spots, but what surprised us not a little was a rather elegantly built Greek church standing in its centre, with no habitations near it, and gradually falling into ruins. So regular and handsome an edifice, isolated in the midst of savage scenery, naturally interested our feelings very much.

This church at Sivri Hissar differs from the cross-in-square plan in several respects. The north-west compartment is more in the nature of an aisle separated from an oblong nave by an arcade: the apse follows directly on the crossing, leaving no room for proper angle-compartments at the eastern end. The point, however, is that it does show an angle-space completed and this reveals how the transition of a cruciform into a cross-in-square could have arisen earlier in the mind of the Byzantine builders. The much-ruined Church of Tchukurken (also in Cappadocia) presents much the same features in its plan: the apse, however, is rounded on the outside and the vault of the angle-compartment is as high as that of the nave. The horseshoe form of the arch prevailed throughout. A small memorial chapel beside the basilica of Aladja Jaila in Lycia has all the four angle-spaces filled up: it has been dated by its ornament to the fifth century. The angle-chambers at the cruciform church at Ak Kale on the Cilician coast were also filled up, and their condition furnished Miss Bell with the interesting and significant comment that "indeed, though at Ak Kale they have all fallen, the essential parts of the building remain standing". The Church of S. Eustathios at Miram near Konia (69) has its western angle-spaces completed: so wide are the openings to the cross-arms that the L-shaped portions of the walls supporting the dome have been reduced almost to the proportion of piers. The larger of the two churches on Mahaletch already mentioned had its western angle-spaces filled up. These angle-compartments are in no way necessities from a constructive point of view: they are separated from the western arm of the cross by a solid wall, and they were entered by doors leading from a narthex on the west.

Many *cross-in-square* churches existed in Anatolia. A large number of them were hewn out of the solid rock and of those which stood above ground some perhaps have perished. The dates of their erection are most uncertain, though some of them may go back to the eighth or ninth centuries. Late dates have indeed been assumed for all of them on the ground of the general destruction wrought by recurrent Arab invasions. Yet it is not safe, for that reason alone, to refuse an earlier date to any of them. Moreover, when rebuilding took place the former plan may well have been followed: the walls were built of stone and the vaults were likewise of stone; they could not suffer like the structure with a wooden roof from fire, and destruction might only be partial. For these reasons it is unwise to be dogmatic about lateness of date.

Many of the cross-in-square churches, nevertheless, are in a sadly ruinous state, like those on Tchet-Dagh (near Bin-bir-Kilissé) on Ali Summasi Dagh (Ala Kilissé) and in Bin-bir-Kilissé itself: they were of simple cross-in-square plan, built of squared stone with four strong central piers supporting the dome and with apse of semicircular or horseshoe plan following immediately on the eastern arm of the cross. Better preserved is one at Firsandyn, which may date from the ninth century, but has long been used as a mosque. Of the cross-in-square churches in Lycoania the most admirably constructed is that of Tchangli-Kilissé, which may belong to the eleventh century and which stands on a hill-side near Akserai above the rolling plain. The elegance and firm beauty of its architecture are enhanced by its prominent situation on the wide and open slope. Though built of stone, much brick has been employed in its construction for decorative effect. The south wall is adorned with broad flat niches surmounted by concentric arches of radiating tiles. Tile bands run along the walls, cutting across the niches and the narrow windows which they contain; tile decoration fills up the spandrels of these arches. Arched niches break the sides of the polygonal drum which was supported by means of pendentives on four square piers—the plan being of the Type IIB (p. 57). A narthex in two stories ran along the west end and a parecclesion adjoins on the north. The apses were also decorated with niches and with courses of brick. Traces of frescoes are preserved inside. Ilanli Kilissé—the "Snake Church"—which is not far distant has the extra bay in the eastern arm before the apse. As the hill-side has slipped away, the church is in a much ruined state.

The Church of S. Gregory Nazianzen at Gelvere in Cappadocia is of the same cross-in-square type as Ilanli Kilissé, but it has undergone a considerable amount of restoration. All these churches have arches on the gables marking the interior curve of the vaults a familiar feature in Constantinople. The Church of S. Amphilochius at Konia—known locally as "The Clock"—was greatly altered on its transformation into a mosque. The square-headed windows and a wooden erection on the roof were of modern date. The original church was of the cross-in-square plan, with the dome supported by pendentives on two piers and the antae of the apse. A deep bay precedes the single round apse. As long as Iconium was a city of the Byzantine Empire, this was an important church, distinguished as the sepulchre of S. Amphilochius. When it was converted into a mosque it was held in equal veneration by the Moslems as supposedly containing the tomb of Plato, whom they held in high esteem. A cross-in-square church at Silleh has a dome on pendentives and a rect-angular drum. There are also two cross-in-square churches at Triglia near the Sea of Marmora of considerable interest. The dome of one of them, S. Stephen (c. A.D. 800), is intermediate between the low dome and the later type on a high polygonal drum. It is of the plan IIA (β) (p. 57). The other church, the Panagia Pantobasilissa, is of type IIA (α) (p. 57).

But it is in the churches hewn out of the rock that the cross-in-square plan is most abundantly represented in Asia Minor. These strange rocky sanctuaries are to be found in different places in Anatolia, but it is in Cappadocia that they are most plentiful. In a barren region to the south-west of Kaisarieh in Cappadocia, where the mountains are intersected by desolate valleys, a great collection of isolated rocks rises above the surface of the ground. From fifty to two hundred feet in height, they are shaped in the forms of cones or cylinders and the landscape is made fantastic by their presence. This remote countryside became a refuge for thousands of monks and hermits, who, in the course of time, excavated in the isolated cones and in the rocky hill-sides innumerable churches and habitations. These extraordinary remains of the Byzantine Middle Ages were studied for many years by Father Guillaume de Jerphanion, who illustrated the results of his researches with a magnificent series of photographs and water-colours. Many of these monolithic churches are of the typical cross-in-square plan. With their domes and vaults, their pendentives and piers, their apses and nartheces, they reproduce the familiar type of structure in the village square and open countryside. A simpler plan would have entailed far less toil and one feels that the symbolism of the cross-in-square and its component parts must have become almost sacrosanct to the devout monastic builders. The façades are sometimes decorated with a series of horseshoe arches. But these strange sanctuaries do not rely for interest only on their location and plan: many frescoes clothe the plain or plastered surfaces of their rocky walls. Representatives of a more popular and monastic art, they afford a striking contrast to the official art of the metropolis. Simple in tendency and narrative in style, they can be most expressive. The earliest examples have been much affected by Syrian influence, while those of succeeding ages conform more closely to the later Byzantine tradition. They date (like the churches) from the ninth to the thirteenth centuries, and contain scenes from the life of Christ and the Virgin and numerous episodes from the stories of the saints. S. George of Cappadocia, mounted on his white horse and slaying the dragon, is naturally a favourite subject.

Other regions in Asia Minor as well as Cappadocia contain churches, sometimes of cross-in-square plan, excavated out of the rocky hills. Others, like one at Ayasin in Phrygia, where the dome and vaults were built of masonry, were only partially rock-cut.

It will have been realised how important was the role which Asia Minor played in the story of Byzantine Architecture. The great cities of the luxuriant coast testify to the early development and to the spread of the domed basilica, the progenitor of Santa Sophia. The wide uplands of the interior show what it could achieve in stone, with its solid barrel-vaults, its simple adornment, its horseshoe arches and its wide variety of plan. The monolithic chapels reveal what a hold the cross-in-square plan had upon the ecclesiastical mind, and, though now the plan is scarce in free-standing structures, its prevalence in the rocky cones is evidence that other churches of the familiar plan may once have stood on Anatolian soil.

It may be convenient at this point, also at the risk of repetition, to refer to another theory about the origin of the cross-in-square. This is the theory that it developed in Anatolia out of the domed basilica. It was found that the simple arches to north and south of the dome did not sufficiently counteract its thrust: the arches were therefore prolonged as barrel-vaults to the exterior walls. Thus the cross-domed basilica was formed. Finally, it is said, the removal of galleries, the lowering of the aisles to one story and the shortening of the nave led to the formation of the classic cross-in-square plan. Such a development is of course quite within the bounds of possibility, but it seems simpler to derive the cross-in-square from the very popular cruciform plan, especially when the possible influence of pagan prototypes may sometimes have been present.

CYPRUS

Cyprus is more renowned for its Gothic cathedrals—picturesque monuments of an alien architecture transplanted to an Eastern soil—than for the little Byzantine churches which rear their domes from its villages and plains. Yet these latter buildings are of importance in the history of the style and possess their own peculiar interest. Overrun by Moslems in the seventh century, Cyprus was alternately Arab and Byzantine until 1191 when it was seized by Richard Cœur-de-Lion in the course of his memorable voyage to the Holy Land. Shortly afterwards it passed into the hands of the Lusignan dynasty, and under its Western rulers became a prosperous kingdom with a high prestige among the nations. The Genoese occupied the flourishing port of Famagusta from 1372 until 1464 when they exercised great control over the island. From 1489 until the Turkish conquest of 1571 Cyprus belonged to Venice.

The Church of Cyprus has from early times enjoyed a position of independence under its own Archbishop, free from the control of any Byzantine Patriarch. The few churches surviving from the period before the Latin conquest include one within the precincts of the romantic Castle of S. Hilarion, for in building their fortress on its precipitous height, the regents carefully preserved the church of the former monastery. There is also a church in the monastery of Antiphonïtïs with the same oblong plan and a dome on six engaged and two free-standing piers: it received about 1500 the addition of an elegant Gothic porch.

The early history of Byzantine Architecture in Cyprus is very obscure and widely separated dates are assigned by different authorities to many of the churches and to types of plan. During the worst period of Arab invasion few new churches would be constructed, but a new era dawned with the Byzantine reconquest after the middle of the tenth century.

In the period of the Lusignan kingdom, when the Latin Church held a position of complete predominance, the village churches, though profusely adorned with frescoes, were poor and humble structures, amply significant of the depressed state of the natives under their feudal lords. In the latter part of the fourteenth century the Greek Church began to be viewed more tolerantly by the Latins, so much so that Pope Urban V in 1368 protested against Latins attending the Orthodox services. A fifteenth-century traveller even tells us that "the clerk indifferently performed the service in either rite . . . he first said mass in the Latin church. . . . This done he went over to the Greek church and consecrated as do the Easterns. . . . Which thing displeased me mightily."

The character of Cypriote architecture is often marked by an interesting admixture of Gothic and Byzantine traits. In the thirteenth and fourteenth centuries the Greeks, in their unpretentious village churches, followed a modified Byzantine plan, but copied details from the splendid Gothic edifices, like the Cathedral of Famagusta, which the Latins had erected for their worship. During the fifteenth and sixteenth centuries much more imposing structures were built in a Byzantine-Gothic style. The Gothic cathedrals of the former age, with their soaring arches, their long aisles and their lofty piers, were worthy objects of emulation.

The pointed arch and vault were often made use of by the Greeks, and the dome was employed in conjunction with the long nave and aisles. In the centuries of Ottoman rule, important churches were erected, some of them displaying Turkish traits.

As already said, many of the Byzantine churches of Cyprus are of most uncertain date. One of the oldest, situated at Kiti, has, since its mosaics were cleaned, been assigned to the sixth century. The central crossing is covered by a dome, the apses are round and the angle-spaces are vaulted at a very low level. Its apse contains a fine mosaic of the Virgin and Child escorted by angels. Attached to the church is one of those "Latin chapels" which were a feature of other Greek churches in Cyprus. The Latin chapel at Kiti, which has ribbed vaulting, was built in the beginning of the fifteenth century and belonged to the noble family of Gibelet.

The Church of SS. Barnabas and Hilarion at Peristerona is an important example of a type which is notable in Cyprus (61). It is a cross-in-square church with five domes on cylindrical drums so arranged as to form a cross, one dome standing over the centre of the building and one over each cross-arm. However, the western cross-arm is prolonged, so as to give the church a basilical form with nave and aisles. Yet the nave is not separated from the aisles by arcades as in a basilica, but by solid walls pierced with arches. This type of plan has been described as "the most peculiar in Cyprus" and assigned to the late tenth or the eleventh century. It occurs also in the five-domed Church of Hieroskypos near Paphos. Another type of plan is that in which the nave is covered by three domes in a row. It is represented by the Church of the Holy Cross at Nicosia, by that of S. Barnabas at Salamis (62) and by that of S. Lazarus at Larnaca. The Holy Cross at Nicosia has Gothic buttresses and some Italian Renaissance carving. S. Barnabas at Salamis had pointed arches; a large building, but of mediocre construction, its easternmost dome fell and a modern apse occupies the place it covered. Of S. Lazarus at Larnaca, a description may be quoted from Pietro della Valle, who visited the city in the seventeenth century:

> It is very ancient, entirely of stone, its arrangements fantastic, though common among the Greeks, for there are three aisles with a roof supported on four piers only, and three domes in a row over the middle aisle and three apses without. . . . Behind the altar there is shown underground, a tomb like a small grotto. . . . This, they say, is the grave of Lazarus.

117

Tradition has it that Lazarus, having been raised by Christ, laboured for the Gospel and died in Cyprus, where he was buried. The Church of S. Lazarus was rebuilt in the eighteenth century, but the original plan was followed.

The three-domed churches of Cyprus possess a particular interest owing to the influence they may have exerted on a group of churches far removed from the Levantine island. In the villages which nestle on the fertile fields of Aquitaine, in south-western France, there are churches covered by three domes in a row. If a tenth-century date can be assigned to these Cypriote churches, it is quite within the bounds of possibility that pilgrims, halting at Cyprus on their way home from the Holy Land, brought the idea of the three-domed church to the West. The subject will be reverted to in the chapter which deals with the churches of Aquitaine.

It was in the flourishing commercial port of Famagusta that the Gothic principles of construction were most avidly borrowed by the Byzantine builders and that the interpenetration of the two styles reached its height. Famagusta was a famous and opulent city. It is narrated that the houses of its wealthy citizens were full of gems and pearls and gold and that it was the great outpost of Western culture in the Orient. The wealthy Greek merchants of the city had every temptation to emulate the splendid Gothic buildings which their Frankish rulers erected in their midst, and when at last a greater degree of toleration was achieved they were not slow to seize their opportunity. It was those merchants who at the end of the fourteenth century erected the now-ruined cathedral of the Greeks. Built in the Gothic style but crowned with a dome, it strove to rival the Latin cathedral of the city. An ambitious structure, one of the largest Greek churches ever built, it succeeded a cathedral of humble proportions, which was retained upon its southern side as an honoured shrine. The semicircular apses of the new cathedral were covered by pointed semi-domes and the long nave was roofed with quadripartite vaulting except in the central bay, where it was interrupted by the dome. The plain exterior was enlivened with Gothic pinnacles. The ruins of the fifteenth-century Church of S. Anthony, which stand beside the walls of Famagusta, also illustrate the fusion of the Byzantine and Gothic styles: it was of cross-in-square plan but had pointed vaults.

The Church of S. Michael at Nicosia has a domed nave and

118

cross-vaulted aisles, in these respects resembling that of Morphou. The latter church is probably no earlier than the beginning of the eighteenth century, though its Gothic capitals have been taken from an earlier buildings. It was a famous pilgrimage church, and Sir George Hill says of it that "the architect has striven not very felicitously to imitate Frankish sculpture and fine building".

The admixture of styles is represented also at Nicosia in the Church of S. Nicolas of the English, known as "the Market". It was originally erected in the thirteenth century for the Order of S. Thomas of Acre, and at a later date adapted for the Byzantine rite. The fourth of the five bays in the nave is covered by a dome with a polygonal drum on pendentives. Ribbed vaults prevail throughout the church, and the nave is terminated by a five-sided apse. The north aisle and the two south aisles belong to the original church: the rest was built in the sixteenth century.

Another interesting feature of the Cypriote churches is represented in the Church of S. John Lampadistes at Kalopanayiotis. Three churches stand side by side, one a domed church, a second a restored barrel-vaulted one and a third a "Latin chapel". At a later date they were all covered by one steeply pitched roof, reaching almost to the ground and completely concealing the outline of the dome and vaults. This kind of roof was added to many churches and seems to have its origin in the East. This type of church has been called the "Enclosed Church". It is also to be found, for example, at Lagoudhera in the Troodos, where it covers a domed Byzantine church. The dome projects through the roof, which rests on a latticed screen.

The ordinary cross-in-square plan is also common in Cyprus, the pointed arch gradually displacing the round. Attractive examples of the plan are to be found at Lambanaka and in S. John, Trikomo, with its pointed doors and windows.

A mixture of types is to be seen in the monastic Church of Acheropoietos, which is of cross-in-square plan but has three domes in a row. Much altered in the sixteenth century, it has a Gothic porch on the west with ribbed vaults.

As a result of Italian influence, many Greek churches in Cyprus contain intramural sepulchres, of which a number still survive. The island has little to show of Byzantine mosaic, but in addition to that at Kiti, already mentioned, there is one in the Church of the Kanakaria Monastery in the long north-eastern peninsula, a district rich in ruins and once very prosperous. It is in a somewhat decayed condition, but dates from the ninth century and represents the Virgin and Child. The churches of the island, however, are profusely adorned with frescoes, many of which are of considerable merit and have been the subject of increased study in recent years. A few fragmentary specimens are said to have been painted before the Arab conquest, but the vast majority were executed from the eleventh right down to the eighteenth century. They depict the usual scenes from the life of Christ and of the Virgin, while figures of individual saints are often distinguished by their dramatic quality and decorative effect. Early Cypriote paintings resemble the Cappadocian frescoes; later ones revive the Hellenistic tradition; and still later ones testify that the paintings, like the architecture, were affected by Western influences and an Italo-Byzantine school took its rise. It is possible only to mention some of the churches where the later examples of Cypriote frescoes exist—the Virgin at Lagoudhera in the Troodos (1193), the Holy Cross near Platanistasa, whose paintings were completed in 1466 and signed by "Philip the Painter", the "Latin Chapel" at Kalopanayiotis, mentioned above, and Asinou (paintings, 1106).

TREBIZOND

After the Latin conquest of Constantinople in 1204, and the subsequent dismemberment of the Empire, there arose, on the southern shore of the Black Sea, a Byzantine state which had a remarkable life of two hundred and fifty years. "The strange and romantic Empire of Trebizond", as one of its historians has called it, was founded by Alexios Comnenos, a grandson of the Emperor Andronikos I. Possessed of a mild climate and a fertile soil, its steep hill-sides were richly clad with the olive and the vine. Its busy harbour loaded the rare products of the East on the ships which conveyed them to Byzantium. Strong in its natural defences and guarded by a castle and lofty walls, it protected a large and prosperous population of natives and of foreign merchants. Throughout the whole course of its history it was fortunate in being subject to the rule of a single dynasty, and as many of its sovereigns were able and conscientious rulers, it attained a high level of culture and ordered life. Alexios III, whose long reign lasted for more than forty years and whose

portrait with that of his wife and mother could be seen in the
Theoskepastos church until 1843, was distinguished as the founder
and benefactor of monasteries and churches. The emperors were
patrons of literature and art and encouraged learning by inducing
scholars to lecture in the schools. The fame of the empire and
city of Trebizond extended to the far-off regions of the West.
Colonies of Genoese and Venetian merchants were established
on its quays: envoys from Edward I of England halted in its
dwellings; John XXII, the Avignon Pope, whose tower stands
high above the river in his native Cahors, wrote a letter to "His
Magnificence the Emperor of Trebizond", and the foreigners who
visited the city could be impressed by the frescoes which illustrated the triumphal events in the nation's history on the palace
walls.

This palace, built in the fortified citadel above the town, is of
considerable interest as it is one of the few important monuments
of Byzantine secular architecture whose walls have survived. The
first part was called the Golden Palace of the Comnenos and
contained the great hall, the archives and the refectory, the hall
being adorned with portraits of the emperors.

> From the sea [writes Professor Talbot Rice] what remains of these
> walls presents a most imposing sight, arches and windows towering
> up above the roofs and the ramparts over the town and the bordering
> ravines. From near by the palace seems even more formidable, for
> the inaccessible nature of the cliff on which it
> stands is stressed again by the walls that over-
> hang it.

The churches in the city of Trebizond are
built of stone, and mostly belong to the
thirteenth century, though former churches
with similar dedications are known to have
occupied many of their sites. Those of S. Basil
and Moum-hané are of cross-in-square plan.
That of the Panagia Chrysokephalos, "the
golden-headed Virgin", is a cross-domed
basilica (67), which was the coronation church
as well as the sepulchre of some of the Trapezuntine Emperors. Rows of piers divide the
nave from aisles whose galleries run into the
north and south arms of the cross. The dome

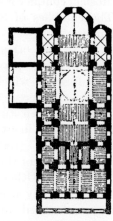

67 The Chrysoke-
phalos, Trebizond

121

rests upon a high and narrow polygonal drum. A narthex and an exo-narthex extend along the western end of the church, while beyond them lies an open porch of later date. A peculiarity of the Chrysokephalos and of certain other churches in Trebizond is the presence of a lateral porch; here it abuts on the northern wall. The presence of the cross-domed basilica at this late period in Byzantine Architecture is an interesting phenomenon and its existence at Trebizond may be compared with its vogue at a still later date in Greece.

The Church of Santa Sophia(68) has the lengthened western arm characteristic of the basilica: in it, however, the extra pair of piers in the nave does not occur; instead, engaged piers are attached to the western wall and the corresponding piers of the central square are prolonged to carry the vault. The dome is covered with a pointed roof, and to the west of the church there stands a detached bell-tower, square in plan and built in 1427. The first story of this tower forms a little apsed chapel, the remains of whose frescoes still survive. On the south wall of the church there abuts a porch with three open arches whose sculptures are thought to recall thirteenth-century work in France. The Church of S. Eugenios is of the same type as Santa Sophia. A rich and important foundation, it was dedicated to the patron saint of Trebizond, whose aid the citizens so often sought in times of national or individual need. Within its walls, in 1350, Alexios III was crowned Emperor of Trebizond, and there too in 1461 the Moslem conqueror said his first prayer after the capture of the city. The churches of S. Philip and of the Evangelistria are domed squares.

These and other churches belonging to this remote and forgotten Empire play another role in the history of Byzantine Art. The frescoes which decorated their walls are of much iconographical interest and sometimes of considerable artistic merit. They have been studied by Professor Talbot Rice, whose researches are embodied in a volume with many plates—"Byzantine Painting at Trebizond" (Gabriel Millet and D. Talbot Rice). The frescoes in the chapel of the bell-tower at Santa Sophia have already been mentioned. Other churches in the city and its neighbourhood were profusely decorated with frescoes depicting saints and the scenes of sacred story: these churches include S. Eugenios, S. Anne and the Panagia Evangelistria. Many of the paintings have been plastered over and whitewashed by the Turks, but as Professor

Talbot Rice has written, "The little that is to be seen in the Church of Santa Sophia, in S. Eugenios and in the Chrysokephalos suggests that the style will be an extremely individual one and will prove . . . of the first importance in the history of East Christian painting." Very interesting is the representation of the Transfiguration in the Church of Santa Sophia, where Our Lord is accompanied not by Moses and Elias, but by two angels clad in white.

CHAPTER VII

Mesopotamia, Armenia and Georgia

MESOPOTAMIA—HISTORICAL SKETCH

IT must never be forgotten by the student of Byzantine Art that the Christian religion, while it spread towards Rome and the West, was also, at a very early stage in its history, carried with rapidity and success across the Syrian plains to the populous cities of the East. As far back as the second century it was established in the Principality of Osroëne, which lay in a loop of the Euphrates to the east of Hierapolis. Legend indicates that Christianity penetrated the country at an even earlier date, for Abgar the King is said to have entered into communication with Our Lord Himself and to have received from Him a letter and His portrait "painted in choice colours". The capital, Edessa—the modern Urfa—for long rejoiced in the possession of this sacred relic, which was deemed to make its walls impregnable. Although Edessa became an important Christian centre, its Church tended to pursue a course independent of that which was followed by the communities of the West. Its liturgical language was Aramean (Syriac), and Tatian's *Diatessaron* or *Harmony of the Four Gospels* (c. A.D. 180) was in use as its evangel. On the other hand, the occupation of Osroëne by the Romans in 210 increased the influence of Antioch over the local Church. This influence continued to make itself felt and is revealed in the Hellenistic nature of the decorative sculpture of Mesopotamian churches, which, though of a later date, faithfully retains the designs of an earlier age.

From Edessa Christianity spread eastward through northern Mesopotamia to the regions around the town of Nisibis, upon the Tigris. It was the Persian conquest which gave the impetus to its supreme expansion. The Edessene church had adopted the Nestorian heresy, which had been condemned by the Council of Ephesus in 431 and which, in spite of its official condemnation by the Roman authority, continued to flourish in Edessa; but in 489 the renowned theological school, called by Gibbon the "Athens of Syria", was closed, and many Nestorian Christians migrated into Persian territory. There, in the lands adjacent to the upper

124

68 TREBIZOND: S. Sophia

69 MIRAM: S. Eustathios

70　ANI: the Cathedral

71　ANI: Church of
the Redeemer

reaches of the Tigris, they built up a powerful Church. The skill of their artisans brought prosperity to their new settlements and the Persian monarchs welcomed immigrants who were bitterly opposed to the Orthodox creed of their Roman enemy. The Nestorians of Persia were not content just to enjoy the free practice of their faith; their zeal prompted them to spread their doctrines far and wide; their emissaries penetrated as far as China and their missionary enterprise is one of the romances of the history of religion. A Nestorian theological school had already been established at Nisibis in 435, and in 498 the Nestorian Archbishop, with his seat at Seleucia (Ctesiphon) on the Tigris, assumed the proud title of "Patriarch of the East". Monasticism, spreading early into the Middle East from its home in Egypt, cast its ascetic spell over the Mesopotamian Christians and for centuries exerted a powerful and increasing sway. Among the monks there were scions of noble Persian and Arab families and the standard of their learning was often high. It is narrated that in the seventh century, after certain dissensions had ceased, "they filled the country of the East with monasteries and convents and habitations of monks, and Satan who had rejoiced at their discomfiture was put to shame".

The sixth century saw the rise of the Jacobites called after Jacob al Bardai, a native of Tela (Constantine), about fifty miles to the east of Edessa. They adhered to the Monophysite heresy, condemned by the Council of Chalcedon, and attracted numerous converts in the East. They still comprise a remnant in Mesopotamia, especially at Mosul.

During the same century the great Justinian, as Procopius narrates, left his imprint on these wide-stretching lands. It has already been mentioned that he reconstructed the walls of Dara on the Upper Tigris: he also formed a reservoir "very close to the Church of S. Bartholomew the Apostle", and built a barrier to stem the river, summoning Anthemius and Isidorus, the architects of Santa Sophia, to his aid. He rebuilt the mountain forts between Dara and Amida, transforming them into "an impregnable line of outposts along the Roman frontier". Nor did he confine his attention to works of military importance. He built two churches at Dara and one at Rusafah (Sergiopolis) which received so many offerings as to become powerful and famous throughout all the land. The Christians of Mesopotamia enjoyed toleration during the period of Moslem dominance, which began in the seventh century, but they have suffered under terrible outbreaks of persecution and only scattered communities survive at the present day to represent the churches which once flourished so abundantly in the early ages of the Christian era.

THE CHURCHES OF MESOPOTAMIA

The most interesting group of churches in Mesopotamia is situated on a hilly plateau in a bend of the Tigris called the Tur-Abdin, the "Mountain of the Servants of God". The district is bounded on two sides by the Tigris, and on the south it falls sharply down to the wide Mesopotamian plain. This secluded region was chosen by monks as a place of retreat from the strife and turmoil of the world. When warfare raged around, the Mountain of the Servants of God was a haunt of religious peace and the fortified monasteries which clustered among its oak-groves grew rich and strong.

The churches of the Tur-Abdin have their walls of stone, but their vaults of brick. Some of them were attached to the monasteries and others rise above the hovels of the villages. The oblong plan with a barrel-vaulted roof is represented by such examples as Mar Azaziel at Kefr Zeh and Mar Kyriakos at Arnas. A more interesting type is that which is known as the "transverse-naved", where the barrel-vaulted nave runs from north to south, with its greater length in that direction. Of such a plan is the monastic Church of Mar Gabriel, and that of Mar Yakub at Salah, which has a finely carved door and bold cornices. The transverse-naved plan was combined with a domical superstructure in the well-preserved Church of the Virgin at Khakh, also in the Tur-Abdin(72). The dome covering the centre of

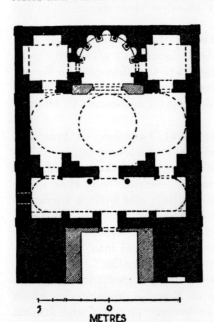

METRES

72 Khakh, Mesopotamia: the Church of the Virgin

the nave is buttressed by two semi-domes. Squinches bring the square to an octagon, and the dome is octagonal in form. A pointed covering roof was replaced by a stone exterior dome in modern times. The octagon above the squinches appears as a square tower externally adorned with arcades. The lintels and arches are sculptured with exquisite carving, and the Corinthian capitals with garlands hanging over their corners belong to a type which is to be found in other churches of the Tur-Abdin. There is a dome in a chamber in the courtyard of the Monastery of Mar Augen, and one over the narthex of Mar Gabriel. Widely different dates have been assigned by authorities to these churches of the Tur-Abdin. Some writers would date them as early as the fifth century, but Guyer's view that they were mostly built in the first half of the ninth century seems more probable.

A little to the south of the Tur-Abdin lay the important town of Nisibis, whose "university" with its thousand students was a renowned centre of learning in the East. Here still stands the Church of S. James, which is one of the most ancient churches in the world, the oldest part dating to 359. It now consists of two contiguous buildings with a round apse at the end of each. The south church consisted of a square space and a porch; the square space is covered by a modern dome, but according to Wigram "it has nothing to indicate conclusively the form of the original roof". The north church dates from the eighth century.

The type of church with nave and aisles of equal height was common in Mesopotamia and occurs among the village churches of the Tur-Abdin. It is also exemplified away to the south in Mosul: one of the churches of that type in the city is Mar Ahudani (thirteenth century?), which like some churches in Egypt has a dome on squinches over the altar-space. An interesting feature of the Mosul churches is their Mohammedan decoration: a doorway at Mar Ahudani is covered with Arabic inscriptions and ornaments. The Church of Mar Petros, which is a long narrow oblong with a north aisle and which De Villard says "is certainly the oldest Chaldean church in Mosul", also has a dome over the sanctuary.

Mention may be made of a type of plan which seems to have been in vogue in southern Mesopotamia at an early date. It was formed of a simple rectangle which comprised a nave and a square-ended sanctuary flanked by two chambers. Two ranges of rectangular piers set close to the nave walls appear to have supported barrel-vaults. Two churches of this type have been discovered at Ctesiphon—one above the other—and two more were found at Hira by Professor Talbot Rice. Those at Hira had also circular-built columns in the nave as well as the rectangular piers, thus forming aisles.

Returning to the north we find at Meiafarqin (Tigranocerta?), on a tributary of the Tigris, a church whose plan resembles that of Santa Sophia, Salonica (45). It belongs to the year 591. The dome rests on four piers strengthened each in the west by three other piers. Between the piers there are arcades on two columns, forming an ambulatory with galleries around the central space. The quatrefoiled-square plan, to be described below in connection with Armenian churches, may be exemplified at Dair-el-Za'aferan, the "Monastery of the Yellow Rocks", the residence of the Patriarch of the Jacobites: it is, however, uncertain whether the church originally possessed a dome or not. A flat niche takes the place of the western foil. The so-called "oval octagon" of Viransheher, between Aleppo and Mardin, is said to belong to the sixth century. It was discovered by Puchstein and has been discussed by Strzygowski in more than one of his volumes. It is in a ruined condition, but it had a dome on eight central arches with an ambulatory around them, and four projections at the ends of the axes. It belongs to that class of church which combines the cross and the octagon and which is exemplified in Palestine and Asia Minor.

A few churches still survive in the ancient city of Amida, or Diarbekir, far up on the Tigris towards its source. The Nestorian church on the citadel is said to date from the sixth century and consists of two domed compartments, the eastern dome being supported by squinches on the outer walls and the western one by pendentives on barrel-vaults. Buckingham, who visited it about 1827, gives an interesting description of this building as it appeared at a time when few travellers from Western Europe penetrated this distant and isolated region: "One of the places used as a stable presents the ruins of a handsome and noble edifice with finely constructed domes of brickwork and a beautiful door with columns and pilasters. Most probably the remains of an old Christian building." Of the Church of the Virgin (El Hadra) at Amida only the choir remains. It was a domed trefoil with an ambulatory and may be compared with the church at Rusafah (Sergiopolis). Mar Cosmo has been much altered. It has piers which may have supported a dome.

One final ruined church demands special mention because of its important bearing on the disputed question of the date to be assigned to the churches of northern Mesopotamia. It is situated at Surg Hagop or Djinndeirmene to the north-west of the Euphrates. The Mesopotamian churches are of very uncertain date, and the most diverse views have been propounded about the period of their origin. On the ground of their decorative features the churches of the Tur-Abdin have been assigned to the sixth century. Strzygowski proposed an early, but Miss Bell and Guyer a much later date. Guyer discovered on the apse of the above-mentioned church at Surg Hagop an inscription belonging to the ninth century. He compares the plan of Surg Hagop to that of one of the churches in the Tur-Abdin and proposes the ninth century for the churches of the area. The decorative details are not themselves early, but merely retained old designs which had been handed down for centuries. The domes were often recon-structions and those at Amida have been dated as late as the Middle Ages. The supporters of a late date for the Mesopotamian churches derive their transverse nave from Persian temples and also point to a strong Syrian influence: their opponents give the plan a Babylonian origin. The transverse-naved church is itself of little importance in the history of architecture. Mesopotamia is notable for its use of the barrel-vault which thence spread far to other regions. It is likewise important for its employment of the dome over the square: the date of the churches has an important bearing on the history of this system, though it must be remembered that a reconstructed dome may have closely resembled an earlier similar feature.

It is unnecessary to dwell further on the dome over the square in Mesopotamia as the subject of that area's relation to its origins has already been discussed in the fourth chapter of this book.

ARMENIA—HISTORICAL SKETCH

For long centuries Armenia, either as an independent country or as a province of the Byzantine Empire, played an important part in the political, cultural and commercial life of the East. Its geographical situation, the fertility of its soil, its wealth of minerals and the ability of its inhabitants combined to raise its citizens to a high position in world affairs, and though for long periods it was subject to different foreign yokes, in the days of its inde-pendence it was distinguished for its wealth and culture. Nor was its influence confined to its immediate surroundings. The enterprise of its inhabitants constrained them to seek fame and fortune in other lands. In the eighth and ninth centuries they contributed in no small degree to the revival of Byzantine strength. The military power of the Empire at this period was due to the Armenian influence which had completely permeated the army.

Armenia lies to the south of the Caucasus Mountains and to the west of the Caspian Sea. It consists mainly of a rugged plateau cleft by valleys which were rich in corn and vine. The Araxes is the most notable of the streams which water its soil, and its most famous feature is the double peak of Ararat, raising its snowy summit almost 16,000 feet aloft. It is on the valleys, steppes and hill-slopes of this broken land that some of the more interesting churches of their age are to be found. Throughout the long course of their troubled and tragic history the aspirations of the Armenians centred around their Church. Their culture has been predominantly ecclesiastical; innumerable ruins of beautifully constructed churches testify to the presence of the religious spirit; many ancient monasteries speak of the popularity of the monastic life in days of old; the literature of Armenia was mainly sacred, and the illumination of religious manuscripts evoked high powers of artistic expression. The Katholikos, the head of the Church, held a position of much secular importance; the possessor of wide lands, he wielded, in the eras of independence, an authority as powerful as the monarch's, while in the ages of enslavement he was the religious and political leader of the nation.

Christianity probably spread northwards into Armenia from the populous cities of the south at an early date: tradition ascribes its introduction to S. Bartholomew and S. Thaddeus, the disciples of Christ. Its establishment before the year 300 as the national religion was due to S. Gregory the Illuminator and his convert, King Tiridates, to whom is credited the erection of many churches. In the course of the fourth century, the Armenian Church developed its organisation along Byzantine lines, but its adherence to Monophysitism, condemned at Chalcedon in 451, isolated it from the main body of the Eastern Church. Its independence was finally confirmed at the Synod of Dwin in A.D. 552.

In A.D. 387 a treaty between the Romans and Persians had partitioned Armenia into two vassal states, but the kings of the eastern division, which lay under the suzerainity of Persia, maintained their nominal independence for about forty years. A new line of demarcation in 591 brought the greater portion of the country under Byzantine sway, but by the year 700 the Arabs had subjugated all the land. In 885 Armenia recovered its long-lost independence and was ruled until 1046 by the Bagratid dynasty, which maintained its prestige by a moral sway over a number of noble families; some of these families were virtually independent, and themselves took the title of king.

The last hundred years of this epoch of independence marks the height of Armenian greatness. In spite of internal rivalries, peace and prosperity abounded—churches, hospitals and almshouses were built, scholarship reached a high level, commerce flourished, and artistic impulses found many outlets; the works of the goldsmith and the coppersmith were particularly renowned. In 1071 the Byzantine forces suffered a crushing defeat at Manzikert on Armenian soil at the hands of the Seljouk Turks, who occupied Armenia. At a subsequent period it became part of the Ottoman Empire, its northern area becoming part of Russia at a still later date. It remains divided between Turkey and the U.S.S.R. at the present day. The Armenians have been expelled from the Turkish portion, and the churches there, no longer used for worship, have been turned into storehouses or are falling into ruin.

ETSCHMIADZIN AND ANI

There are two sites in Armenia which demand a special mention for the importance which they hold in the architectural annals of the nation. The one in the Soviet Union is Etschmiadzin, the ancient Vagarshapat, now only a large village where the Katholikos resides. The monastery with its dependent village is set in a spacious walled enclosure upon a wide plain stretching to the distant base of Ararat. According to legend, Christ Himself descended in glory and with flaming light and appeared to S. Gregory the Illuminator in this place. He struck the ground with a golden mallet and a golden pedestal appeared bearing a fiery cross: visions of three domed churches followed in answer to His further summons. In obedience to His commands Gregory built the first cathedral on the central spot and three other churches in the places indicated. Etschmiadzin became the ecclesiastical centre of Armenia, and although for a time it was abandoned for Dwin, it again became the residence of the Patriarch in 1441. Armenians from all parts of the world have visited this sacred spot and their generosity has added modern buildings to the monastery which testify to the skill of the Armenian mason.

The other famous site, which is in Turkish Armenia, is that of the city of Ani, capital of the medieval kingdom of the Bagratids. Long since ruined and deserted, it stood behind a double line of turreted fortifications on a plateau elevated between two deep ravines. An old chronicler who knew the city both in its perfect and its ruined state, speaks of the beauty of its environs, "a resplendent and happy garden, crowned with leaves and rich in fruits". The princes, clad in gay colours, sat upon their thrones to the accompaniment of song and music. So rich in shrines was Ani that it was called the "city of 1001 churches". Now the broken walls of its remaining churches rise amid the debris of the ruined town. Long known to archaeologists, occupying an honoured place in the older histories of architecture, they are worthy memorials of the great era in Armenian history.

THE GENERAL CHARACTERISTICS OF ARMENIAN ARCHITECTURE

It is sometimes stated that the churches of Armenia are built entirely of squared stone; in reality a core of rubble is faced on both sides with blocks of squared volcanic stone, carefully fitted together. They bear the impression of solidity and firmness and are characterised by a severe and simple dignity. In the external plan and elevation the preference is invariable for the straight line. The arms of the cross terminate in angular pediments and the dome is covered with a conical or pyramidal roof to throw off the snow which may fall upon the mountain slopes. The dome rests upon a high cylindrical or polygonal drum. This drum is often of massive appearance, having a dimension which is great in proportion to the building as a whole. It is in large measure this massiveness of drum which gives to many Armenian churches in spite of their modest dimensions an essentially monumental aspect. Many Armenian interiors can have an unencumbered spaciousness, a feature still further emphasised by the general absence of the Iconostasis: the apse is separated from the nave only by curtains, which are drawn together during certain parts of the Divine Liturgy.

Both the squinch and the pendentive were employed to support the drum of the dome. The squinch was the expedient which was most frequently employed: the pendentive came into use at a later date and has a flat and not a curved profile. Exterior ornamentation, at least in the earlier churches, is usually of a simple nature. It often consists of blind arcades with tall slender colonnettes running along the walls and around the drum (71). In one of the churches at Ani, dedicated to S. Gregory, the spandrels are filled with exquisite and delicate sculpture of birds, animals and foliage.

If the buildings thus adorned have acquired a lightness and elegance certain others retain a plain severity. Armenia is a country where the mountains dominate the scene. The snow-clad peaks of Ararat and subsidiary ranges cut across the land. It is possible to imagine that the nature of the landscape as well as the quality of the material has impressed itself upon the monumental and clear-cut structures which were erected upon the hills and in the broad valleys between the towering mountains. Tall V-shaped niches were often employed to break the exterior surfaces of the walls; they terminated in arched heads which were sculptured, sometimes with rich and varied carving, but more usually with scallops or fluted decoration (70). These angular niches are cut into the walls in such positions that they serve summarily to indicate the divisions of the interior. One of the most remarkable features of Armenian churches is the lack of correspondence between inside and outside plan: apses are concealed in the thickness of the walls; a quatrefoil interior plan may appear as a rectangle externally; the inner disposition is hidden from without. The niches, then, serve to give some indication of the inner arrangement. Aesthetically they form a striking contrast to the flat surfaces of the walls. Among the interior features of the churches to be noted are the round columns engaged to the walls or piers as arch-supports. They bear circular, roll or cushion capitals (often with an impost) and are occasionally sculptured with geometrical designs. Windows are small and narrow and are usually round-headed: they may be surmounted by arched mouldings sometimes sculptured with floral decoration and turning away horizontally at the sides. There was much elaborate decoration distributed over walls of some of the later Armenian churches.

In Georgia decoration is sometimes spread over the walls in a haphazard fashion. Some of the Georgian carving, as at Mzkhet and Ananur, is of a quaint but rich description, displaying the vine and crude figures of animals. Both in Armenia and Georgia numerous inscriptions can be found incised upon the buildings.

Many Armenian churches have received additions in the shape of contiguous structures. Among these additions was the zamatun, a large fore-hall, which could be used as a place of sepulture. Its size might be altogether disproportionate to that of the church: before the principal church in the monastery of Varak there is a zamatun in nine domed bays which is larger than the church itself. In monastic churches the zamatun would be used for the recital of certain offices by the monks. Other additions to the churches were the charming belfries which rise from their roofs. They consist of a circle of open arches surmounted by a conical roof and resting on a low base. They appear to have been built in the thirteenth century, their form being derived from the kiosks over minarets.

CHURCHES IN ARMENIA AND GEORGIA

In the churches of Armenia there is to be found a great variety and ingenuity of plan.

The *basilica* occurs in the country, both the true basilica and the basilica with nave and aisles of equal height—the so-called "three-naved hall-church". But the preference of the Armenian architect was always for the dome. He took the dome over the square as his original unit and with facile ingenuity he adapted it to suit his purpose and his fancy. He buttressed it with apses or, as we may call them, foils; he rounded off angles into circular form; he multiplied the foils as his fancy dictated; he added chambers and he masked the structure in straight walls. He was contented with nothing stereotyped, but delighted in every device by means of which he could develop the original features of his plan.

It will be convenient to record the domed churches of Armenia in several classes.

The Quatrefoil. In this type the ends of the foils touch each other and the dome covers the central square, resting on corbels across the angles. The foils show externally in the eleventh-century Chapel of S. Gregory, one of a picturesque group of churches at the Monastery of Sanahin, south of Tiflis. More often the plan is complicated by the presence of chambers abutting on the walls, as at Sarindsch (eleventh century) and at Agrak near Tekor (seventh century), where there are side-rooms to the eastern apse. The Monastery of Chtonsk, in a rocky valley near Tekor, possesses two churches of eleventh-century date, each of which has a chamber between each pair of foils; in one of them, the Church of the Virgin, the outside form is brought to the plan of an irregular polygon, while in the other one, dedicated to S. Sergius, it is brought to that of a rotunda. The latter church is a singularly attractive building; a round-headed arcade encircles the lower story, the arches resting on engaged and coupled columns. An arcade of high pedimental arches surrounds the drum, the arches cutting into the roof and forming a series of ridges on its surface. The ruined church of the Holy Apostles at Ani also had four chambers. The outside plan is brought to a rectangle, with angular niches marking the junction between chambers and foils: a porch of later date is distinguished for its striking Saracenic decoration. In another type of quatrefoil church a circular wall surrounds the quatrefoil, which is usually composed of columns; between quatrefoil and outer circle an ambulatory is formed. The ruined Church of S. Gregory which King Gagik built at Ani in the year 1001, and the tenth-century church at Bana, are of this type. They should be compared with the Cathedral of Bosra in Syria. Of the same type is the much-ruined but once-splendid Chapel of the Palace of Zwarthnotz near Etschmiadzin (seventh century). The Katholikos Narses III, whose Greek monogram appears on one of the capitals, built it "with high walls and all sorts of marvels worthy of the divine honour to which he constructed them". Numerous carved fragments lie about its site, consisting of deeply cut mouldings and vine-patterned archivolts and capitals that display basket-work and eagles with outspread wings. These types clearly show Byzantine influence.

Hexafoils and Octofoils. The quaint and attractive Chapel of S. Gregory at Ani, which was built in the eleventh century on a cliff overlooking the river, has six foils within and twelve sides without. Every second side is broken by an angular niche with a strongly projecting cornice above; by means of these niches an indication is therefore given of the interior hexafoil.

There are three other small hexafoils at Ani and one at Kazkh in Georgia, where bold pointed arches form pediments around the drum, the main body and the porch. The Cathedral of the Redeemer at Ani, built in 1035, has eight foils inside and sixteen sides outside (71). It has characteristic blind arcading round its lower story and its drum. The walls of the arcades are covered

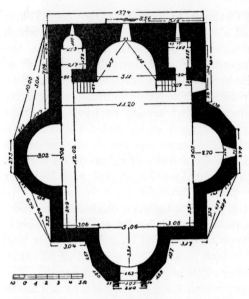

73   Plan of the Cathedral of Mastara, Armenia

with inscriptions, one of which records that, in 1034, Prince Aplgharib, having brought a piece of the True Cross from Constantinople, built this chapel to contain it and decreed that services be held every night therein until the Second Coming of Christ. The ruins of another octofoil lie at Irind.

Trefoils. In the trefoil a rectangular nave is substituted for the western foil. The nave is covered by a barrel-vault buttressing the dome on the west. The Church of the Virgin at Talin and that of S. Ananias at Alaman are of this type.

The Quatrefoiled Square. The ends of one foil, in a quatrefoil church, meet those of the adjoining foils. In the quatrefoiled square, on the other hand, the foils stand out from straight walls which extend beyond each of them to right and left: the basis of the plan, in other words, is a square from each side of which an apse or foil projects (73). The dome, covering the square, is supported by squinches at the angles. The plan is a development of the domed square, the apses or foils being introduced to provide abutment for the side thrust of the dome. As we shall see, irregularities often modify the square. Though these churches are of modest dimensions, their interiors are characterised by a fine sense of space. Externally their drums have a broad and massive appearance. The Cathedral of Mastara (*c.* A.D. 650) (73) is dignified, simple and compact: it has little ornament except naturalistic vine leaves and grapes on arches above the windows. A straight wall outside encloses the apse and its side-chambers in the east. The ruined church at Artik (seventh century) had a similar general plan. The tenth-century Church of the Apostles at Kars—a city

136

which at one time was a centre of great cultural importance—has a massive dodecagonal drum, with quaint figures in long robes in the spandrels of its arches.

The quatrefoiled square plan underwent a further development by the rounding-off of the angles at the corners of the square; four niches were thus formed, each three-quarters of a circle in plan(79). In this type also side-chambers flanked the foils and passages led from the side-chambers into the circular niches. It occurs with four side-chapels at Mzkhet (seventh century) and Ateni (eleventh century) in Georgia. One of the most remarkable examples of this plan is to be found at Awan. The four side-chambers are circular in plan; the angles of the square are rounded into three-quarter circles; four foils spring from the central area. Nevertheless the exterior walls form an unbroken rectangle. There could be no greater discrepancy than that between the complex interior and the simple exterior, hiding all that is within. In the Church of S. Hripsimeh at Etschmiadzin(79) the four chambers are square in plan, while in the exterior rectangle V-shaped niches indicate the terminations of the foils. This church was built by the Katholikos Komitas in the year 618, but it has been much restored.

The beautiful tenth-century Church of Achthamar on an island in Lake Van has long been one of the most sacred spots in Armenia and a monastic abode from early times(74). It has side-chambers only at the east end and the angles of the square are rounded off. Various additions, including a large nine-bayed porch, abut on the walls of the church, which is remarkable for its external decoration. The whole of the walls is interspersed with sculpture, often in high relief. The figures from the Bible story and from hagiography are crudely carved, but the ornamental designs are rich and intricate. Grotesque animals recall the winged quadrupeds of Assyria; lions, gazells and hares form friezes; heads of birds and beasts jut out from the surface of the walls; King Gagik, the founder, clad in a gorgeous robe, offers a model of his church to Christ; here are figures of saints, prophets and evangelists and there are the twisting branches of the pomegranate and the vine. The iconographical cycles containing the stories of Jonah and Isaac are reminiscent of those on the walls of the Catacombs of Rome and are thought to have been derived from Egypt. The style, on the other hand, is akin to the Sassanian Art of Persia. The numerous animals may have reference to the story of the

Creation. Lynch points out that the attraction of this famous Armenian shrine is enhanced by its island situation and the beauty of its pink volcanic stone. It may be of interest to note that the architecture of the Armenian church in Paris is based on that of Achthamar.

Of quatrefoiled square plan is also a church in the Monastery of the Seven Churches at Varak near Lake Van, where another church, used as a library, contained some primitive illuminated texts. The ruins of other churches lie scattered round about.

The Quatrefoiled Cross-in-Square. Among the vineyards on the banks of the Arpa Chai, to the south of Ani, there stands a ruined church which has been rescued by Strzygowski from obscurity and placed among the most important monuments of East Christian Art. It is the cathedral of the ancient city of Bagaran, by whose scattered ruins it is surrounded. It was explored and studied by an Austrian expedition in 1913, and following upon these investigations Strzygowski assigned it a leading role in the history of Byzantine Architecture. An inscription is said to date its erection to the years 624–631, but the accuracy of this dating has been suspected. In plan it is a cross-in-square church with each arm of the cross terminating in a projecting apse— what we have called, for convenience, a quatrefoiled cross-in-square. The dome rests on a drum carried on squinches and broad pointed arches supported by square piers. The cross-arms, with their pointed vaults, terminate in triangular gables and the eastern angle-spaces are cross-vaulted. The round, horseshoe, pointed and oviform arches are all to be found in the church. Hood-moulds above the windows display the vine and other ornaments. Two side-chambers of a later date appear in the east. Bagaran (or an earlier prototype) has been thought by Strzygowski and his followers to mark a definite stage in the evolution of the cross-in-square plan, by the introduction of free-standing piers for the dome. According to him the original basic plan from which the cross-in-square sprang was the simple domed square. The domed square was succeeded by the quatrefoiled square—a square with an apse on each side to buttress the dome. But builders wished to construct churches with domes of a less diameter. They solved their problem by the introduction of piers within the building to support the dome. The quatrefoiled cross-in-square plan was thus evolved. The final stage was the omission of all the apses (or foils) except the eastern apse and the consequent formation of the standard cross-in-square plan. Strzygowski suggests that the idea of forming the cross-in-square may have been derived from its use as a *ground-plan* in Persia: thence it passed over to Christian architecture. He instances the employment of the cross-in-square *ground-plan* in a hall in the Palace of Sarvistan.

In earlier chapters it has been argued that the cross-in-square church may have developed in a simple way out of the cruciform. As has been said, the date of Bagaran has been disputed. The plan may have reached Armenia from Asia Minor and Syria. Even if it developed independently on Armenian soil, there is no proof that it was the prototype of the Byzantine church of cross-in-square plan with its dome on pendentives.

The Cathedral of Etschmiadzin (75) is another quatrefoiled cross-in-square, but it has been reconstructed. It appears to have originally been a quatrefoil with four side-chambers, the whole forming a square externally. Some features of the present plan may go back to the seventh century, but numerous alterations have been effected upon the fabric of the famed Armenian shrine throughout the long course of the centuries. Portico and belfries date from the seventeenth century. A chamber for relics was added in the east end as recently as 1881. This is the patriarchal church of the Armenian people, and is said to occupy the exact place where S. Gregory beheld his vision and built his church.

The Cross-in-Square. As the intervening vaults buttressed the dome sufficiently, three of the foils were dropped and the cross-in-square plan was reached. The cross-in-square plan of the two-piered type as described in Chapter IV occurs in two tenth-century churches at Akori and Astapat. Four central supports appear in S. Gaiane, Etschmiadzin, which was built in 630 but restored in the sixteenth century. With its conical roof over its dome, its polygonal drum, its high pointed gables, and its poverty of decoration, it is of the same simple bold and clear-cut style which has already been described as so typical of Armenia. The Cathedral of Mren (*c.* 640) also has four free central supports for the dome: in the tympanum of its west door it possesses a feature which occurs in other Armenian churches, a sculptured representation of the donors meeting Our Lord. At Mren, the donor and his wife clad in fur coats advance towards Christ, who is accompanied by three saints holding books. More familiar than either of these churches is the Cathedral of Ani, which has long been renowned as one of the most illustrious and remarkable monuments in

Armenia (70). An inscription records its completion in 1010. Travellers who penetrated to Ani in bygone days were impressed by the Gothic appearance of its pointed arches and the clustered columns which supported its dome. The horseshoe arch appears in the western arm, and even the pointed arches have a slight horseshoe bend in their lower courses. The rectangular frames of the windows are sculptured with intricate and delicate inter-lacings which show a kinship with Saracenic designs. To early travellers the Cathedral of Ani was something of a mystery, and it was thought that it underwent a reconstruction at the hands of Western architects who followed the Crusaders. The cathedral with its pointed arches is, however, an undoubted product of native growth. How far this building and other buildings in Armenia affected the use of the pointed arch and ribbed vault in the Gothic architecture of Western Europe is a subject outside the scope of this volume. The case for Armenia is admirably stated by M. Rey in his *L'Art roman et ses origines*. In any case the Cathedral of Ani is in itself a notable building and, as Miss Der Nersesian truly says, "deserves to be listed among the important examples of medieval architecture". The cross-in-square plan did not obtain the lasting hold upon Armenia which it did in Greece and the Balkans. Nevertheless it had a considerable popularity in Georgia, especially in the twelfth and thirteenth centuries. Georgia, or Iberia, occupied a region of varying extent among the mountains and valleys of the Caucasus. It adopted Christianity about the sixth century and, unlike Armenia, adhered to the Orthodox faith of Byzantium. For long centuries it retained in whole or in part a virtual or legal independence but finally became part of Russia in the early nineteenth century. Its churches show strong affinities with those of Armenia. The arcade on the outside of the walls is a common feature. Mention may be made of the churches in the Monastery of Gelati in the Caucasus. They show the familiar conical roof and the largest of them is adorned with frescoes inside. There is a two-column cross-in-square church at Pitsounda on the shore of the Black Sea with a round apse and a curving roof over its dome. Other Georgian churches have been or will be mentioned in the course of the description of Armenian churches.

The Cross-domed Basilica. (Reference should be made to Chapter IV, p. 56.) The cross-in-square and the cross-domed Basilica of Armenia merge into one another, the latter being

74 ACHTHAMAR

75 ETSCHMIADZIN: the Cathedral

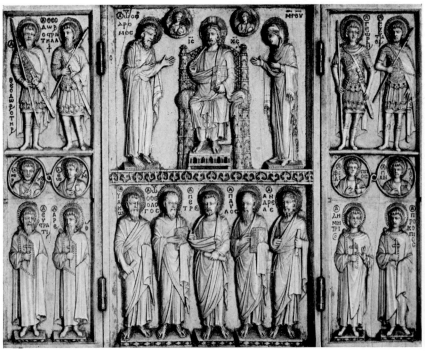

77 HARBAVILLE TRYPTYCH

distinguished only by its greater length and by the narrowness of its aisles. The Church of Dwin (seventh century), the Cathedral of Thalin and the Cathedral of Kutais (eleventh century)(78) retained the apses at the ends of their north and south arms, as in the quatrefoiled cross-in-square.

At Thalin the side-chambers to the eastern apse are separated from it by unbroken walls, the only entrance to them being from the aisles: this disposition occurs in other Armenian churches. The east apse is, as usual, polygonal on the exterior. The outside is adorned with arcades, carved archivolts and V-shaped niches. A barrel-vault covers the prolonged west arm and the dome with its circular drum rests upon pendentives. The church at Dwin, once a great ecclesiastical centre and the residence of the Katholikos for many years, has been almost completely destroyed. The Cathedral of Kutais is the most important monument of ecclesiastical art in Georgia. The traveller Freshfield described it in 1869 as "the ruins of a very fine Byzantine cathedral. Four lofty pillars, still remaining, once supported a central dome. The porch is very curious and we remarked the ram's head introduced into its sculpture as though the legend of the Golden Fleece has been known and appreciated by its builders." The Cathedral of Mokwi, now in ruins, was once another important example of Georgian architecture. A cross-domed basilica with double aisles, it dates from the early eleventh century and in plan resembles the Cathedral of Santa Sophia at Kiev in Russia.

Usunlar (Odzun) (eighth century) and Bagawan (seventh century) have no "transeptal apses". The former is supposed to show the oldest existing example of a polygonal drum of considerable elevation with the cupola covered by a conical roof. There is an interesting

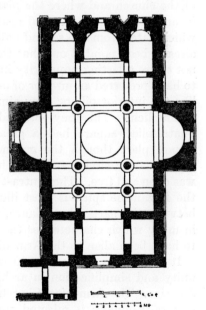

78   Plan of the Cathedral of Kutais, Georgia

141

cross-domed basilica at Tekor (Dighour), noted last century in the works of Fergusson and Texier and agreed to be one of the oldest churches in Armenia. It has undergone a reconstruction and the nature of the alterations has suggested that the cross-domed basilica of Armenia may have developed out of the "three-naved hall-church" characteristic of the Mesopotamian area. Tekor was originally of this type with three naves vaulted at equal height: at a later date a dome with lateral cross-vaults was "superimposed" upon it. It will be seen that the substitution of a dome with cross-vaults for part of the vaulting on the latitudinal axis of a three-naved hall-church would lead to a cross-domed basilica. The dome of Tekor, which was, like early Eastern domes, conical in shape and which was enclosed by a square tower in its lower courses, was struck by lightning and collapsed in 1912.

The Domed Oblong. One other type of plan may be mentioned, a type which after the tenth century became very popular and tended to supersede more complex plans. This was the domed oblong, where a dome rests on broad piers engaged on the walls of the church and where the plan is a simple oblong terminating in an eastern apse. A good example is the Cathedral of Talish, which dates from the second half of the seventh century. It has already been pointed out that the Greek cross-in-square plan did not enjoy a lasting popularity in Armenia. The Armenians seem to have preferred an interior of unencumbered space: they did not like the interior pillars; they aimed at spatial unity, at freedom, at simplicity. This they obtained in the domed oblong. Even the quatrefoiled square had a greater freedom than the cross-in-square plan: though the ground-plan became complex by the three-quarter circles and side-chambers, the whole central area was open and free. The contrast between the Armenian spirit and the Byzantine spirit is most illuminating. The close connection between the parts, the balance, the equilibrium, the complexity in unity which characterises the Byzantine cross-in-square, seem to have been alien to the Armenian spirit.

It is perhaps interesting to compare this Armenian spirit of unity and simplification in architecture with the same spirit in doctrine. The Armenian Church adheres only to the first three General Councils: it rejected the Council of Chalcedon with its balancing and subtle definitions about the person of Christ—the two natures divine and human in the One Person. It is true that its apologists often protest that they are really orthodox. Nevertheless the Armenian Church has been permeated by Monophysitism which sees in Christ one divine-human nature, merging the human in the divine. The spirit of unity and simplification is thus apparent alike in its doctrinal and architectural outlooks.

THE RELATION OF ARMENIA TO BYZANTINE ARCHITECTURE

The relative position of Armenia in the history of Byzantine Architecture is a subject which has raised problems not easy of solution. It is now clear that Armenian Architecture is not a mere provincial offshoot of Byzantine, but the mutual influences exercised by one upon the other are not so easy to assess. In the opinion of some authorities Armenian Architecture, though truly national and individual, owes much to Byzantium: others believe that the current ran in the opposite direction and that both in the sixth and the tenth century Armenia moulded the art of the Empire. The decision depends to a great extent on the dates which may be assigned to the Armenian churches. The dates given in this chapter follow the indications of Strzygowski in his *Die Baukunst Der Armenier*, but his views have been combated by Diehl, Macler and others, who believe that he antedates some buildings. They would assign most of them to the tenth and eleventh centuries. That Armenia played a great role in the history of the Empire in the eighth and ninth centuries is a fact which is indisputable. It has already been pointed out that Emperors of Armenian descent occupied the throne and that the army was filled with Armenian troops. They were stationed all over Asia Minor, and it seems highly probable that the stone churches of Asia Minor borrowed features from Armenian settlers who followed them. On the other hand, in Constantinople itself where Greek influence was predominant, there was bitter opposition to Armenian infiltration, and the Greek influence finally got the upper hand. The bureaucracy and to a great extent the church were proud of their Hellenistic tradition, and though Armenians flocked to the capital as merchants, monks and students, the hostility which their presence may have aroused should not be minimised. It is true that some Byzantine plans, such as S. Mary of the Mongols at Constantinople and Nea Moni at Chios, would appear to have an Armenian origin, but to derive the typical

Byzantine plan from the Armenian plateau seems an unwarranted hypothesis.

On the other hand, influence from Byzantium and Anatolia must have found its way to Armenia from the days of Justinian. The prestige of the capital was too potent to be denied. Even when the Arabs held so many of the Eastern provinces, Byzantine Art exercised its sway in the conquered territory as the Mosque of Omar at Jerusalem so amply testifies. Armenia cannot have escaped this influence. But the influence was mutual and the Armenian took his share in the artistic life of the capital and many other cities. Among the architects who were employed to repair Santa Sophia after the great earthquake of 989 was Tiridates the designer of the Cathedral of Ani. Byzantium was much affected by the culture of this versatile and skilful race whose genius and initiative carried its influence far beyond the narrow confines of its own mountain land.

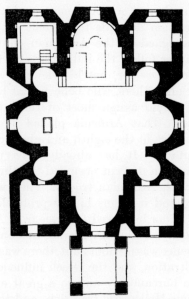

79   S. Hripsimeh, Etschmiadzin

CHAPTER VIII

Palestine, Syria and Egypt

PALESTINE AND SYRIA IN EARLY CHRISTIAN DAYS

IT was only natural that many churches should have been erected in the Holy Land after Christianity had spread throughout the country of its birth. The discovery of the True Cross by S. Helena, mother of the Emperor Constantine, fixed the attention of believers still more upon Jerusalem, and pilgrims were led from far and near to visit the sites which were hallowed by their association with events in the life of Christ. The Emperor Constantine himself made it his aim to endow such sites with buildings worthy of their sanctity. His Church of the Holy Sepulchre at Jerusalem was the most famous of all these erections. "He judged it incumbent on him to render the blessed locality of our Saviour's Resurrection an object of attraction and veneration to all. He issued immediate instructions therefore, for the erection on the spot of a house of prayer." In a letter to Macarius, Bishop of Jerusalem, he signified that the church both as a whole and in its details should be of surpassing beauty. Constantine's buildings included a rotunda which encircled the rock-hewn tomb. Time and time again they have been damaged and rebuilt, and only a western segment of the rotunda remains of the original foundation. The Crusaders made important additions, and reconstruction did not cease with them. The present buildings give no idea of those of Constantine, but the lights of Easter still blaze out year by year in a venerated shrine, and the plan of the round Church of the Holy Sepulchre has been imitated as far away as Orphir in the distant Orkney Isles.

Almost equally celebrated was the Church of the Nativity which Constantine built over the cave at Bethlehem. The existing church was erected by Justinian and was described by the eighth-century traveller Willibald as "a glorious building in the form of a cross". It has a long nave terminated by a round apse, double aisles and apses finishing off its transepts. The roof is wooden and the Corinthian capitals show transition to the Byzantine impost-capitals. The surviving mosaics date from the twelfth century and include pictures of domed cross-in-square churches. It is believed that the church was once adorned with mosaics externally and that the Persians when they invaded Palestine in the early seventh century spared the Church of the Nativity because one of these mosaics depicted their fellow-countrymen, the Wise Men of the East.

In 1934, excavations having been undertaken beneath the floor of Justinian's church, the foundations of the basilica of Constantine were brought to light. It comprised an atrium, a basilica, and, in line with them, an octagon which stood over the Holy Cave. A representation of the church is to be seen in the beautiful fourth-century mosaic in the apse of the Church of S. Pudenziana at Rome. There the octagon stands out prominently with the basilica on its right. Constantine also built a basilica on the Mount of Olives and one at Mamre at the site of Abraham's oak. Other sacred localities were early commemorated: among them may be mentioned the traditional spot by the shores of the Lake of Galilee where Christ fed the Multitude. A large stone lay in the field upon which Our Lord is said to have sat when He performed the miracle. A tiny church was at first built around the stone, to be followed by a basilica of a grandeur more compatible with the fame of the place. This basilica, which may date from the beginning of the fifth century, finished off square like many other basilicas of Palestine and Syria. In other words, the apse, round in plan, did not project externally, but was "inscribed" within the rectangle, two small chambers or spaces separating it from the lateral walls. The Church of the Multiplication of the Loaves and Fishes is specially distinguished for its splendid mosaic pavement with storks, peacocks, geese and other birds perched on branches among various flowers.

During the Byzantine period Syria and Palestine became rich in ecclesiastical buildings. A great development ensued towards the end of the fifth century, and in the next two centuries every village had its church, and every important town boasted not only of its cathedral but of a dozen other churches. In monasteries, clinging to the sides of precipitous ravines, monks wrote hymns which are sung in English-speaking churches at the present day. Strange ascetics dwelt in remote seclusion or drew multitudes to revere their self-denial. Chief among them was S. Simeon Stylites, who for years lived on the top of a lofty column around which was built a great church extending in four directions from the central octagon. Travellers from the West began to visit the scenes associated with the life of Christ and to record the wonders they had seen. If travellers from abroad flocked to Syria, her own citizens penetrated to distant regions. Her enterprising mariners ventured forth in their little sailing ships with their freights of wine and salted fish, of pistachio and embroidered fabrics and Damascus blades to be bartered for the products of Italy and Gaul. Her colonists settled in groups as far as Bordeaux and her wandering artists set their stamp upon Constantinople, Ravenna and Rome. Syrian scholarship was famous and many students attended her schools of rhetoric and law. Eusebius, the Father of Ecclesiastical History, was Bishop of Caesarea and Chrysostom, one of the world's greatest preachers, was educated at Antioch.

CHURCHES IN SYRIA

Of the considerable number of churches whose remains exist in Syria and Palestine few, if any, can be classified as Byzantine in the strictest sense of the term. Mr. J. W. Crowfoot says, "The central churches (of Palestine) which fall within our chronological limits show no sign that we can discern of Byzantine . . . influence. Enough remains for us to justify us in claiming for the churches of Palestine a separate niche . . . in the history of religious architecture." Nevertheless, as Syria and Palestine were from the fourth to the seventh century an important part of the Byzantine Empire, it is impossible to omit all mention of the buildings which were erected then upon its soil and a brief record is demanded to complete the picture. Among central-planned churches that of S. George at Ezra, long familiar in histories of architecture, has been already mentioned (p. 45). Ezra is a village situated some forty miles east of the northern end of the Lake of Galilee and its church is of modest dimensions. It consists of a square naos containing the eight-fold dome sup-port, a bay between two rectangular chambers and a projecting apse be-yond. The present dome is a modern one; the original was perhaps of wood (80).

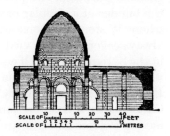

80   Ezra: longitudinal section

Very much grander and larger was the Cathedral of Bosra, once a populous city over twenty miles

147

south-south-east of Ezra, and the seat of an archbishopric (81). The cathedral, dedicated to SS. Sergius, Bacchus and Leontius and now in a ruined state, was erected in 512. It is a plain structure built of the local basalt, but contains carved material from classical buildings. In the centre of its square naos stood four exedrae of columns separated each by a pier. An ambulatory was thus formed between the central area and the outer walls. An apse and side-chambers projected from the eastern end. It was roofed in wood.

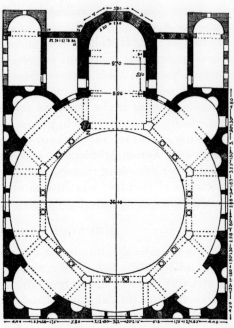

81   Plan of the Cathedral of Bosra

Antioch, the place where, as we read in the Book of Acts, the disciples were first called Christians became renowned in due course as a Christian centre. There the Emperor Constantine built an octagonal church "of surpassing size and beauty". Set in the midst of a great enclosure and rising to a lofty height, it was profusely adorned with gold and other precious materials. This church was not a memorial one but was erected for congregational purposes: the problem of the location of the altar faced the builder of a circular or octagonal church, but we do not know where it stood in Constantine's church at Antioch. Justinian, always eager to build, vied with Constantine in his noble churches in the Syrian capital. Of equal distinction were the churches which were erected away to the south, at Gaza on the sea-coast of Palestine. A sixth-century church in that city was described by Choricius as a combination of the circular and octagonal plans, having a dome on eight arches in the centre, "four of which were prolonged to the walls". It was richly decorated with mosaics. Pendentives seem to have been employed in the propylaea, for we read of the spaces between the arches being "roofed with four concave triangles". An earlier church at Gaza (c. 400) was built by Bishop Porphyrius on a cruciform plan after instructions sent by the Empress Eudoxia. "And there was in another paper within the letter a plan of the holy church shaped like a cross even as now with God's help it is to be seen, and it was written in the letter that the holy church should be founded according to the plan." At Khan-el-Ahmar, a place on the road between Jericho and Jerusalem which has been claimed as the site of the Inn of the Good Samaritan, a church dedicated to S. Euthymius was excavated in 1928–9. A dome on pendentives over its nave seems to have replaced an original wooden roof in the second half of the seventh century. Far more extensive are the excavations which have been conducted at Jerash, the ancient Gerasa, once a populous and flourishing city some twenty miles to the east of the Jordan, on a latitude about half-way between the Dead Sea and the Lake of Galilee. Rebuilt by the Romans, it was situated in a fertile country intersected by a running stream, and the ruins of its temples, its amphitheatres, its colonnades, and its streets fully attest its importance and prosperity. The site has been excavated and described by the Yale University, the British School of Archaeology in Jerusalem and the American School of Oriental studies in Jerusalem. Earthquakes shattered the stately buildings in the eighth century, and the place was abandoned until comparatively recent times.

Gerasa became celebrated in Christian days for a miraculous fountain in front of which stood the cathedral. Dating from the third quarter of the fourth century, it was a basilica with each aisle separated from the nave by a row of ancient Corinthian columns carrying an architrave. The apse, which is "inscribed", is of a less width than that of the nave, a characteristic of basilicas of early date. It has two small square side-chambers within the rectangle. During the course of the next three centuries numerous other structures clustered on or near the atrium on which the sacred fountain stood—churches, atria, baths, baptisteries, dwelling-houses, stairways, chapels, porticoes: the whole elevated site was crowded with ecclesiastical buildings. One of them is the Basilica of S. Theodore, built in 494 with the material from a classical building. Its apse, which projects externally, spans the whole width of the nave. In another part of the town stood the Church of SS. Peter and Paul to which a date about 540 has been assigned. In this basilica the side-chambers of the apse have developed into veritable apses with round ends. These side-apses cannot be described as prothesis and diaconicon for the change in the liturgy which brought about the prothesis did not take place till the reign of Justin II. The chancels of these Palestinian basilicas like those of S. Clemente and S. Maria in Cosmedin at Rome extended down the nave. Mr. Crowfoot thinks that the chambers took the apsidal form simply for effect, as a pleasant way of closing the vista down the aisles. There were other plans at Jerash. A cruciform church, dedicated to the Prophets, Apostles and Martyrs dates from the middle of the fifth century. It had a semicircular apse. Each arm of the cross was divided into a nave and aisles by rows of columns, and the angle-spaces of the cross were filled up with rooms. The church, which was constructed mainly of material from classical buildings, would be roofed in wood, though the angle-chambers may have been domed.

The centralised plan is also to be found in the Church of S. John, which bears a close resemblance in plan to the Cathedral of Bosra. Four central columns, however, take the place of the colonnaded exedrae of Bosra. It had a wooden roof. Of special distinction is the mosaic pavement of S. John with its representations of famous cities. Among them is Alexandria with its walls and towers, its colonnades and churches, its famous gates of the Sun and Moon and its palm trees bearing clusters of red dates; away to the left in the open country is a shrine that was both a beacon for mariners and a famous place of pilgrimage.

Enough perhaps has been said earlier to give a slight indication of the churches of Palestine built during the Byzantine era. As has already been stated, there was a great number of churches in the country, and even after the Arab conquest, a period of toleration permitted the further erection of Christian places of worship. Within recent years the patient labours of archaeologists have shed a flood of light on the Christian architecture of the Holy Land, and many edifices in a more or less ruinous condition have been carefully studied and described.

It is impossible to close without reference to the most famous series of Christian edifices in Syria. It is true that they are not in any strict sense specimens of Byzantine Architecture, but they were erected on Syrian soil when the land was part of the Byzantine Empire, and they are of so remarkable an interest that they cannot be passed by. In North Syria to the south-east of Antioch and in the region of the Hauran, east of the the Jordan, stand the marvellous remains of flourishing towns whose buildings date from the fourth to the sixth centuries after the Birth of Christ. Abandoned by their inhabitants in the seventh century, when the hosts of the Persians and Arabs invaded the country, they remained for centuries forgotten and desolate amid the vast expanse of the desert. At last, in the mid-nineteenth century, a French archaeologist, the Comte de Vogüé, brought the knowledge of these remarkable ruins to the scholars of the West. American expeditions, under Howard Crosby Butler of Princeton, completed the work which de Vogüé had begun. Beautifully constructed of stone, these buildings are both of a religious and a secular nature and are gracefully adorned with sculptured ornament. The churches are nearly all of the basilical type. Their apses are internal in earlier examples and project in the later ones from the rectangle. The façades are imposing, with an open porch under a great arch, flanked by two towers and approached by a flight of steps. Above the open vestibule between the towers, a gallery extends. The apse is flanked by side-apses. In later buildings the horseshoe apse is common. These basilicas reveal a combination of Oriental and Hellenistic elements; the open porch between the two towers and the horseshoe arch are Eastern; from the Hellenistic cities is derived the general feature of nave and aisles. Among these buildings may be mentioned Roueiha, Baquouza and Tourmanin, which was destroyed by the Turks as late as the nineteenth century after it had been seen by de Vogüé, and of which he gives a reconstruction in his book. Most imposing of all are the ruins of Qalb Louzé with its fine mouldings, its great arches, its twin towers and its range of rectangular windows in the clerestory. The churches in Hauran follow the same general plan as the above churches of northern Syria, but, owing to the scarcity of wood, were roofed in stone: among them are those of Tafka and Qannaout. Built of a hard basalt, the churches of the Hauran have well been fitted to endure the ravages of time. No less remarkable than the edifices themselves is the decoration with which their lintels, capitals, arches and mouldings are so richly and profusely sculptured. Hellenistic and Oriental influences combined to fashion this ornamental style; the classical acanthus is bent and twisted into new shapes; stars and rosettes and other devices separate floral patterns; birds are perched on the branches or stand fronting one another.

151

Away in the northern desert at Kasr-ibn-Wardan, there stands a group of lonely and imposing ruins. It consists of a church, a palace and barracks, and dates from about A.D. 564. The church was a domed basilica with a narthex, a north-west stair-tower and an apse with side-rooms, showing a straight wall outside. In style and plan it bears the influence of Constantinople. Constructed of brick and a local basalt, it was adorned with frescoes, mosaics and yellow marble columns and its capitals belong to a fine Byzantine type. Mesopotamian influence is evident in the pointed arches of the dome, which was still standing in the nineteenth century. Its system of construction was remarkable, for above the arches there rose walls between which the pendentives were placed, and the pendentives were pierced with windows.

EARLY CHRISTIANITY IN EGYPT

In the seventh century, Syria was overrun by the Moslems and ceased to form a part of the Byzantine Empire. Later in the same century Egypt, apart from Nubia, also fell under Arab sway. The loss was a severe calamity for the imperial power. For centuries Egypt had been a proud and flourishing province of the Roman and Byzantine Empires. From her great port of Alexandria the grain which had been grown in the fertile valley of the Nile was carried across the sea to feed the teeming population of Constantinople. Commerce flowed across Syria to the distant East and over the Mediterranean to Italy and Gaul. For hundreds of years Alexandria remained one of the most wealthy and luxurious cities of the known world. Noble buildings adorned her streets and her palaces were filled with costly works of art. Her famous library and her museum brought innumerable scholars to her class-rooms, and her school was graced by the presence of S. Clement, whose theological writings are revered as among the greatest treasures of early Christian literature. Yet between Constantinople and Alexandria there always existed a latent resentment which burst into open antagonism when passions were aroused. It was with envious eyes that the Patriarch of Alexandria watched the growing prestige and power of the Patriarch of Constantinople. Alexandria was the birthplace of heresies and although in the Christological controversies of the fifth century it was S. Cyril of Alexandria who supported the orthodox position, Egypt eventually adopted the Monophysite heresy, and fell into schism to form the Coptic Church.

Alexandria had been a Hellenistic city, impregnated with the culture of Greece, though modified by considerable Oriental influences. In the spheres of painting, decoration and the illumination of manuscripts she contributed in no little degree to the development of Byzantine Art. But behind the refined city of the coast lay the country district and the desert, where native and Eastern habits of thought were strong. In the spiritual realm these elements were of major importance for the Empire. Egypt was the birthplace of the Christian monasticism which spread with such rapidity over all Byzantine territory and which exercised so powerful a sway over the minds of men and the fabric of society through all the centuries of Byzantine history. Fleeing from the corruptions of the world, thousands of hermits betook themselves to lead solitary lives in the Thebaid. To one of these hermits came a certain Roman soldier called Pachomius who had been converted to the Christian faith. By grouping some of these hermits in a colony on an island of the Nile he became the founder of Egyptian monasticism. In addition to spending long hours in meditation and prayer they occupied their time in farming, basketmaking and the building of boats. By the end of the fourth century there were eight monasteries in Egypt. Thousands of monks and hermits populated the Egyptian desert, spending their hours in fasting, prayer and labour, but issuing from their solitudes to plunge into the theological disputes which raged in the city. They painted the frescoed walls of their churches and embellished sacred manuscripts which were conveyed to distant cities, and from their Egyptian fastnesses they radiated an influence and set an example which was felt throughout the length and breadth of the Eastern Empire.

In spite of these facts the connection which can now be traced between the architecture of Christian Egypt and that of Byzantium is very slender. Alexandria, hallowed by its associations with S. Mark, must have possessed churches of great size and beauty, but all of them have long since disappeared. The marble capitals which have been discovered seem to have been imported from Constantinople. Christianity early spread up the Nile Valley, where it found many adherents. It was the official religion of Nubia—from Assuan southwards—from the sixth to the fourteenth century, but the Christian enclave was separated from the Empire by the Moslem power.

EGYPTIAN CHURCHES

As the Church of Egypt was the Coptic Church, so its architecture was Coptic Architecture. The dome, placed upon a square substructure, was a common feature of its churches; the squinches which supported them were derived from the same common Eastern source as those employed in other parts of the Byzantine Empire.

Egypt must once have possessed many splendid churches but most of the extant ones are of small size and poor material. In one type the whole area is covered by a series of domes. There are churches of this sort north of Assuan at Edfu, Medinet Habu, and other places. The Church of SS. Cyrus and John at Cairo has twelve domes and that of S. Pachomius at Medammot has no less than thirty-three. Another type, found at Gendal Irki, Serre, Madeyq, and Kasr Ibrim (all south of Assuan) has a central dome with parallel barrel-vaults on north and south.

There are also churches of a basilical plan in Egypt, finished off square in the eastern end. Among them are those of four monasteries which stand surrounded with high walls amid wide stretches of desert sand in the Natrun Valley to the north-west of Cairo. These monasteries were sacked in 817 and their churches belong to a later date (82). At the east end, which finished off square, there extends the "haikal" or sanctuary, in three domed parts. It is preceded by a domed or transversely vaulted choir, the disposition recalling Mesopotamian plans. The choir is separated from the three-aisled nave by a wall. Butler, who visited the monasteries in the later nineteenth century, describes them as "veritable fortresses . . . with blind walls rising sheer out of the desert sand". He goes on to describe the courtyard with its churches, chapels and domestic buildings and the large tower which housed the vestments, the sacred vessels and the ancient books, among which Curzon discovered such treasures on his famous visit to the Monasteries of the Levant.

The Egyptian dome shows a brick or plastered surface on the outside. A common position for its employment was over the "haikal". A familiar example is at the Church of S. Sergius

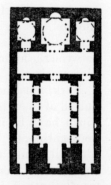

82 Dair-al-Baramus,
Natrun Valley,
Egypt

at Cairo, built on the spot where the Holy Family is said to have rested after the Flight into Egypt. Some churches have an east end which is of a trefoil form internally. They include those in the monasteries of Amba Saman, near Assuan, and those in the much-discussed Red and White Monasteries near Sohag in the Thebaid. The White Monastery was visited by Curzon, who was greatly impressed by its appearance.

> The peculiarity of this monastery is that the interior was once a magnificent basilica while the exterior was built by the Empress Helena in the ancient Egyptian style. . . . The monastery stands at the foot of the hill on the edge of the Libyan desert where the sand encroaches on the plain. It looks like the sanctuary or cella of an ancient temple and is not unlike the bastion of an old fortification: except for one solitary doom tree it stands quite alone and has a most desolate aspect backed as it is by the sandy desert.

The churches of the White and Red Monasteries are of basilical plan and carry domes on squinches over the haikal. These domes with their squinches have been the subject of much discussion, but it has now been proved that the towers which carry them were originally roofed with wood and the domical coverings were not substituted until a much later century.

The remains of the great Monastery of S. Menas in the Maareotis desert belong to an imperial foundation erected by Arcadius in the fifth century. With its great basilicas it must have been an imposing place of pilgrimage, visited by tens of thousands of devotees every year. It contained a baptistery in the form of a domed square, brought to an octagon by niches in the angles between engaged columns.

EGYPT AND CONSTANTINOPLE

The churches of Egypt are to be classified in a style of their own, in that of Coptic Architecture. Their plan was dictated by their own liturgical and ecclesiastical customs and their structure bears the stamp of native feelings. Yet, as always, influences penetrated from without and those of Syria and the Orient are evident. Nor does it appear unjustifiable to trace a connection with Byzantium, and it is not unreasonable to suggest that it was from there that the idea of placing a dome over a square was derived. The dome itself seems to have been familiar in Egypt many centuries before the birth of Christ, and it was used in Roman times to cover a circle in a great building in Alexandria. Byzantine influence has been minimised. It is true that none of these churches are true examples of Byzantine Architecture, but it is possible to appreciate the views of Statham when he speaks of the square domed compartments being "obviously of Byzantine suggestion". At the same time, in existing structures the Byzantine influence has become derivatory and remote. The dates of many of these churches are uncertain and possibly much later than once they were believed to be. Somers Clarke thinks that all the many-domed churches mentioned above were later than the Arab invasions. Many others may have been restored after that date. Cresswell has quoted an Arab author of the thirteenth century to prove that three churches, originally roofed otherwise, were fitted with domes in the twelfth century.

Yet it is possible that the extant churches ultimately owe their system of domical construction to Byzantine influence emanating from the capital or Asia Minor. When the regular commercial intercourse between Alexandria and Constantinople is considered, when it is known that architectural ornaments were shipped from there to Egypt, it is surely natural that the churches should have felt the influence of the capital and that Alexandria could boast of domical churches in the true Byzantine style. From Alexandria the idea would spread to the country districts. The passage of the years would bring about modifications: local and Arab feeling would leave their impress upon the design. Nevertheless Byzantine Architecture played its part in the original suggestion and the domes of the Egyptian churches may be described as distant and indirect descendants of Byzantine types.

CHAPTER IX

Later Churches in Constantinople

THE BASILIAN AND COMNENIAN EPOCHS:
AN HISTORICAL SKETCH

D URING the first half of the ninth century the armies of Byzantium were able to hold its enemies at bay, both in the Balkans and Asia Minor; but the constant raids and sporadic victories of Bulgar and of Arab caused widespread misery and destruction, while the loss of Sicily and Crete to the Moslems deprived the Empire of two valued islands. The capture of Crete brought a continuous series of tragedies in its train, as the Arab pirates issued from their island fortress to harass the routes of commerce and despoil the industrious towns of the mainland. The advent of the Basilian dynasty led to an improvement in the fortunes of the Empire. Basil I was born in Thrace, the son of a Slavonic peasant. He found his way to Constantinople, where he obtained employment as a groom in the household of the Emperor Michael III the "Drunkard". Appointed first to be Chamberlain and then to be co-emperor, Basil slew his dissolute benefactor, and reigned as sole monarch with the tacit approval of the populace. The new emperor proved himself to be an able general and an efficient administrator. In 876 he recovered a portion of southern Italy, which, as the theme of Longobardia, continued to be an imperial possession for almost two hundred years. He did not suffer the depredations of the Moslem pirates to remain unchecked. He reformed the financial system and codified the laws. His policy was maintained by Leo VI (886–911), a scholarly and philosophic ruler who was surnamed the "Wise" and who strove, like others of his dynasty, to protect the small proprietors from the growing encroachments of the powerful landowners of Asia Minor. In the reigns of Constantine VII Porphyrogenitus (912–959) and the co-Emperor Romanus I Lecapenus, the soldiers of Byzantium penetrated far into the Moslem East, raiding the ancient cities of Nisibis and Amida, where they exacted tribute from the enemy. Armenia freed itself from Mohammedan rule and accepted Byzantine suzerainty.

The authority of the Empire extended to the far-off shores of Lake Van.

Throughout the Basilian period the strength of the Empire can be ascribed not only to the wise administration of talented sovereigns and the invulnerable stability of a complex bureaucratic system. Fortunately for the Empire, its neighbours were weakened by the spirit of decay and internecine feuds. The West was in a state of chaos and the East was rent by civil wars. The times were favourable to Byzantium and the Emperors wisely seized the opportunity which was offered them by fortune. Under the rule of the Basilians the Byzantine Empire reached the very zenith of its fame and was acclaimed as the most cultured and civilised country in the known world. Constantine Porphyrogenitus, an author of distinction and a patron of letters, strove to ease the lot of the peasants while the recapture of Crete by the ability and determination of Nicephorus Phocas in 961 protected the navigator of the adjacent sea and removed a perpetual threat to peaceful commerce. Nicephorus Phocas (963–969), who succeeded Romanus II (959–963), was a strange character, an ascetic who dreamt of renouncing the world to become a monk, a general whose armies drove the infidel far beyond the Taurus Mountains, an administrator who strove to conserve the finances of his country. His career and the whole contemporary life of the Empire have been described in a sumptuous and richly illustrated volume by the late M. Gustave Schlumberger. John Zimisces (969–976), the assassin and successor of Phocas, also penetrated Mesopotamia and inflicted heavy defeats on the Bulgarians and Russians, who were menacing Constantinople from the north.

But it was under the Emperor Basil II, surnamed Boulgaroktonos, "the slayer of the Bulgarians", that the Byzantine Empire reached the summit of its power and the farthest limits of its territorial aggrandisement. In the course of a hundred years it doubled its area, and its prestige among the nations was paramount. It was against the Bulgarians, who had been a thorn in the side of the Empire for many years, that Basil most persistently launched the weight of his victorious armies, decimating his enemies with ruthless severity, and in 1048 completing their subjugation. His Empire now stretched in unbroken extent from the Euphrates to the Danube. So great were the exploits of this austere and incorruptible sovereign, who had taken monastic vows and beneath his imperial robes wore the habiliments of a monk.

But the glory achieved by the Byzantine Empire was destined all too swiftly to be dimmed. Basil's brother, Constantine VIII, reigned only three years, to be followed by the Empress Zoe from 1028 to 1050, her successive husbands sharing her imperial crown. Stable administration and good government declined, while the intrigues of palace officials and the promotion of unworthy favourites sapped the integrity of the State. At this time also, new external foes threatened the ailing Empire. By the time William the Conqueror had landed in England, Norman knights had established themselves in southern Italy. Surely and steadily they encroached upon the Byzantine possessions in the peninsula until, in 1071, Bari on the heel of Italy, the last stronghold of the Empire, had capitulated to the predatory and astute adventurers.

In the East the position was still more serious. The Seljouk Turks, pouring down from their home in Central Asia, had in 1055 occupied Baghdad. Thence they swept over Asia Minor in repeated incursions, bringing devastation in their wake. These inroads, moreover, changed the population, for the Turks who infiltrated the country settled down in abandoned regions. For a long time the character of the peasantry had also been changing in the retained areas. The small proprietors were being crushed out by the accumulation of land in the possession of powerful nobles. These feudal lords, with armies of serfs, attained a semi-independent status, weakening the central authority at Constantinople. The diminution in the number of free peasants also meant a serious loss of revenue through taxation, and a decrease in the available recruits for military service. All these causes, coupled with many years of insurrection and internal strife combined to hasten the decline which the Byzantine Empire suffered in the eleventh century. But the age-long Empire had marvellous powers of recuperation, and the skill of a sovereign who knew how to turn the circumstances to the advantage of his country, raised it once more towards the level of its former glory. The sovereign was Alexius I of the great Anatolian family of the Comneni. When he ascended the throne in 1081 he found the Empire at the nadir of its fortunes. Ten years previously a rash though intrepid Emperor, Romanus IV, had fallen prisoner to the Turks, with the annihilation of a great army, in the fatal battle of Manzikert (1071), one of the most disastrous in the history of the Empire. The Turkish hosts swept over Anatolia to the very shores of the Sea of Marmora and established a large Sultanate

159

with its capital at the ancient Christian city of Nicea, hallowed to every Greek by the memory of the first General Council of the Church, held within its walls seven hundred years before. Such was the position of affairs which Alexius faced. An unexpected ally came to his assistance when in 1096 the armies of the First Crusade encamped outside the walls of Constantinople on their way to the Holy Land. The Crusaders marched through Asia Minor; Nicea fell to their victorious armies, then Antioch and then Jerusalem, Latin kingdoms and principalities being formed out of former Moslem possessions. The forces of the Byzantine Emperor followed the Crusaders, and he was enabled to regain a great part of Asia Minor. The Empire had got a new lease of life. But the territorial aggrandisement was counterbalanced by commercial loss. Alexius had been forced to concede valuable trading rights to Venice, which was granted freedom from dues in imperial ports and a privileged quarter in Constantinople. The successful rivalry of the Venetian Republic began to sap the prosperity of Byzantium, whose merchants felt a bitter hostility to their determined competitors. Although John II Comnenus (1118–43) wisely strove to improve the lot of his subjects, trade continued to decline and taxation to be a grievous burden. Under Manuel I Comnenus, a brilliant but erratic sovereign, all but the coast of Asia Minor fell into the hands of the Turks. Nevertheless he staved off complete disaster. But the terrible blows which the Empire had suffered had a permanent effect. The claims of a deposed and blinded Emperor Isaac II Angelos and of his son offered a pretext to Dandolo, the Doge of Venice, to divert the Fourth Crusade from a war against the infidels to an attack on the capital of the Christian Empire of the East. In 1204, with their fleet anchored in the harbour, the Crusaders stormed the opulent but feeble city, massacring its inhabitants and pillaging its priceless treasures. Tremendous fires, vividly described by the Latin chronicler Villehardouin, devastated its northern and western quarters. Great numbers of precious objects, reliquaries, icons, processional crosses, were carried off to Western Europe, where many of them are still preserved in the treasuries of churches and in the galleries of museums. But those which have been preserved are as nothing to the quantities which have disappeared.

A great part of the Byzantine Empire was parcelled out among the Latin conquerors, the capital and its environs being subject to Baldwin, Count of Flanders, first Latin Emperor of the East. From the very beginning the Latin Empire was a pitiable affair. It struggled on, in its ruined and decimated surroundings for little more than fifty years, reverting in 1261 to the Greeks under Michael VIII Palaeologus, sovereign of the Empire which had been established at Nicea during the period of the Latin occupation of Constantinople.

COMMERCE, LITERATURE AND ART

The political power and economic prosperity of the Basilian epoch gave an impetus to every form of intellectual and artistic pursuit. Fair and opulent, dowered with the glory of the purple and hallowed with the presence of a thousand sacred relics, the great and populous city on the sunlit shores of the Sea of Marmora was the cynosure and admiration of mankind. Basil I proved to be not only a capable general and administrator, but an emulous patron of the arts, embellishing his capital with magnificent buildings, most lavishly adorned. Many of his successors were quick to abide by his tradition and the light which he kindled, though dimmed by the period of anarchy, shone with a refulgent brilliance until far into the Comnenian epoch.

From about the middle of the ninth to the end of the eleventh century, Constantinople reached a level of culture and fame attained by no other city of the time. Travellers who wended their way to the shores of the Bosphorus were dazzled by the luxury and splendour of the metropolis of the Eastern Empire. In the opinion of Benjamin of Tudela, who visited the Orient in the twelfth century, its only equal in the world was Baghdad, capital of the Arab Empire. According to Benjamin, the streets of Byzantium were thronged with men clad in sumptuous raiment "who all looked like the sons of kings". Private habitations were filled with objects of inestimable worth; palaces and churches displayed an incomparable beauty. A cosmopolitan city, it attracted the representatives of many different races. The royal authoress Anna Comnena, in her history of the reign of her father, the Emperor Alexius, mentions the numerous Armenians who dwelt in the city. The Empire itself was a heterogeneous admixture of races, bound together by the ties of a Hellenistic culture and the Orthodox Church. It was inevitable that all these races—Greeks, Syrians, Anatolians, Armenians, Slavs and others—should gravitate towards the capital. Foreigners attracted by motives of commerce or study or by the sheer beauty of this resplendent town, formed their dwellings within its circuit. Russian merchants under stringent rules were permitted to settle at the city while colonies of Venetians and Genoese were, in the twelfth century, assigned their separate quarters. Monks from many regions of the Orient settled in the numerous monasteries which abounded in Byzantium, and students from distant places in East and West attended the lectures of its university.

The centre of a flourishing commerce, Constantinople brought traders from all parts of the world to its busy markets, and as a centre of exchange transmitted the luxurious products of the Orient to the barons, ecclesiastics and wealthy burghers of Western Europe. The Arab occupation of Syria had seriously curtailed the profits of Greek merchants, but the intercourse of commerce between Arab and Byzantine states was maintained. Gold and silver, pearls and amethysts and other precious stones, aromatic unguents and healing herbs, were shipped to the marts of Constantinople. An extension of trade was developed to the North, and down the long course of the Dnieper honey and leather and furs were carried from the inhospitable regions of the North to the Black Sea and the Golden Horn. From the Byzantine Empire itself came the grain grown on the wide cornfields of Anatolia and Thrace, and the rich silk from the looms of Larissa and Thebes.

During this period literature, nurtured by classical study, continued to flourish within Constantinople. The Emperors, Constantine VII and Leo VI were themselves authors: encyclo-paedias were compiled which gathered together the facts and traditions of the past. The events of the reigns of Emperors were duly chronicled by contemporary historians like Leo the Deacon and Michael Psellus and the lives of the saints and the narration of their miracles made a vivid appeal to the heart of the devout. Poetry and science, grammar and literary criticism had their representatives while the stirring exploits of Diogenes Akrtas, a hero of the Anatolian frontier, were glorified in all the excitement of a popular romance.

In this rich and cultured city the artist found a ready field for his talent. Wealthy nobles and proud officers of state, elate with the dignity of their grandiloquent titles and their gorgeous robes, filled their palaces with the treasures of art. There was a wide demand for costly fabrics richly woven with designs of Eastern origin, birds, animals and fruit. Most gorgeous of all were the silken fabrics destined for imperial display or personal use, and on which representations of eagles or lions or fabulous monsters glistened in purple, green and gold. Among the fabrics of this period preserved in European museums perhaps the most celebrated is the so-called shroud of Charlemagne at Aix-la-Chapelle with its encircled elephants. Even more precious from both the artistic and iconographical standpoints were the illuminated manuscripts. Of the many examples belonging to this epoch one may cite the celebrated Menologium of Basil II, which was prepared for the piety of that Emperor by several different artists towards the close of the tenth century. Containing lives of the saints, it is embellished with over four hundred miniatures relative to its subjects. As one turns over the precious leaves of this treasure of the Vatican Library, one is impressed, despite a certain sameness of treatment, by the glowing richness of the colour, the interest of the architectural settings, the dignity of the figures and the detailed skill of the execution.

Diptychs, tryptichs and coffers of ivory delicately carved with subjects both sacred and secular also continued to be produced in vast numbers. Among the numerous ivories which have found their way into the museums of Western Europe may be mentioned the beautiful Harbaville Triptych in the Louvre, depicting the scene known as the Deisis (the enthroned Christ between the Virgin and the Baptist), with military saints and apostles standing grouped in the other compartments (77). The Victoria and Albert Museum in London has an ivory relief of the tenth century showing the Dormition of the Virgin in the top panel and saints fronting the spectator in characteristic Byzantine attitudes in the panels below. Reliquaries, crosses, icon-frames and plaques, embossed and jewelled and enamelled, were produced in large numbers for the use of the Church. An illustration is given of a plaque in gilded copper now in the Victoria and Albert Museum (76). It depicts the Virgin and Child and is executed in repoussé. Of considerable grace, it is stated to have once been preserved in the Cathedral of Torcello near Venice. The inscription is in Greek.

After the troubles caused by the Iconoclastic Controversy had ceased and the Basilian dynasty had been established on the throne the arts of fresco and mosaic were impelled to a new life, and pictures in these media clad the walls of the sacred buildings.

In Constantinople itself some of the mosaics which have been uncovered in recent years at Santa Sophia date from this period. The frescoes in the strange rock-churches of Cappadocia have already been mentioned as examples of a popular art.

Nor was the talent of the architect and artist requisitioned only for the purposes of religion. The Basilian and Comnenian monarchs erected or restored magnificent habitations which they adorned with sumptuous grandeur. Constantine VII has meticulously described the Palace of Basil I, the Cenourgion, with its columns of onyx and Thessalian marble, its sculptured ornament and glittering mosaic. Nicephoras Phocas transformed the Palace of Boucouleon into a powerful and lavishly decorated fortress. The Comneni built the Palace of Blachernae, which lay just beside the land wall of the city and which was said to have been filled with "painting in colour and in gold". This was the residence of the later Emperors: from it they issued to ride and hunt in the spacious park outside the gate with their retinue of attendants; it was the starting-point of the solemn processions which the Emperor and his courtiers made to visit some hallowed shrine on an annual festival; it was the scene of imperial receptions when the emissaries of barbaric nations were dazzled by the magnificence which greeted them. Of the great Palace of the Blachernae there remains only a forlorn and dilapidated pavilion which goes by the Turkish name of Tekfour-Serai. It is traditionally connected with the name of the Emperor Constantine VII Porphyrogenitus and is an interesting example of Byzantine secular architecture. It has a façade pierced with windows and arches and encrusted with brick and marble. The older palace on Seraglio Point, known as the Sacred Palace and sumptuously adorned by Theophilus in the ninth century, was further embellished by Basil I. But when the soldiers of the Fourth Crusade entered the city they found the Sacred Palace in a state of considerable decay, a condition which became complete in the last stage of the Empire's history.

FEATURES OF THE ARCHITECTURE

The churches under review were with one exception converted into mosques by the Turks, who altered the structures and covered most of them with a thick coating of plaster and whitewash. It appears, however, that the earlier churches were built of thin bricks and the later ones of stone varied with thin brick courses. The beds of mortar in the joints are usually of considerable thickness. Vaults and domes were built of brick, vaults being of the barrel, domical, or cross type. Cross-vaults in the angle-spaces and in the side apse-chambers are especially characteristic of Constantinopolitan churches. As has been already stated in Chapter IV, when dealing with the varieties of the cross-in-square plan these plans in Constantinople show additional bays before the apses, the central one vaulted at a lower level than the eastern cross-arm (type IIA (β), p. 57). This lower vaulting adds considerably to the aesthetic effect. The additional bays have often niches in their side-walls internally, giving a trefoil plan. The apses, three in number, were round in the inside and showed several faces of a polygon on the outside. They were often decorated with arcading and with tall narrow round-headed niches. Arches on the outer walls of the gables articulated the curve of the interior vaults. As time advanced more and more care was expended upon the external appearance of the edifices, which were enlivened with bands and arches of brick. The heightening and multiplication of the drums which supported the domes became more and more characteristic of churches of a late period. The original use of a drum doubtless arose from constructive reasons, but it was a desire for external effect which prompted its greater elevation and increased the numbers of the domes. The lofty central dome was a bold and effective crown to the building and the subsidiary ones added to its importance and to the picturesqueness of its silhouette. The drums were polygonal in plan externally and circular within. Pilasters might decorate the interior or they might be concaved into a number of compartments. Decorated on the outside with angle-columns tied together by arched cornices, they became highly ornamental features. Windows were round-headed and invariably occupied sides of the drums, and the apses. In the drums they were single, but elsewhere they were often of double or triple form, the lights being divided by slender marble shafts with carved capitals. A semicircular window divided by vertical shafts into three lights often appears in the gable. Carved marble slabs were employed to occupy the lower part of the windows and to serve as balustrades. The square-headed doors often carried carved marble architraves. The type of capital most usually employed to crown the columns of the later churches of Constantinople was the Byzantine Corinthian impost-capital with its details sculptured in various and elaborate forms. This summary of the main characteristics of the Byzantine churches of the capital may serve to introduce the description of the individual churches, in the course of which further allusions will be made to them.

A familiar feature of these churches was the gynaeceum or the gallery for the use of women worshippers. In the earlier churches it formed a gallery within the church, in the later it was placed over the narthex. The narthex was an important feature in all the churches. Additional accommodation was provided by an exo-narthex, by side-chapels or even by contiguous churches. It is interesting to note the different methods adopted to secure increased space in the Byzantine Church and in the Romanesque or Gothic Church of the West.

It has already been pointed out that attempts have been made by scholars to trace a definite evolution from the domed basilica through various stages to the four-columned cross-in-square plan. According to the views of these scholars this development took place in Constantinople itself: the domed basilica, through the prolongation of its north and south dome-arches to the exterior walls evolved into the cross-domed basilica. Then, by the elimination of the galleries and their supporting arcades, the cross-domed basilica became the cross-in-square church with a dome supported on piers. Finally, by the substitution of columns for the piers, the four-columned cross-in-square plan was achieved.

Against these views the following facts may be pointed out. In the first place, the vast majority has disappeared of those innumerable shrines which once graced the city and which might have accurately attested the development of ecclesiastical architecture within its bounds. The extant churches are not sufficiently numerous to demonstrate with accuracy the development of the style. It seems to the present writer that the available evidence is not sufficiently strong to prove these theories in their entirety. In the second place, many of the churches in Constantinople are of so uncertain date that they cannot be evidenced as fixed stages in a gradual evolutionary process within the capital. The passage from the domed to the cross-domed basilica may have taken place in Asia Minor. On the other hand, the cross-in-square plan, as has already been pointed out in a previous chapter, may with the greatest reason be considered a development of the cruciform. Once the cross-in-square type had been evolved—also in Asia Minor—the transition to the four-column plan is straightforward.

This transition can now be seen in Constantinople itself. The earliest cross-in-square church, SS. Peter and Mark, of ninth-century date, has for its dome-supports sections of wall, angular in plan. The transition from such a church to the Myrelaion, where the supports of the dome are piers, and then to the south church of the Pantocrator, where they used to be porphyry columns, is obvious (see below). All that can be said about the development of church architecture in Constantinople is that the general tendency as time proceeded was to free the nave from encumbering elements and transform it into a clearly defined and well-knit unit.

The progress of the centuries also indicates a greater appreciation of elegance in the exterior. A somewhat heavy cubical elevation gives place to one which is more shapely and more harmoniously defined.

DESTROYED CHURCHES

The most important church of the period was the famous "New Church", built by the Emperor Basil I and glorified in a panegyric of the Patriarch Photius at its consecration in A.D. 881. It has long since disappeared. Its rich interior glittered with silver and gold. The columns and steps were inlaid with rare varieties of stone and the walls gleamed with panels of coloured marble. The floor was so paved with marble and mosaic that it seemed covered with a carpet of silk and purple. The upper walls were adorned with fine mosaics. Christ Pantocrator surrounded by a guard of attendant angels looked down from the dome; the Virgin was in the apse, and prophets, patriarchs and saints stood in the nave. The church retained a reminiscence of the basilica in a spacious atrium, where two fountains played, but in itself was probably of the Greek cross-in-square plan. The outward aspect must have been brilliant and imposing, for its roof and five domes were covered with gilded plates of bronze, which scintillated in the sunshine. The "New Church", which stood within the palace precincts, was a typical expression of the proud Byzantine autocracy. It is significant that Photius should declare in his panegyric that the Virgin in the apse is extending her arms in prayer, not for the community of Christian people, but for the safety of the Emperor and his triumph over his foes. The greatest church built in Constantinople during this period was essentially an imperial shrine.

Emperors of a later date than Basil were equally ready to

signify their devotion by the erection of magnificent temples to the glory of God. We are told that Romanus II thought that nothing in the whole world was good enough for a church which he built and dedicated to the Virgin. There flowed into it from the royal revenues "a golden river", and the Emperor could scarcely abandon the contemplation of the work. In the construction of a church dedicated to S. George, Constantine IX employed every resource of art. Gold gleamed upon the roof and precious marbles encrusted the floor and walls, resembling "flowers set in alternate hues". Constantine built another church "in a circle on a magnificent and lofty scale". Psellus says that it was decorated with golden stars throughout, issuing from its centre as a never-ending stream. The surrounding ground was levelled "like a race-course" as far as the eye could see, and other buildings were erected within the sacred precincts. Of particular interest and significance is the description given by Psellus of the care which was taken to provide a beautiful natural setting for the church. It was encircled by lawns of dewy grass covered with flowers and shaded by trees, where streams ran and fountains played. It was all like the perfect and unparalleled vision which should meet the eye at the end of a pilgrimage.

As for the church itself it is said by Psellus to have been of dazzling beauty. As the visitor gazed on the details, he was always delighted by some new discovery and when he looked upon the structure as a whole he marvelled at the beautiful harmony and symmetry of its parts.

The scanty references which have survived the passage of time throw some light on the most illustrious of the churches, but the city possessed hundreds of others. Almost all the Byzantine churches of this city which so impressed the mind of medieval pilgrims have perished in fire or crumbled to decay, and only a handful of them survive to attest the beauty of the vanished sanctuaries.

THE SURVIVING MONUMENTS

The Church of Theotokos Pammakaristos, the All-Blessed Virgin, which occupied a commanding position overlooking the Golden Horn, has been assigned a date varying from the eighth to the thirteenth century (84 and 87). It is said that an inscription which occupied a place on its former apse ascribed its foundation or restoration to a certain John Comnenus, who may have lived in

83   CONSTANTINOPLE: S. Theodosia (*Gul-djami*)

84   CONSTANTINOPLE: S. Mary Pammakaristos (*Fétije-djami*)

85, 86 CONSTANTINOPLE: S. Mary Diaconissa (*Kalender-djami*)

the eleventh century. The elegant Parecclesion on the south side of the church is a fourteenth-century addition and will be dealt with later (p. 183). After the Turkish conquest of Constantinople in 1453, the Greek Patriarch, Gennadios, refusing the splendid Church of the Holy Apostles, was content to accept from the Sultan the humbler shrine of the Pammakaristos as his cathedral. The Patriarch resided in the adjacent monastery, and for over one hundred years his throne was permitted by his Moslem master to stand

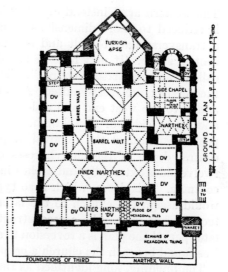

87 Pammakaristos (*Fetijé-djami*), Constantinople

proudly within the church. In the days of Mahommedan rule, the Greek Patriarch exercised considerable power among his Christian followers, and the Church of the Pammakaristos was an object of interest and veneration to pilgrims and travellers from many parts. The awe of the visitors was quickened by the collection of royal portraits, sacred pictures and precious relics, which had been conveyed from the Church of the Holy Apostles, while a permanent congregation of worshippers was ensured by its situation in the midst of a large Greek colony brought into the depopulated city by the Turkish Sultan. But the Pammakaristos was eventually doomed to become the shrine of an alien faith. The golden cross no longer flashes back the sunlight that streams upon its dome. The occupation of Georgia by the victorious troops of Sultan Murad II was commemorated by the transformation of the Church of the All-blessed Mother of God into Fetijé-djami, the Mosque of the Conqueror. It suffered considerable alterations at the hands of its new owners, especially at the eastern end, where its apses gave place to an uncouth angular projection surmounted by a Turkish dome. The church may be described as an abbreviated form of the cross-domed basilica. A domed central area is surrounded on three sides by rectangular spaces from which it was at one time probably separated by arcades.

The western arm, instead of being long, as in a normal basilica, is reduced to short dimensions vaulted on its lower story with a transverse barrel-vault and separated by an arcade from the central space. (It may here be noted that the type is sometimes called "an ambulatory church".) The western angle-spaces, like the narthex, are cross-vaulted. At a later date an exo-narthex was added to the west end and aisles were extended along the north and south sides of the church. The still later Parecclesion(87) probably entailed the removal of part of the south aisle. The central dome of the church rests on an attractive drum with twelve sides externally and arches in two orders resting on angle-columns. This drum, which is so typical an example of its style, would assign the church to the later period of Byzantine Architecture, but it may be a reconstruction. If the church is of the later period the plan is a reversion to an earlier type. In 1940 there was found beneath the church a crypt with a vault on columns.

The building, long identified as the Church of S. Mary Panachrantos, the "Immaculate", and secluded in the heart of the old town, is now thought to have been the church attached to the famous Monastery of Lips. After the Turkish conquest it became the mosque Fenere-issa-mesjedi. It consists of two contiguous churches of different dates with access from one to the other through the common wall(88). A later exo-narthex runs along the whole length of the western front and is returned along the south side. The complex of buildings is an interesting example of how the need for additional space, caused doubtless in this instance by increased numbers in the monastic community, was met. In a cathedral of Western Europe the problem might be solved by building a new and larger chancel. In the Byzantine East the result was achieved by the construction of a contiguous church (parecclesion) and nartheces. The south Church of S. Mary Panachrantos was of abbreviated domed basilical plan, but its present dome is a Turkish work. The apses were decorated with niches and with pilasters that carried capitals in low relief. The northern church, which dates from the tenth century and was originally of cross-in-square plan, has undergone considerable alteration at the hands of the Turks, who removed the central pillars and built a new dome on four pointed arches. The side-apses have not the low elevation normal in a cross-in-square church, but are as high as the central one. The apses are less elaborately decorated than those of the southern church.

The setting-out of the northern aisle of the southern church raised some intricate problems, which were for many years a source of perplexity to archaeologists. The eastern portion of the south wall of the north church was used to form part of the wall of the south church. It looked as if the north church were the earlier building. This opinion was opposed by other authorities who held that the southern church was the earlier building, but that its eastern part was reconstructed when the north church was built.

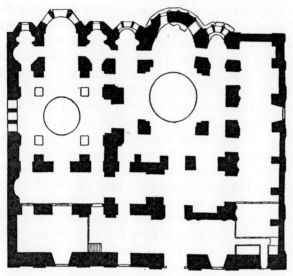

88   S. Mary Panachrantos (*Fenari-issa-mesjedi*)

However, the clearance consequent on a fire which occurred in 1918 seemed to show that the northern was the older of the two churches. The north church had an additional south aisle which was used to form the north aisle of the southern church when the latter came to be built. There are also traces of a northern aisle to the north church, which was therefore of the so-called "five-aisled" cross-in-square plan. It has been averred that this was the normal type of cross-in-square plan in Constantinople and that it passed thence to Kiev in southern Russia, where it is to be found in the famous Cathedral of Santa Sophia. The presence of walled-up entrances in the outer walls of other cross-in-square churches in Constantinople seems to bear witness to the fact that at least several churches in the capital possessed these additional aisles.

These Panachrantos churches were placed under the department of museums in 1947 and will be repaired.

The Church of S. Theodosia (*Gul-djami*) (83), long employed as a store-house for naval equipment before it became a mosque, may be assigned to the tenth or eleventh century. Its dedication recalled the Iconoclastic Persecution under the Emperor Leo III. A crowd of citizens attacked the soldier who had mounted a ladder to destroy the sacred mosaic over the Palace Gate. Theodosia, who was prominent among the assailants, was arrested and suffered martyrdom in the cause of images. It was on the Feast-day of S. Theodosia, 29th May 1453, that the Ottoman Turks burst into Constantinople and brought an end to the Byzantine Empire. They found the Church of S. Theodosia crowded with worshippers, and it is said that its name of Gul-djami, the "Rose Mosque", came from the garlands of roses with which it was enwreathed on that tragic and memorable day. The building, high and heavy-looking, has been considerably marred by the Turks, who removed most of the decoration on the outside of the central apse and substituted pointed arches for some round ones inside. The tall narrow niches, of a much later date than the original building, that adorn the side-apses must have been repeated on the central apse. The church is a shortened cross-domed basilica. The massive dome-piers are of irregular ground-plan and tall triple arcades divide the central area from the lower stories of the cross-arms except on the east. The angle-chambers rise high. Curious chambers were hollowed out of the eastern piers. They housed the relics of saints, and that on the south is supposed to have contained the remains of Constantine, the last Emperor of Byzantium, who perished in the vain defence of his city. The Church of S. Theodosia is a good illustration of the stages through which the plan and elevation of Constantinopolitan churches passed in the course of their development. The domed basilica has given place to the cross-domed basilica with its galleries extending to the tympanum of the outer wall. Everything is becoming more opened out and yet at the same time reaching towards a greater sense of unity. But, admirable though the lines of its repeated curves may be, it has not the full perfection of the cross-in-square. With its heavy piers, its high angle-chambers, its arcades and galleries, and its various irregularities it has many features alien to the symmetrical and open plan which was destined to predominate.

The Church of S. Mary Diaconissa (*Kalender-djami*), with its rich revetment of coloured marble, must once have been a shrine of great loveliness (85, 86). Yet the date and even the identification of the building are most uncertain. The very existence of the Mosque of Kalender-djami seems to have escaped the notice of European travellers for centuries, until in 1880 it was identified with the Church of S. Mary Diaconissa and its rediscovered beauty was made known. The Church of S. Mary Diaconissa was of considerable importance in Byzantine days and was visited by the Emperor every Easter Monday, as he moved in solemn procession on his way from the Palace to the Church of the Holy Apostles. A church so honoured by the Emperor would be richly adorned, and a great deal of its marble panelling admired by Gyllius in the sixteenth century still remains in position. The church itself may date from the ninth century, but it was not panelled till a later period. Most beautiful among the remains are two marble slabs on the eastern piers, set between columns of verd-antique and below a cornice of acanthus. The church may originally have been a cross-domed basilica, but if any galleries occupied the cross-arms they have been removed. It evidently once had additional aisles on north and south as in the case of the north Church of S. Mary Panachrantos. It has a narthex and also a later exonarthex. Changes were effected on the building by the Turks, but it appears that alterations were also made in Byzantine days, especially at the eastern end, where the plan is very irregular in form.

There is no church in Constantinople richer in historic memories and artistic treasures than S. Saviour in the Chora (*Kahrié-djami*) (89). The first church upon the site was erected when the vicinity still lay outside the walls and was distinguished by the indication "in the Chora"—"in the country". Long after the extension of the city beyond the original fortifications and the erection of the Theodosian walls the rebuilt church retained its title. In building the second church the Emperor Justinian presented it with a hostel for the accommodation of Syrian monks, a provision which illustrates the close relationship between the capital and the influential territory of Syria. It is therefore not surprising that artistic motifs from that province should have spread to the Church of the Chora: the design of a lintel over the central door sculptured with enwreathed foliage and a central vase between two peacocks bears a resemblance to one from Syria and is definitely of Eastern origin. The monastery and its church

173

rejoiced in being the frequent subjects of imperial patronage, and its proximity to the Blachernae Palace aided its enrichment. In 1081 the church, which had fallen into disrepair, was restored by the mother-in-law of Alexius I. In 1278 it was again restored after falling into decay during the Latin occupation of Constantinople. Distinguished citizens finished their days in the Monastery of the Chora, among them Theodore Metochitis, statesman and scholar, who magnificently adorned the nartheces and parecclesion and died in 1331. He is represented in a famous mosaic in the narthex, kneeling before Christ and offering Him a model of the church. Clad in gorgeous robes, he wears a fantastic bulging hat. The Chora was the first church to fall into the hands of the Turkish besiegers, who broke the miraculous icon of the Virgin and converted the building into the Mosque of *Kahriédjami*. It was restored by the Turks in 1860. The Chora stands at the foot of a steep hill lined with the typical wooden Turkish houses. Its many domes with windows ringed around the drums, its simple arcading on the façade, its low whitewashed walls and its setting between tapering minaret and stately cypresses combine to make it one of the most picturesque exteriors in the city. It has no less than six domes, most of them being later than the thirteenth century. The church is therefore an excellent illustration of the desire of the later Byzantine builders to demonstrate the importance of a church exterior by a multiplicity of cupolas. In Western Europe the builder might gratify his wish to emphasise the exterior of a church by the erection of a loftier spire; in the East he does so by the addition of domes.

The original plan of the present church seems to have taken the form of a domed central square with a rectangular area set on each of three sides and three apses on the fourth. The plan bears a resemblance to that of Santa Sophia, Salonica. But a great many alterations were made on the structure in later Byzantine days. The northern aisle and front of the narthex have been rebuilt. An exo-narthex was extended all along the western end of the church and was returned along the whole length of the southern side as a parecclesion terminating in an apse. The beautiful series of fourteenth-century mosaics in the narthex and exo-narthex brilliantly testify to the high level of culture in Constantinople when the Empire was only an attenuated state and surely approaching the end of its long career. The majority of these mosaics portray events in the life of Christ and the Virgin

174

from the canonical and apocryphal gospels (90). Several miracles are depicted, such as the healing of the two blind men at Jericho, but the concentration rests almost entirely on incidents connected with the Nativity of Christ and the Nativity of the Virgin Mary. Christ Pantocrator surrounded by Old Testament patriarchs occupies one of the domes of the narthex, and the Virgin with Old Testament kings and prophets has a place in another. In the Miracle of the Turning the Water into Wine at Cana of Galilee appears in Arabic letters the date 6811 (i.e. A.D. 1303). The mosaics of the Chora are characterised by a picturesque feeling, an expressive realism, and an amplitude of familiar detail. While their themes are inspired by Syrian sources, the treatment carries on the Hellenistic tradition. A liveliness of gesture and sense of naturalism are evident. At the same time they possess features which are specially characteristic of the period when they were made. The figures are set in front of a profusion of architectural constructions, walls, porches, houses, roofs and domes. There are beautiful decorative sculpture and fine marble panelling in the Chora. The parecclesion is adorned with frescoes of great beauty and of the same date as the mosaics in the main church, for many years hidden beneath whitewash. They are now being uncovered.

The Mosque of *Atik-Mustapha-djami* was a cross-in-square church whose dedication is supposed to have been to SS. Peter and Mark. It represents an intermediary stage in the development of the type as the dome-supports are not yet columns or piers but L-shaped portions of wall. It has no galleries and no additional bay before the apse. Probably of ninth-century date it bears a resemblance to Anatolian plans; it seems reasonable to affirm that it was from Asia Minor that the cross-in-square type of church passed over to Constantinople. The exterior aspect is quite Moslem owing to the Turkish dome and roofing and infilling of the windows. The church was not built to accommodate large numbers of worshippers at a service, but for the special purpose of housing a sacred and highly venerated relic. The robe of the Virgin Mary, having been abstracted from Palestine and conveyed to Constantinople, was held in such esteem that a special shrine was deemed necessary for its worthy preservation. The function for which the Church of SS. Peter and Mark was built has a bearing on its features of construction. It is of small dimensions —only about fifty feet long—and has no galleries. It did not require wide unencumbered spaces or an open vista. A shrine was required where individual worshippers could come in to halt in devotion before the holy relic and then pass out again to the busy street. The liturgy had of course also to be celebrated in the church, but accommodation was necessary for only a small group of worshippers. The little building admirably fulfilled its primary purpose. But the Robe of the Virgin reached such a level of fame that its original home in the city no longer sufficed for the multitudes who thronged for its veneration. It was believed to have saved the city from the ravages of plague and calamities of war, and was granted a more magnificent home in a church dedicated to the Virgin but long since destroyed.

The Mosque of *Bodroum-djami* has been identified with the Church of the Monastery of the Myrelaion which was restored by the Emperor Romanus Lecapenus in the first half of the tenth century and became the final resting-place of that monarch and members of his family. A cross-in-square church with a narthex, its dome supports are simple piers. The arms of the cross were roofed with cross-vaults instead of with the usual barrel-vaults. It has the additional lower-vaulted bay between the apse and the eastern cross-arm (see p. 57). The Myrelaion clearly marks the growing sense of harmony and elegance in the ecclesiastical architecture of Constantinople. The considerably lower elevation of the angle-spaces and the loftiness of the drum give a grace to the general form of structure that is very different from the heavy aspect of a cube. The elements mount up pleasingly to the central dome. The walls are more freely decorated with arches and cornices, though the profuse elaboration which characterises churches of later centuries is not yet achieved. The Myrelaion was seriously damaged by fire in 1912.

Valuable archaeological excavations have been conducted by Professor Talbot Rice below and around this church which showed that it stood above a substructure or lower church of identical plan. Extensive substructures of this type seem to have been very important in Constantinople; they were much less usual elsewhere.

The little Mosque of *Ahmed-Pasha-mesjedi*, perhaps the Church of S. John the Baptist in Trullo, was also of cross-in-square plan, but its columns have been removed by the Turks. It is probably of eleventh-century date and differs from the ordinary type in having its apses round instead of polygonal on the outside.

The Church of S. Saviour Pantepoptes (the "All-seeing")

89   CONSTANTINOPLE: S. Saviour in the Chora (*Kahrié-djami*)

90   THE CHORA. Mosaics: Nativity and the Miracle at Cana

92   CONSTANTINOPLE: S. Saviour Pantepoptes
(Eski-Imaret-Mesjedi)

91   CONSTANTINOPLE: S. Saviour Pantocrator
(Zeirek-Kilissé-djami)

(*Eski-Imaret-mesjedi*) (92) is another example of the cross-in-square type with an additional lower-vaulted bay before the apse. It was built at the end of the eleventh century by Anna Comnena, the mother of the Emperor Alexius I. This brilliant and able princess, one of the most outstanding and remarkable figures in Byzantine history, assisted her son in the administration of the State for over twenty years. At the end of this period she relinquished her exalted position and returned to the Monastery of the Pantepoptes, where in 1105 she died and was buried. The church occupies a hilly site above the Golden Horn near the place where the Latin Crusaders first invaded the city and where the Emperor Alexius Comnenus had pitched his vermilion tent. The church, well built of courses of brick and stone, is an example of the Greek cross-in-square plan with the additional bay intercalated before the apse (93). The piers on which the dome rests had their angles splayed by the Turks. The prothesis and diaconicon have got niches hollowed out of their side-walls so as to provide additional room for the priest in these confined spaces, when he conducted the preface to the liturgy or robed for the service. Over the narthex, which runs along the western end, was a gallery for the women at worship while beyond the narthex there was constructed a later exonarthex. There are some fine carved string-courses inside the church. The graceful dodecagonal drum is decorated

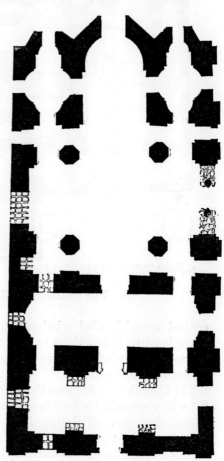

93   S. Saviour Pantepoptes
(*Eski-Imaret-mesjedi*)

with engaged angle-columns carrying arches which surmount the windows and penetrate the roof of the dome, which, like those of some other Constantinopolitan churches, has interior ribs meeting in a central medallion.

Typical Byzantine features are further to be found on the exterior in spite of the damage which it has undergone. Such is the fenestration of the wall of the cross-arm, which shows a

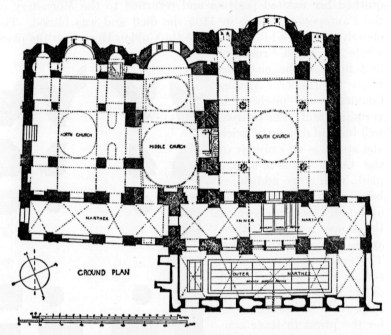

94   The Pantocrator (*Zeirek-Kilissé-djami*)

central round-headed window flanked by two similar ones of lower height. Below them extend three windows of equal height, the whole six windows being enclosed in a great semicircular arch on engaged columns.

The Church of S. Saviour Pantocrator (*Zeirek-Kilissé-djami*)(91, 94) was a remarkable building, consisting as it did of three conti-guous churches, all dating from the twelfth century. These churches were the property of a famous monastery which was founded in the twelfth century by the Hungarian princess, Irene, the wife of the Emperor John II Comnenus, and were perhaps completed by her husband before 1136.

95 CONSTANTI-
NOPLE:
S. Theodore
(*Kilissé-djami*)

96 (*Below*)
The Interior

97   ATHENS: Capnicarea

98   SKRIPOU

Of all the later churches of Byzantium none was more celebrated than that of the Pantocrator. It gloried in the possession of countless sacred pictures, richly set in jewelled frames. Its chased and enamelled reliquaries, its rich sacramental vessels and its ornaments of silver and gold, excited the cupidity of the knights and ecclesiastics of the Fourth Crusade, who deposited some of the precious spoil in the churches and cathedrals of the West.

A royal foundation, the monastery was plenteously endowed by imperial benefactors. Enriched with money and vineyards, it was granted freedom from taxation, and independence of the Patriarch. Most important of all, at least in the estimation of the populace, it was the owner of the wonder-working icon of S. Demetrius which had been conveyed from his city of Salonica and brought to the Pantocrator amid a great concourse of adoring worshippers. Nor was the monastery indifferent in maintaining charitable activities; a hospital, a home for the aged and a guest-house for strangers were part of the monastic possessions. Finally, the Pantocrator was not only patronised by the Imperial family during their lifetime: it was also their mausoleum. Emperors and empresses, princes and princesses, were laid to rest in splendid tombs within its walls. It is these facts—the royal patronage, the possession of a famous icon, the consequent popularity of the church, the royal mausoleum—which help to explain both its gorgeous adornment and the triple nature of its plan.

During the Latin occupation of Constantinople the Pantocrator fell into the hands of the Venetians who celebrated the Latin rite within its walls. It was wantonly damaged by their rivals, the Genoese, after the Byzantines recovered the city in 1261. But the Emperors of the Palaeologian dynasty took an interest in its welfare and a scion of the house became its abbot. Its last abbot, Gennadius, became the first Patriarch of Constantinople under the Turks. Some thirty years after the Turkish conquest a devout Moslem called Zeirek transformed it into a mosque.

The southernmost church is probably the oldest of the three: it is a cross-in-square with the extra bay before the apse. The dome, which has been subjected to Turkish modifications, rests on four fluted pillars, which have replaced the "porphyry columns" seen by the traveller Gyllius. A narthex in five bays extending along the west wall projects beyond it to north and south. Beyond the narthex is a five-bayed exo-narthex. Over the narthex rests the gynaeceum. As the central bay of the narthex opened right up to the roof of a dome which covered it, the gynaeceum was divided into two parts. The central bay was floored in Turkish times to provide accommodation for the Sultan when he attended the mosque for prayer.

The dome of the church and that of the narthex rest on polygonal drums which have had some alterations made on them by the Turks. The apses have characteristic niches and arcading outside and the line of the vaulting is pronouncedly articulated on the exterior by recessed arches. The church still retains some of the marble which so richly clothed its walls in the days of its imperial splendour. Marble panelling is preserved on the apse and beautifully carved fragments have been used in the construction of the Turkish pulpit. The doors in the narthex and exo-narthex are still framed in green, white or red marble and the floors of these adjuncts are paved with broad marble slabs. In the southern church there are remains of a pavement in *opus sectile* showing a representation of the Labours of Hercules and other themes.

There is free access from the middle church to the north and south churches and their nartheces. In a sense, therefore, the three churches are one. The church was in an abandoned state, but repairs have recently been put in hand. It was a royal mausoleum containing among other tombs the magnificent sarcophagus in black marble which contained the remains of the Emperor Manuel Comnenus. Beside this tomb there was a relic which attracted the devotion of many pilgrims, the porphyry slab on which the body of Our Lord is said to have been laid after His Deposition from the Cross. The sarcophagus now stands just outside the western doors of the church, a plaything for children.

The northern church is of the cross-in-square type with an additional bay before the apse. The exterior of the apses is decorated with characteristic arches and niches. There is a gynaeceum over the cross-vaulted narthex. The dome with its square piers is a Turkish restoration; Gyllius speaks of "the hemisphere" sustained by four arches supported on four columns of Theban marble. Within the church there is a Mussulman chair made out of a curious mixture of Turkish and Byzantine fragments.

These three churches in spite of the mutilation and disfigurement, to which they have been subjected, form a group of buildings of very great interest. They claim to possess notable historical associations and memories of a widespread and enduring sanctity. Their architecture is characterised by a simple dignity and charm, and the remains of their marble embellishment are a sufficient testimony of the rich beauty which once was theirs.

CONSTANTINOPLE UNDER THE PALAEOLOGI

It was to a poor and attenuated country that the Byzantine Emperors returned when they expelled the Latin usurpers from the venerable metropolis which they had occupied for less than the normal span of a single life. When the Emperor transferred his seat of government from Nicea to Constantinople in 1261, the Byzantine Empire, which had once extended from the Euphrates to Italy now comprised little more than Constantinople, Thrace, Macedonia and a part of north-west Anatolia. The realm of the Paleaologi has been described as the successor not of the far-flung Roman but only of the tiny Empire of Nicea.

In spite of its diminutive size the Empire did not fail to secure a minor aggrandisement by a signal victory over the Franks. In 1281 Michael VIII secured the cession of part of the Morea. But this success was offset by the relentless advance of the Turks in Anatolia. As we have seen, a new branch of the Mohammedan invaders, the Ottoman Turks, had settled before 1280 in Asia Minor. Their descendants were destined to rule in Byzantium. Constant Turkish aggression whittled away the shrunken possessions of the Empire. Ephesus, once the splendid city of the distant Hellenistic age, fell in 1308. During the long reign of John V Palaeologus (1341–91) the process of attrition, helped by a civil war, went on apace.

The Turks crossed over into Europe. A brief breathing-space was granted to the Greeks when Timour the Tartar swept down on the Turks, but it passed away all too quickly. By the repulse of a Turkish attack on Constantinople in 1422, the Byzantines won their last victory. By this time the once great Roman Empire had become only a tiny dominion. It comprised only the city with South-east Thrace, the Morea, and a few Aegean islands. John VII (1425–48) strove like his predecessors to enlist the support of the strong Western Powers on behalf of the doomed Empire of the East. These efforts were of no avail and in 1453 Constantine XI, the last "Emperor of the Romans", died fighting the soldiers of Mahommet II, who were pouring through the gates. The great metropolis on the Bosphorus which for over a thousand years had been the home of Christian civilisation and culture fell under Moslem sway, and the Byzantine Empire passed away from the stage of history.

STATE OF CONSTANTINOPLE

The descriptions of travellers testify that Constantinople under the Palaeologi was still a beautiful and illustrious city, though it was sadly diminished in population and contained many vacant spaces. The Spaniard Ruy de Clavijo wrote of its wonderful churches, marvellously rich and artistically embellished. A literary revival took place and art was patronised. Beautiful fabrics continued to be made in the city, among those being the so-called "Dalmatic of Charlemagne". This superb piece of work is now to be seen in the Sacristy of S. Peter at Rome. One side shows the Transfiguration and the other a magnificent rendering of Christ in Glory surrounded by angels and other figures (152). The scenes are embroidered in gold and silver on a soft blue ground.

Critics, like M. Millet, distinguish two schools in the frescoes of the period, a Macedonian and a Cretan. Both of them follow the methods of Hellenistic practice, but also reveal a Western influence. The Macedonian school, however, shows a strong Eastern influence in its realism, in its iconography and in the setting-out of its pictures in long continuous friezes. The style of the Cretan school is elegant and picturesque and seems to have been affected by the meticulous art of the icon painter. It produced admirable work in the monasteries of Mount Athos as late as the sixteenth century, long after Constantinople had been occupied by the Turks.

THE CHURCHES

The little mosque which is known as *Kilissé-djami* (96) was once a Byzantine church. Travellers and scholars have held different opinions as to whom the church was dedicated, but probably it was S. Theodore the Tiro, or recruit, a soldier who was martyred in 306 by the Emperor Maximian for his refusal to persecute the Christians. The church is a charming example of the later Byzantine style (99). A cross-in-square church of eleventh-century date with additional bay before the apse, it shows how much attention was being directed towards the treatment of exteriors in the period when it was built. The walls are enlivened with thin red tiles set in beds, in saw-toothed cornices, and in arches.

182

The strongly projecting cornices of the polygonal drum over the crossing surmount windows set in several orders of arches. The apses were adorned with niches and decoration of tiles. The roofs of the cross-arms finish off as angular gables, but the curve of the vaults is strongly articulated on the exterior by recessed arches below. A passage or aisle used to run along the south wall and a similar construction probably also ran along the north wall. Brunoff thought that a domed basilica originally occupied the site. The church, although

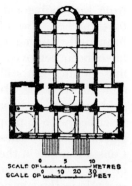

SCALE OF 0 5 10 METRES
SCALE OF 0 10 20 30 FEET

99 *Kilissé-djami*

of the eleventh century, is noticed here because its outstanding feature, the exo-narthex, was added to the narthex about the fourteenth century; this exo-narthex is a most pleasing composition although alterations have been effected in the drums of its three domes (95). Five arches recessed in several orders frame the windows in the upper story of its façade. The lower story has niches and two triple arcades resting on columns with old capitals. The lower part of these arcades is filled in with slabs taken from older buildings and carved with lozenges, circles, rosettes, crosses and other typical Byzantine designs. Some of the mosaics that decorated the exo-narthex have recently been uncovered; they are to be dated to the fourteenth century, but are coarser and less accomplished than those of the Church of the Chora.

In spite of the changes which have arisen by the transformation of the building into a mosque, the exterior decoration of S. Theodore and the well-proportioned symmetry of its interior still compel our admiration.

Closely connected with this exo-narthex in the style of its exterior decoration is the pareccelesion which was added to the south side of the Pammakaristos Church in the fourteenth century (84). It was in this chapel that Mohammet the conqueror of Constantinople entered into discussion with the Greek patriarch about the teachings of Christianity. The pareclession of the Pammakaristos is an attractive and elegant little building. A mortuary chapel connected with the adjacent church, it takes the form of a small cross-in-square church preceded by a narthex. Externally it is richly adorned with niches, arches and brick decoration and it has finely sculptured pilasters on its apse. The dome springs

183

from high polygonal drums, with cornices set in orders of saw-tooth arches. Two of the green marble columns which with their beautifully carved capitals supported the dome of the church have been removed and replaced by a Turkish arch, but the fine mosaics are still in place on the upper levels of the walls and in the dome. In the dome the Pantocrator is shown on a gold ground, surrounded by twelve prophets holding scrolls inscribed with appropriate texts. These mosaics, like those of the Chora, are a witness to the artistic skill which prevailed in Constantinople in the last age of the Byzantine Empire. The face of Our Lord is dignified but tender. The prophets are highly realistic in their varied attitudes, in their vivid individuality and in their graceful sense of movement.

One final church in Constantinople is of peculiar interest, both historically and architecturally. S. Mary of the Mongols (S. Mary Mouchliotissa) was founded towards the end of the thirteenth century by Maria, daughter of the Emperor Michael Paleologus and widow of a Mongol prince. It was preserved as a Christian building because it was presented by the Sultan to Christodoulos the Greek architect of the Mosque of Mehemet, as a token of his imperial gratitude. S. Mary of the Mongols was never appro-priated by the Turks as a mosque, but has remained a place of Christian worship throughout the course of its history in spite of efforts made to secure its alienation. Nevertheless it has under-gone at least as much change as churches which were adapted to the requirements of the Moslem faith, including a final looting in the anti-Greek riots of 1955. Along with the church Maria founded a convent which she endowed with a considerable amount of landed property, both inside and outside the city. She was herself mentioned in an inscription and depicted in a portrait recently discovered in the Church of the Chora. In plan the Church of S. Mary of the Mongols is a quatrefoiled square, consisting as it does of a central square covered by a dome in the centre and buttressed by an apse on each side. It is true that a narthex on the west side has prevented an apse being formed there, but the dome is buttressed by a semi-dome on that side as well as on the others. A large quadrangular addition on the south at some time necessitated the destruction of the southern apse. The drum of the dome, unlike that of many later Constantinople churches, has a horizontal cornice. There is a close connection between the architecture of S. Mary of the Mongols and that of Armenia. The sojourn of its foundress in the East, the quatrefoiled square plan, and the use of the pointed arch all point in the direction of Armenian associations.

GENERAL CONCLUSIONS

The Byzantine churches of Constantinople are only a remnant of those which existed there in the palmy days of the Eastern Empire, when the city was the proud possessor of innumerable hallowed shrines. Ducange in the seventeenth century gives the names of four hundred, and many more must have been in existence some centuries before he wrote.

Earthquake, war and fire have wrought their toll of havoc and destruction. The irreparable disaster of the Latin Conquest in 1204, with its terrible conflagrations and ruthless despoliation, was the genesis of a gradual decay. The revived Empire of the Palaeologi presented but the strange spectacle of a proud and historic metropolis, rich in the storied treasures of the centuries, presiding in the sadness of its decline over the territory of a tiny state. Though art and learning flourished in this last period of Byzantine history and though Western eyes were still dazzled by the glory of Constantinople, the Empire had for ever fallen from its ancient state of power and glory. Buondelmonti of Florence writes of the many ruined churches which he saw in 1422, and under the Palaeologi the material of churches was used to construct buildings like the Citadel, erected near the Golden Gate. The Ottoman conquerors continued the work of destruction and many churches were swept away to provide vacant areas for their palaces. Many of the later churches of Constantinople were of no great dimensions. The Chora is approximately seventy-five feet in length, the North Panachrontos a hundred feet and SS. Peter and Mark less than fifty feet. As we have seen, a church might be small in size for different reasons. It might be attached to a monastery with few inmates or it might be in the nature of a sacred shrine hallowed by the memory of some healing saint of a distant age, whose potent influence might be sought by the little group who gathered at the liturgy or sought cure in individual prayer. Or it might be, like a rich and precious reliquary, fashioned to enshrine some famed and miraculous icon, reverenced by the constant stream of pilgrims who passed through the ever-open door.

But the elegant charm of these last Byzantine churches atones for their want of a more imposing scale and the picturesque silhouettes of their multiplied cupolas was an emphatic substitute for the monumentality of the ruling central dome. Bejewelled with marble panels in soft and varied colours, in pink, grey and green, glittering with mosaics in purple and in gold depicting the sacred story, theirs was the preciousness and loveliness like that of the enamelled casket of the goldsmith. The soft curved lines of their exteriors and the meticulous elaboration of their walls were a true expression of the spirit of the opulent and ceremonious city which overlooked the fair and placid waters of the Sea of Marmora. The few survivors, transformed and despoiled though they be, indicate the choiceness of the art which flourished so copiously and enduringly in the fertile soil of the Byzantine capital.

CHAPTER X

Greece

THE GREEK SCENE

GREECE is so famous for its treasures of classical antiquity that it is easy to minimise the heritage of its Byzantine era. There is no land richer in Byzantine churches than Greece. In the midst of her modern streets and squares and near to the marble columns of her antique temples, Athens preserves some fascinating old churches, rare and precious monuments of her Middle Age. Dispersed throughout the country, in town and village and lonely field, in the valleys of Laconia and on the shores of Messenia, on the hill-sides of Phocis and the plain of Attica—in every region of Greece Byzantine churches diversify the landscape with their distinctive domes. As they nestle in their sequestered valleys or repose on their quiet hill-slopes, the appeal of their well-wrought masonry and attractive form is enhanced by the loneliness of their position, the beauty of their environment, and the classic traditions which haunt their sites. They are often built in places which have been hallowed by an immemorial sanctity. Fragments from ancient temples are embedded in their walls; a broken cornice with its crisply cut acanthus lies close by upon the ground; the capital of an Ionic column serves as the base of the Christian altar; a legend of pagan divinity is immortalised in the locality; from an antique spout there gush the waters of a sacred spring, the reputation of whose healing virtue extends through all the Christian era to remote ages of antiquity.

Greece seems to have left its own peculiar impress upon its churches. Their exteriors do not show the same number of soft curved lines as do the churches of Constantinople. They are neither so severe as those of Armenia nor so ornate as those of Serbia, but exhibit a quiet charm and a classic restraint which seems native to their soil.

As a secondary province of the great Byzantine Empire, Greece acted a minor part in the drama of history. Before the ninth century she had suffered greatly from poverty and depopulation, and had been considerably affected by Slavonic immigration. The close of that century ushered in a brighter period and she became rich and flourishing. To her olive-groves, her vineyards and her silk factories she owed a high measure of prosperity, and, although no resident emperor could endow her with buildings on the magnificent scale, her wealthy monastic foundations were embellished with sumptuous mosaic and rich sculpture, while the even tenour of her life permitted the erection of many churches which were carefully constructed and choicely adorned.

Many ancient Greek temples were transformed into Christian churches, the most celebrated of them being the Parthenon itself. Faint traces of the frescoes on the walls of its cella may still be seen. They have been assigned to the eleventh century, when the Emperor Basil II visited Athens and enriched the church, but they may belong to an earlier date.

CHURCHES IN GREECE

A church of heavy appearance at Skripou in Boeotia (873–874) is a transitional form to the cross-in-square(98). It is built largely of antique stone blocks. The arms of the cross rise high above the angle-chambers, which, as is normal in churches in Greece, are roofed with barrel-vaults; on north and south the arms of the cross project beyond the line of the angle-spaces, so as to make the ground-plan cruciform. The three apses are round, and the dome rests on a sixteen-sided drum. The vaults are massive, and thick walls separate the east and west arms from the angle-spaces, cramping the interior with their bulk. The scanty sculpture includes a frieze with animals in enwreathed foliage.

Very different in aspect is the so-called Small Cathedral at Athens, otherwise known as the Church of the Virgin Gorgoepikoos or of S. Eleutherios. It is well set off in its open square, and in its diminutive charm forms a striking contrast to its large and unattractive neighbour, the early nineteenth-century Byzantine cathedral. The Small Cathedral is an admirable example of the classic cross-in-square type(8). The dome rests on four piers which replaced marble columns in 1833. The drum belongs to a type characteristic of the Athenian churches and imitated elsewhere in Greece; its angle-columns support simple semicircular arches over archivolts of radiating bricks, while its tiled roof adheres closely to the form of the dome inside and sinks down into the spandrels of the arches; there is therefore no projection of the roof to form eaves. Built for the most part of white Pentelic marble, the Small Cathedral contains about ninety sculptured slabs and fragments in its walls, the spoils of older buildings long since destroyed. The antique and the Christian pieces have been placed side by side, though a certain attempt at symmetry can be detected in the arrangement. A frieze represents the months of the year by pagan festivals and the signs of the zodiac; a slab depicting a couple of wrestlers is built sideways into the apse; upon some fragments the familiar egg-and-dart ornament of antiquity is displayed. Oriental influence is evident in those Christian slabs which show sphinxes, lions, eagles, fighting dragons and affronted gryphons at a fountain. There are many different crosses.

The Small Cathedral, so compact in form, so clear in structure, so interesting in its sculptured walls, is of modest dimensions. The smallness of their size is a noticeable feature of many Greek churches, and some scholars have seen in it a reminiscence of the cella of the pagan temple.

Many old Byzantine churches in Athens were unhappily destroyed in the third decade of the nineteenth century, when the newly established kingdom, eager to preserve the classic inheritance, did not set sufficient store on that of the Byzantine Age. Among the few surviving examples of medieval churches is that which is dedicated to the two warrior saints Theodore. The church was long thought to date from 1049, but the inscription in the west wall is now read as 1065. It presents many features typical of the class to which it belongs. It is built, like many other Byzantine churches in Greece, of squared stones with a tile in every vertical and horizontal joint. The round arches over the lights of its double windows rest on the capital of a slender shaft: the windows occupy favourite positions on the apses and the drum, and have brick ornaments in their tympana. Saw-tooth bands run flush along the walls and around the windows. The three apses are polygonal on plan outside and all project externally. The church as a whole, however, is not a completely evolved example of the cross-in-square plan, for the western supports of the dome are not columns, but walls which separate the western arm from its adjacent angle-spaces. The eastern supports to the dome are the *antae* of the bema. The central bay of the narthex, unlike that in the Small Metropolis, is vaulted at a lower level than the western cross-arm, each terminating in its own gable. The drum is of the same variety as that of the Small Cathedral, but has double windows. There is a characteristic bell-tower on the southern side.

Standing in the middle of the modern Hermes Street, the Church of the Capnicarea with its old brown walls is a quaint relic of bygone days (100). Built in the eleventh century, it was enlarged in the thirteenth by a parecclesion, an exo-narthex and an elegant porch (97). The church is of the four-columned type. Masonry blocks are arranged to form a cross pattern on some of the walls. A similar motif is to be found at Daphni and was also employed in the lower part of SS. Theodore Athens, but there it has been much obscured by repairs.

The Church of the Asomatoi—the Angels, the "Bodiless Ones" —has been much altered in modern times but has retained its typical dome. The Church of the Holy Apostles was a quatrefoiled cross-in-square but has undergone alteration at its western end. Belonging to the first quarter of the eleventh century, its high accentuated drum rests on four columns with antique capitals; its bricks are cut out in patterns after the style of Kufic lettering. The Frankish Duchy of Athens has left traces of its existence in some heavy-looking ribbed Gothic vaults in the Church of the Purification (Hypapanti) of the Virgin.

Mount Hymettos, the range of rounded hills which commands so beautiful a prospect of Athens, with its white houses spread over the Attic plain and the Acropolis rising proudly from its midst, became the dwelling-place of monks at an early date. The monks have long since disappeared, but their churches and monasteries remain. That of Kaisariani (103) still reposes in a secluded valley, verdant till recent years with a grove of olives, cypress, laurel and pine. Before the First World War the valley was quiet and remote, although so near the city, but a crowded new suburb has crept near its solitude. The site was renowned in classical mythology as the scene of the death of Procris at the unwitting hands of Cephalos, and Ovid sings of its soft green sward, its sacred spring and its wooded glade (102).

The dome rests upon four marble columns which with their debased Ionic capitals came from a pagan temple that stood in the locality, and various carved fragments, classic and Christian, serve as lintels or lie upon the ground. Gigantic cypresses tower above the old monastic buildings and the ochre walls of the little church face a sunlit court. On the eastern boundary wall the

100   ATHENS: Capnicarea

101   OMORPHI ECCLESIA, ATTICA; showing the later Narthex

102 KAISARIANI

103 KAISARIANI
(*from a water-colour
by Mrs. C. Hamilton*)

waters of the spring, sacred in Christian as in classic days, gushed from a marble spout fashioned into the head of a ram.

The present church, which may date from the eleventh century, is of the four-column cross-in-square type (23). The dome was damaged during the Turkish period and has undergone some alteration. The drum finishes off horizontally to meet the projecting roof. It is less decorated and has no angle-columns. The church itself is constructed of rubble, but its eastern end and part of its north and south cross-arms are beautifully faced in courses of squared stone and thin tiles, the brown colour of the porous stone and the deeper red-brown of the tiles blending in an effective harmony. Vertical tiles between the joints are more infrequent, and their rarity has suggested an early twelfth-century date for the church. The narthex, which has a dome over its central bay, and a parecclesion with a bell-tower are built of uncoursed rubble and belong to a date later than that of the rest of the church.

The interior is adorned with frescoes arranged generally in accordance with the usual late Byzantine scheme. The Divine Liturgy and the Communion of the Apostles (9), both in the central apse, may be singled out for special mention. The Divine Liturgy is the heavenly counterpart of the liturgy on earth, celebrated by Christ and His ministering angels; beneath a triple arch stands the altar upon which the Gospels are set; a cherub holding a fan in either hand hovers above; Christ is twice represented, clad in the rich vestments of an Orthodox bishop—a purple stoicharion and over it a pink-and-white saccos; from below the saccos appears the epitrachelion, a gold stole with tassels; from around His neck there hangs down in front the omophorion, adorned with crosses; other vestments He also wears. On His right we behold the first of the advancing angels who approach from the left carrying chalices, censers, fans and other articles. Below this fresco there is to be seen Christ giving the Bread and Wine to His apostles who reverently bend to receive it.

A marble slab built into the wall of the narthex is illustrated (104). It resembles slabs in the Byzantine Museum and in the Small Cathedral at Athens. Beneath an arch it shows a cross with acanthus leaves springing from its base and filling the lower angles, while the upper angles contain rosettes.

Higher up on the slopes of Mount Hymettos there is the four-column cross-in-square Church of the Monastery of Asteri. Picturesquely situated on the gently rising plain, there stands

191

the monastic Church of S. John the Theologian whose cross-in-square plan is obscured by surrounding outbuildings. A ruined Church of S. George, nearer Athens, is of the domed hall type. Perhaps the most charming of the Byzantine churches of the Attica countryside is Omorphi Ecclesia, the "Beautiful Church", which stands solitary in the plain beyond Patisia (101). The dome with the angles of its drum enriched by marble colonnettes is of the Athenian type. Marble saw-tooth bands frame the windows and extend along the walls. A parecclesion shows Western traits that date from the epoch of the Duchy of Athens. The church with its parecclesion is beautifully constructed of squared stones and tiles (31), and some of the vertical tiles have their faces cut into dia-

104　Carved slab in the narthex, Kaisariani, Attica

mond and rectangle patterns. As we shall see later, this cutting of the tiles to form patterns is a feature of other Greek churches. The building rests on a plinth of rubble. It has been assigned to the eleventh or twelfth century and the parecclesion has been thought either contemporary or later. The narthex, as is sometimes the case, is an addition built of uncoursed rubble. Faded frescoes, including one of the Ancient of Days, adorn the roof and walls.

There is a curious church of another plan at Daou-Mendeli in Attica. The naos is squinched out to form a hexagon for the dome with its dodecagonal drum.

There are many cross-in-square churches to be found in the Morea or Peloponnese. Among them are three of the twelfth century in Argolis—at Merbaca, Areia and Chonica—which possess many common features. They rest on massive substructures of marble blocks and are meticulously decorated outside. Merbaca, especially, displays an elaborate adornment, the façades being enriched with saw-tooth bands and archivolts, limestone cornices, coloured faïence discs, and broad meander friezes of brick (106).

As often happens in Greek churches the radiating brick arches round the windows are flanked with quadrant arches of a similar nature. Sculptures in the walls include a Byzantine sundial, a frieze with grapes and an antique votive-relief. At Merbaca, as well as at Chonica and Areia, the Capnicarea at Athens and other churches, tiles in courses are cut out in patterns to form continuous friezes along the walls. The scrupulous care and thought employed in the elaboration of these brick patterns flush on the walls of the Greek churches are well deserving of praise. In the earlier churches the bricks were arranged to form Kufic lettering, a form of Arabic used to transcribe the Koran at Kufa on the Euphrates, and afterwards employed for architectural decoration. It passed from the Orient to Greece. In the twelfth century the patterns became simpler, but in all their forms they are admirable for their purpose. In Merbaca as in so many other Greek churches the wise employment of detailed ornament, the accurate fitting of masonry, the symmetry of plan, the clarity of outline, the economy and restraint, and the well-determined proportions induce the belief that something of the old Hellenic spirit survived among the Greek builders of the Middle Ages. All three churches have the eastern arm prolonged, Chonica possessing the lower vault (see Chapter IV, p. 57). They all have niches in the side-walls of the bema, three projecting apses, nartheces and bell-towers of later date. There were at Merbaca and there still are at Areia, porches before the door, and Areia has a later exo-narthex. Chonica and Areia have, in addition to the familiar brick orna-mentation, tall plain marble crosses embedded in their walls. Of the Byzantine-Corinthian impost-capitals in Merbaca and Areia, one shows a ring of channelled leaves surrounded by broad, open, acanthus leaves. All three churches belong to the twelfth century. That at Areia—which, it should be said, is known simply as the Church of the Hagia Moni, the sacred monastery—is known by a document at Turin and an inscription on its walls to have been erected in 1143 and dedicated in 1149.

Of all the churches in the Morea it is those of Mistra which have attained the highest level of distinction in the history of Byzantine Art. Mistra is a ruined city of the Middle Ages, clustered on a steep and rocky hill, about two thousand feet above the level of the sea and some two or three miles from Sparta, whose broad streets lie embosomed among the olive-groves of the wide Lacedaemonian plain. The hill of Mistra stands detached at the base of Mount Taygetos, the great range that sweeps down so majestically through the land. Its churches form one of the most remarkable and attractive series of monuments in the eastern Mediterranean. The chance of historical events had elevated Mistra to a position of unexpected importance in the final epoch of the Byzantine Empire. At the beginning of the thirteenth century the Morea, conquered by crusading knights, entered on its career as the Frankish Principality of Achaia. At the battle of Pelagonia in 1262 its Prince William de Villehardouin was captured by the Byzantine Emperor, and was compelled to cede the south-eastern portion of the Morea to the victor as the price of ransom. The Byzantines took possession of Villehardouin's fortress on the summit of the hill, and on the lower and middle slopes they built a town which became the capital, first of the Province, and then of the Despotate of Mistra. As in the middle of the fourteenth century the rest of the Empire comprised little more than Constantinople and Thrace, the Greek territory attained a position of unwonted importance. A son of the Emperor resided as Despot in Mistra, where in the Upper City the walls of his ruined palace bear silent witness to regal splendour. There was great intercourse between Constantinople and Mistra, which became a flourishing city and could boast a school of philosophy and a cultured life. The social and political importance of Mistra was equalled by its ecclesiastical predominance. Many religious establishments were founded within its walls and the Monastery of the Brontocheion was endowed with lavish grants of fertile vineyards throughout the province.

The churches of the Evangelistria (beginning of the fourteenth century), Santa Sophia (c. 1350) and the Peribleptos (end of the fourteenth century) are of the two-column cross-in-square plan. Their *western* cross-arms with the adjoining angle-spaces are slightly prolonged. The Peribleptos (109) is partially hollowed out of a cliff (B) and has a strangely irregular parecclesion (D). It would only be natural to expect a strong connection between the architectural style of Constantinople and that of Mistra: the Peribleptos reveals the influence of the capital in the concentric projecting arched cornices which surmount the windows of the drum and support the tiles of its roof. Some western traits in the building are derived from the adjacent Principality of Achaia—a fleur-de-lis between two rosettes on the central apse and a trefoil window within the Gothic arch of a tower. A porch extends down

105   MISTRA: Evangelistria

106   MERBACA

107　Mistra, Pantanassa: the Tower

108　Mistra, Pantanassa: the Apse

one side and a refectory abuts on the apses. The church contains admirable frescoes which have been compared with those of thirteenth-century Italian masters. The work of different artists, they have been connected with the Cretan and also with the Macedonian school. The frescoes are full of life; the treatment is refined and the colouring is delicate and subdued. Prominent among them is the Divine Liturgy in the prothesis: carrying censers

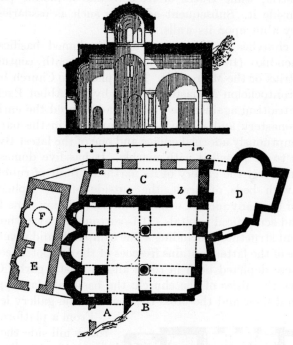

109   Peribleptos, Mistra

and other Eucharistic vessels, the angels advance towards Christ at the altar with rapid and silent motion. The Transfiguration shows Christ, a noble figure, surrounded with a great mandorla.

The Evangelistria (105) seems to have been a cemetery chapel. The apse shows five sides of a polygon below, which merge into a semicircle above. Like the Peribleptos, the Evangelistria is built with the familiar squared stones framed in tiles. The octagonal drum has alternate niches and windows, the latter being surmounted by strongly projecting archivolts and cornices. A later porch and other buildings abut upon its walls.

195

High up on the hill-side and above the Palace of the Despots there stands the ruined Church of Santa Sophia. Built, as a monogram attests, by the Despot Manuel Cantacuzenos, it appears to have been the court church; in following the example of Justinian's great church at Constantinople in its dedication to the Holy Wisdom it shows how the Despots of Mistra imitated the precedents of the capital. In general features it resembles the Evangelistria, while traces of frescoes and a mosaic pavement remain inside it. Subsequent additions such as ossuaries and a baptistery abut upon its walls.

Three churches at Mistra are of cross-domed basilical plan, the Aphendiko (1312), the Pantanassa (fifteenth century) and S. Demetrius or the Metropolis. The Aphendiko Church belonged to the Brontocheion Monastery. Built by the Abbot Pachomius, whose patriotism against the Franks had secured the enrichment of his monastery and whose portrait appears in the narthex, it was a sumptuously adorned edifice and one of the latest Byzantine churches to be panelled with marble. It has five domes, and a sixth dome over the gallery of its narthex. Built of rubble interspersed with beds of brick, the outside of the Aphendiko is enlivened by many niches, while its interior retains some frescoes, panels and sculptured capitals. It is surrounded by a whole series of adjacent structures, including a fine campanile and several ossuaries: one of the latter contains frescoes of the Despot Theodore II, who is here depicted both in royal and monastic garb. Galleries run above the aisles of the church: the basilical plan appears on the ground floor and the cross-in-square at the gallery level.

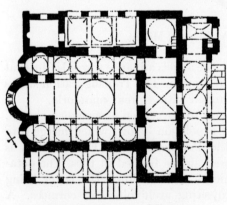

110   Pantanassa, Mistra

From a platform on the rocky hill-side the Monastery of the Pantanassa commands a magnificent view over the wide plain of Lacedaemonia far below (107), fertile with its olive and orange groves. The church is a cross-domed basilica resembling the Aphendiko in plan (110). It also has five domes on drums, the central one of which has been restored.

Other compartments are domed internally. Four columns form an arcade on each side of the nave, forming the basilical plan on the ground floor. On the upper story the cross-arms extend to the outer walls. The revival of the cross-domed basilical plan at this late epoch of Byzantine Architecture is of much interest and the mind is carried back to the cross-domed basilicas of much earlier centuries in Constantinople. There are, however, important distinctions between the earlier and later types. In the earlier type the four supports to the dome are continuous piers: in the later type they are columns in two stages. In the earlier type there are more than one column between the dome-supports: in the later type there is but one column on either side. Moreover, the builders of these late cross-domed basilicas had a different outlook from those of an earlier epoch who built the cross-in-square. No longer is the sense of compactness and unity present. The building is no longer the close-knit entity. Utilitarian conceptions and picturesque detail have ousted the sense of balance and proportion.

The Pantanassa is oriented south-east: as the traveller approaches it the first object to meet his eye is the belfry at the northern angle (107). It rises above an elegant loggia running along the wall of the church, which commands the panorama of the plain. Each of the highest stories of this belfry is pierced with openings consisting of three arched lights. They are recessed within pointed arches and on the highest story crowned with a triangular gable. Trefoils pierce the wall above the archway below. The design of this tower bears comparison with that of twelfth-century bell-towers in Auvergne and Aquitaine. The beautiful apses (108) also reveal an admixture of Western and Byzantine traits: an arcade of narrow pointed arches runs around the base; the decoration of the wall-space above this arcade is derived from Western Gothic Art; two broad stones set on the centre of each arch support curved skew-stones terminating in broad, palm-like finials. But the Byzantine mingles with the Gothic, for above this space there is an arcade of round-headed arches with the familiar archivolts of radiating bricks. Along the upper story of the north wall of the church runs a blind arcade, its arches articulating the line of the vaults inside; this is a Constantinopolitan feature. The interior is still covered with frescoes, which, though inferior in style and execution to those of the Peribleptos, are splendid in individual quality and general effect. A sense of religious joy is combined with a vivid appreciation of natural beauty to create their

197

devotional spirit. The dazzling and translucent quality of the varied colours permeates such frescoes as the Raising of Lazarus, the Ascension, and the Entry into Jerusalem. The frescoes of the Pantanassa have been well described as "the very flower of late Byzantine Art".

The Church of S. Demetrius, reconstructed as a cross-domed basilica at the end of the thirteenth century, was originally a wooden-roofed basilica belonging to the eighth century, a time when the cult of the saint spread rapidly over the East. Fragments with designs of an early date have been found embedded in its walls. It contains a mosaic pavement, a richly sculptured iconostasis and a walnut throne, a rare example of Byzantine woodwork. Its frescoes, which belong to the first half of the fourteenth century, are of two schools, the one whose compositions include the martyrdom of S. Demetrius, following in its simplicity the eleventh- and twelfth-century tradition, the other, more complex and impressionistic, following (as in the Last Judgment) the later style. A hall in the courtyard of the monastery houses a museum which contains many sculptures and inscriptions.

The churches of Mistra reveal an admixture of Greek and Constantinopolitan traits. Where the two-column plan is adopted, where the masonry is composed of square stone and thin tiles in the joints, where the cross-arms terminate in angular gables, the Greek influence is evident. Constantinople shows its influence in the form of the drums, in the exterior curves marking the vaults within, and in the domed basilical plan. The Western traits which have already been indicated and which filtered into Mistra from the neighbouring Principality add a note of interest and variety to buildings already distinguished by their varied charm.

Two secular buildings in Mistra deserve attention. The one is the Palace of the Despots, which consists of two parts at right angles, pierced by many windows. Amid the scattered ruins of the Upper City, the great hall, the spacious rooms, the wide courtyard—once thronged with the Despot's followers—stand empty and forlorn. A steep climb leads up to the other building —the fortress on the summit of the hill. A vaulted doorway leads to the outer court, while the inner court contains the princely residence and a little chapel. The fortress was occupied and restored both by its Byzantine and Turkish masters, but the original plan and part of the buildings are the work of Villehardouin, the Prince of Achaia.

Looking from its battlements one views the distant panorama over the Lacedaemonian plain and, on the abrupt hill-side beneath, the ruins of Mistra, the shattered and abandoned relics of the last epoch in the history of the Byzantine Empire. Its domed churches, its alien campaniles, its broken palace, its cobbled streets and its crumbling houses sleep beneath the blazing sunlight in their solitude and their decay. Only a handful of people dwell in the village at the foot, and a few nuns occupy the convent, of the Pantanassa. But the ruined city is for ever memorable in the fortunes of medieval Greece and the slowly dying Empire, while it is justly famed as the repository of beautiful specimens of architecture and precious examples of religious art.

In the very south of the Morea the narrow peninsula of Mani presents its rugged outline to the waters of the Mediterranean. It was a remote and inaccessible countryside, and during long periods of the Byzantine and Turkish sovereignty its turbulent population preserved a virtual independence. It was not until the ninth century that they were converted to Christianity and began to build simple churches of oblong plan in local stone. In the tenth century S. Nikon arrived among them as a missionary from Sparta, and encouraged the construction of churches with domes. A considerable number of Byzantine cross-in-square churches have survived in the villages and countryside of Mani from the eleventh, twelfth and thirteenth centuries. The earliest of them seems to have been at the Church of the Asomatoi at Kako Vouno, which is built of stone and whose dome rests on the antae of the bema and on two piers. The two-columned cross-in-square plan is to be found at Boulari̇oi (22), Kouloumi, Vamvaka, Gardenitsa and Ochia. This is by far the commonest plan in Mani. The four-column type without the additional bay before the apse occurs at Kitta and Koutiphari: with the additional bay it is to be seen at Karouda and Keria. In general, the Maniote churches possess many features in common with typical cross-in-square churches in other parts of Greece. For example, there is to be found in some of them the use of porous stone in squared blocks framed in the horizontal and vertical joints by thin brick; archivolts of radiating bricks are set over the doors; two-light windows separated by a slender shaft, each light surmounted by an arch of radiating brick and by a further arch above, encompassing the whole; brick patterns such as diapers, laid flush with the walls; arched cornices over the windows of the drums; and apses showing sides of a polygon externally. At the same time a local influence has also left its impress upon their structure. The native stone was freely employed and in the generality of cases brick was used for decorative rather than for structural purposes: the dome-arches may be set back over the square and tied with marble beams carved with ornamentation while earthen pots may be set into the base of the pendentives. Most important of all is the relationship of the naos to the narthex: the western arm of the cross is carried right through the narthex to its western wall; the narthex is thus divided into three bays, the central one being vaulted at the same level as the western arm of the cross and having the same breadth. This arrangement means that the central bay of the narthex really forms part of the naos, for, as a rule, the western cross-arm runs right on without a separating wall. (At Vamvaka there is a wall which stops short at the springing of the arch.)

It is probable that the idea of the long continuous western arm was derived from the oblong barrel-vaulted chapels which served as places of worship in Mani before the domed style came into fashion. Some of the churches like Vamvaka and Kitta have their exteriors enlivened with faïence vases set in the tympana or other places. The horseshoe arch of the west door at Kitta is significant of Anatolian influence. Ochia has Gothic-looking gargoyles in its drum. The marble iconostases of the churches are carved with such typical designs as birds pecking at grapes, and the translucent marble closures to the windows, of which there is a set at Vamvaka, are sculptured with foliated crosses and acanthus scrolls.

There are other cross-in-square churches in the Morea, too numerous for mention, most of which have received little study. They are to be found, among other places, at Chrysapha, Perpeni, Scala, Gastouni and Samari, and in the Church of S. Charalampos in Calamata, where the Frankish castle with the lion of S. Mark embedded in its walls overlooks the wide Messenian Gulf. The Church of the Holy Apostles at Kalamata is a simple cruciform. During the tenth, eleventh and twelfth centuries there was great activity in the construction of churches in all the regions of the Morea, an activity which is a clear witness to an active religious and artistic life. These churches were bound to no stereotyped design, but varied much in structure, arrangement and decoration. Nevertheless the cross-in-square is by far the most frequent type.

111, 112, 113   S. Luke, Stiris: carved marble slabs

North of the Gulf of Corinth, in Phocis, there is a monastery which, with its churches, has been fully described by Messrs. Schultz and Barnsley in a sumptuous volume published at the beginning of this century. The monastery is known as that of S. Luke of Stiris, and its two eleventh-century churches stand within its courtyard. The smaller church, dedicated to the Panagia, the Virgin, is of cross-in-square plan. Being of the four-column type with the extra bay before the apse vaulted at a lower level than the eastern cross-arm, and with quadripartite vaults in the angle-spaces, it belongs to the Constantinopolitan tradition. Its large double narthex in six bays and its exo-narthex are probably due to an influence coming from Mount Athos. Its walls are enriched with many saw-tooth bands and patterns in brick. The drum of its dome, a remarkably fine creation, has eight sides pierced with double windows, having slender marble shafts at the angles with lions' heads above. The lower part of the drum is panelled with elaborately carved marble slabs; the floor of the church is beautifully inlaid with slabs and tesserae of coloured marble.

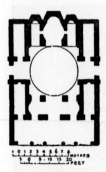

114   Church of the Monastery of Daphni

The larger church, which is dedicated to S. Luke (116), follows a different plan, the central square being bounded by twelve piers—one at each angle, and two tied by an arch on each side between the angle-piers (see plan of Daphni, Fig. 114). The square is brought to an octagon by means of squinches in its angles; at a higher level small pendentives bring the octagon to a circle for the base of the dome. The arms of the cross and the subsidiary spaces are cross-vaulted and galleried. In this type of church the central square opens out into all the three apses and not, as in the ordinary cross-in-square type, to the central apse alone. In S. Luke only the middle apse, whose antae are furnished with niches, projects externally. The low dome is surrounded by a sixteen-sided wall.

The Church of S. Luke has always evoked the admiration of travellers, and in the seventeenth century was thus described by George Wheler in his account of his tour in Greece:

And truly this is the finest Church I saw in all Greece next to Santa Sophia at Constantinople, notwithstanding it is very old and

115   DAPHNI

116   S. LUKE,
STIRIS

118   DAPHNI: Annunciation Mosaic

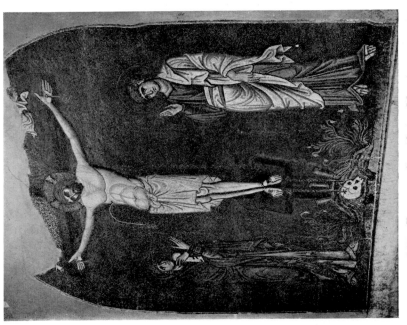

117   DAPHNI: Crucifixion Mosaic

hath suffered much by earthquakes and time. It is built after the Greek manner, almost square. . . . Then there is an indifferent large Cuppalo in the middle and it is proportioned within in the shape of a Cross. All the walls are cased with polished marble.

The splendid revetment of coloured marbles covers most of the lower part of the church, the upper surfaces having been adorned with mosaics. The Virgin with the Infant Christ is seated on a throne in the conch of the apse, and Pentecost fills the dome of the bema. In the diaconicon there are episodes from the Book of Daniel. The squinches are occupied by the Nativity, the Presentation at the Temple and the Baptism, but the Annunciation in the fourth squinch has been destroyed. Throughout the whole church there are numerous figures and medallions of saints. In the narthex there are depicted the apostles, saints, the Virgin, and events in the life of Christ. Over the door from the narthex to the naos the bust of Christ, if completed to form a full-length figure would have covered the door and thus symbolises the Lord's words, "I am the Door". Although the mosaics of S. Luke are sometimes stiff in design, they generally attain a high degree of merit. Individual figures possess a calm dignity, the arrangement of the scenes is harmonious and the colours, set against a gold background, are rich and glowing. The iconostases, lintels, gallery parapets and window closures of the two churches comprise many sculptured pieces and slabs of marble. They are carved with such typical devices as twisting foliage, decorative crosses and intertwining strands arranged in a rhomboid form containing flowers (111–13). The floors are paved in coloured marble.

The plan of S. Luke is represented by other Greek churches, among them that of S. Nicholas-in-the-Fields, at Skripou, in Boeotia, which belongs to a monastery farm dependent on S. Luke. Much smaller than the parent church, it is built of a blue-grey marble and is compact and harmonious in its form. It has no narthex, but a pseudo-narthex is formed by the western cross-arm and angle-spaces running into one.

Better known is the eleventh-century church of the Monastery of Daphni; beautifully situated in a quiet grove upon the Sacred Way between Athens and Eleusis, it is one of the most famous monuments of Byzantine Art which have surivived to the present day (115). It resembles S. Luke in plan, but its bema is cross-vaulted, and all its three apses project externally (114). It is preceded by a narthex in three cross-vaulted bays and by an exo-narthex with pointed arches that belong to the period of occupation by Cistercian monks in the time of the medieval Duchy of Athens. Originally the church had no galleries, but these were added over the narthex and western angle-spaces at a later date. Earthquakes and decay having weakened and endangered this historic church, its walls and mosaics were carefully restored in the closing decade of last century, when the removal of a lower vault in the narthex brought some precious mosaics to light. The mosaics which glow on the walls of the Church of Daphni are of great beauty. Distinguished by their elegance, variety, fineness of modelling and idealistic spirit, the evangelic scenes follow the Hellenistic tradition, showing a greater tendency towards the picturesque and more varied gestures than those of S. Luke. In Grabar's words, theirs is "the suave beauty of a humanistic Christian art". The episodes from the life of Christ and the Virgin, commemorated in the ecclesiastical festivals, contain compositions of the highest merit. Among them is the Crucifixion (117). In the figure of Christ there is a sense of calm and assured triumph, crucified though He be. It is evident in the expression of the face and in the whole pose of the body and proclaims with conviction the fact that He overcomes the sharpness of death. The figures of the Virgin and S. John on either side of the Cross are characterised by a tender and restrained grief, while their attitudes have a noble grace in keeping with the simple greatness of the scene. Equally impressive is the companion picture of the Descent into Hades, where Christ, a splendid figure, tramples underfoot the Prince of Darkness and the broken gates of Hades. As elsewhere, the Annunciation occupies a prominent position in a squinch (118), partly, as Professor Demus shows, because the scene lent itself to being fitted into a curved receptacle. "The Angel stands . . . opposite to the almost frontal figure of the Virgin. The spatial distance between the two figures expresses the theme of the meeting of two different spheres." A colossal bust of Christ the Pantocrator, terrible in its grim severity but intensely powerful in effect, surrounded by sixteen prophets, occupies the centre of the dome. The Virgin with archangels is set in the central apse, and S. John the Baptist, the forerunner of Our Lord, occupies the prothesis where the preparation of the Sacred Elements takes place. Figures and medallions of saints in mosaic are dispersed throughout the church, and marble panels clothe the surface of the walls beneath. The type of plan represented by Daphni and S. Luke is on the whole very satisfying and attractive, although squinches in aesthetic quality fall far short of great pendentives with their upward-sweeping curves. The wide unencumbered central area, sharply defined and surmounted by its overhanging dome so high above, has a wonderful sense of spaciousness and dignity: with the openness of this central area is contrasted the complex mystery of the various compartments which are grouped around it: apses, angle-spaces and cross-arms. Screened by arcades or iconostasis, dim in half-lights and shadows, they make their contrast to the vision. Yet at the same time there is no sense of disparity; the whole structure is bound together by the unifying dome and its subsidiary vaults.

The Church of SS. Theodore at Mistra, which dates from 1295 and which belonged to the Brontocheion Monastery, is of the same type (120), but has barrel-vaults instead of cross-vaults in the angle-spaces and arms of the cross. The angle-spaces were used as ossuaries and, like the rest of the church, were adorned with frescoes, one of which represents the Emperor Manuel Palaeologus kneeling before Our Lord. The church was patronised by the imperial house and its exterior was decorated with great skill and care. The outsides of the apses have spaces on them for marble panels and are enlivened with dentil bands which are carried over the windows. Dentil cornices are also extended below the eaves. The original cupola has been destroyed, but the fine, richly adorned drum with its sixteen arched openings is still preserved. It is interesting to note that while the east and west arms of the cross terminate in triangular gables those on the north and south are curved following the interior line of the vaults; this is a mixture of Greek and Constantinopolitan traits.

There is another church of the same type to be found at Monemvasia. Monemvasia, which has been called the "Gibraltar of the Morea", was a stronghold on the south-east coast of the peninsula, occupying a rocky hill which stands isolated in the sea and connected by only a narrow causeway with the shore. The last place to be captured by the Frankish princes, it reverted after a brief spell to the Byzantine Empire, and then was sometimes under Venetian and sometimes under Turkish and for a short period under Papal rule. Its Church of Santa Sophia (c. 1300) stands amidst the ruins of the military town on the summit of the rocky hill. It belongs to the same type as S. Luke and Daphni,

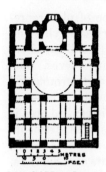

119 S. Nicodemus, Athens

but its narthex is preceded by a loggia of Venetian date. The late Church of S. Nicolas (1703) is of cross-in-square plan, but it has pointed arches and a Renaissance façade with pilasters and a broken pediment.

At Athens the S. Luke type of plan is represented by the Church of S. Nicodemus, originally known as the Panagia Lycodemou (119). An inscription within the building records the death of its founder in 1041. It was built on the site of a Roman Bath and is now the Russian church of the city. It is provided with galleries and its angle-spaces are covered with domical vaults, but it has also certain affinities with basilical plans. The exterior is distinguished by its elaborate friezes of cut brick, with designs in Kufic lettering, derived from contemporary Arab sources: it is interesting to remark that the presence of Arabs in Athens in the tenth and eleventh centuries is attested by a number of inscriptions in the town, including one which records the dedication of a mosque. The Church of S. Nicodemus was drastically restored and its campanile built in the nineteenth century. A ruined church at Christianou in Triphyllia seems to be an early example of the type.

The type of plan which has been under review seems most probably to have had its source in the East. It could have been derived from the quatrefoiled square of Armenia, the foils being replaced by vaults: the use of the squinch also points to an influence emanating from that country. Strzygowski suggests that Tiridates the Armenian architect who undertook the restoration of Santa Sophia at Constantinople in 989 may have been responsible for the introduction of the plan. He concludes that the leading churches of the type were "erected under imperial patronage" and that the adaptation of the Oriental plan was "due to imperial influences at Constantinople".

Oriental influences have also been detected in the remarkable thirteenth-century Church of the Parigoritissa at Arta, which was the royal Church of the Despots of Epirus (121). A massive cube crowned with five domes on drums and a sixth dome on an open arcade, it has none of that elegance characteristic of the Greek Byzantine style. In plan it is a domed square, with triple sanctuary opening off the square and a narthex and parecclesia furnished with galleries; the dome-arches are not prolonged as barrel-vaults to the outer walls. The central dome, elevated to a great height, rests on four stages of corbelled-out columns; Epirus lies towards the west, and perhaps the builders of this church, in aiming for height, were influenced by some Gothic church they had seen in Europe. Though there is a considerable amount of Byzantine brick decoration in the building, Gothic traits are also in evidence, for there are trefoil arches below the drum inside, and corbels shaped like fantastic monsters without.

Greece can boast of other plans—the hall-church, like S. Basil at Arta, with rich faïence decoration: basilicas, some of them of an early date, including the remains of one at Corinth: domed cruciforms, like one already mentioned at Calamata and one at Manolada; trefoils, as at Platani, near Patras.

It is now necessary to move up to the more northerly area of Greece. The churches of the monasteries of the Meteora, strangely perched on the summits of high cylindrical rocks in Thessaly, are of cross-in-square or trefoiled cross-in-square plan. The most important and oldest monastery at Meteora was founded in the fourteenth century, but the church was not completed till the sixteenth century, years after the time when the Empire passed under the sway of the Ottoman Turks. The apses terminating the transepts are derived from the plan customary on Mount Athos. Other monasteries, those of S. Barlaam, S. Stephen, etc., are perched on the summits of these precipitous and fantastic rocks, once the homes of many monks who on their lofty heights had abandoned the world of men. The churches were profusely painted with frescoes of the late Byzantine school.

Farther south, at the hill of Episcopi, overlooking the Gulf of Volo, there have been found some sculptured slabs and fragments testifying to the former presence of an important religious settlement. The designs are familiar to Byzantine Art and include pecking birds, eagles, interlacings and decorative crosses. Some of them are in champlevé and an Arabic influence is evident.

Churches of an earlier period in the great and wealthy seaport of Salonica have been described in a previous chapter. The city is also fortunate in the possession of some beautiful and interesting monuments of the later epoch. Chief among them is the distinguished Church of the Holy Apostles, an erection of the early fourteenth century (122). Situated in a little square in the higher part of the town this charming little edifice, a modified variety of the cross-in-square type, has been influenced in its plan by the earlier Church of Santa Sophia in the same city (see Chapter V). But it is for the richness of its exterior adornment that the church is especially distinguished. The five domes rest on high and elegant brick drums, with angle-colonnettes supporting arched cornices over recessed niches. They have a striking and pronounced effect. The apses are covered with elaborate patterns of brick above and tall niches below. Among the designs employed in this profuse but appropriate ornamentation are diamonds, arches, zigzags and frets. There is no Byzantine church where the elaboration of surface pattern in brick reached a higher level than this small Church of the Holy Apostles. Brick ornamentation is also conspicuous in the cross-in-square Church of Yakub-pasha-djami, which also belongs to the fourteenth century and in that of S. Elias, a domed trefoil. The Church of S. Pantelemon at Salonica has been assigned by M. Diehl to the middle of the twelfth century. It has an elegant central drum with flat niches and windows surmounted by radiating bricks, while the roofs of the cross-arms follow the curve of the vaults.

An earlier cross-in-square church at Salonica is of a simple exterior with little decoration but of bold and pleasing form. This is the Church of the Virgin which an inscription dates to the year 1038 and which became the Mosque of Kazandjilar-djami. The central dome has a flat cornice and two tiers of niches in the drum, but the drums of the domes over the narthex are of the Athenian type with their arches penetrating the roof.

The Salonican churches show how architecture flourished in this important town during the last three centuries of its independence. The period was interrupted by the Latin occupation during part of the thirteenth century, but even after the reconquest of the city by the Greeks Salonica was enabled to fulfil an important role. The elaborate elegance and meticulous workmanship of the Holy Apostles are a clear indication of the refined taste and lavish care which characterised Salonica in its final epoch as the second city of the Christian Empire of the East.

Scanty remains at Philippi have been acclaimed—not without challenge—as those of a sixth-century cross-domed basilica, and there is an interesting twelfth-century church at Feredjik in Thrace, with five domes and double columns to support the central one.

At Molyvdokepastro on the Greco-Albanian frontier there are some churches which have been described by Mr. Donald Nicol. One of them, the Dormition of the Virgin, is a domed trefoiled

120   MISTRA: SS. Theodore

121   ARTA: Parigoritissa

122 SALONICA: the Holy Apostles

123 KUCEVICTE

square with a nave. The centre of the nave is covered by a transverse vault: the transverse vault was common in Epirus. The Holy Apostles is a cross-in-square church with a narthex and south covered portico. Both churches may originally date to the fourteenth century. The Cathedral of Serres in Macedonia—a basilica—has a fine mosaic which represents the Communion of the Apostles and is perhaps of eleventh-century date.

MOUNT ATHOS

As early as the ninth century, hermits were living their solitary lives on the wooded slopes of Athos, the most easterly of the three peninsulas which run out into the Aegean Sea from the broad projection of Chalcidice. In the following century Athanasius the Athonite founded the original community of Lavra beneath the shadow of its mountain on its south-eastern shore. Other monasteries followed upon Lavra, and the sacred mount of Athos has long been occupied by a large population of monks. By far the greater part of the existing constructions is subsequent to the Turkish conquest. Indeed, a considerable proportion belongs to the last few centuries, for periodical fires have swept over individual monasteries and extensive rebuilding has often been required. Each monastery consists of a rectangular court surrounded by the monks' quarters. The refectory stands sometimes separately in the court and sometimes among the surrounding buildings. The church occupies the centre of the court, which may also contain subsidiary chapels and other edifices. In front of the church and covered by a dome on columns there rises the *phiale* or sacred well whose waters are used to bless the rooms on the Festival of the Baptism of Our Lord and on the first day of each month. The danger of attack by corsairs was often so imminent that the monasteries were constructed to act as fortresses and furnished with towers of defence. Therefore, though their elements are picturesquely grouped, their exterior walls present a simple and severe appearance. Their churches, secluded within their courtyards, are plentifully adorned both without and within. Built of rubble, they are normally of the four-column cross-in-square plan with an extra bay of lower height before each of the three apses, which project at the eastern end. The builders, however, borrowed a feature from the trefoil church plan by finishing off the north and south arms of the cross with apses, which were called *choroi* and were reserved for readers, singers and dignitaries. The churches of Athos are distinguished also by the largeness of the narthex, which usually has six bays in two rows. Certain monastic offices were recited in the narthex and a larger space than usual was required for the monks who were to participate in these services. In later days nartheces were built in two divisions, the outer of which was called the *liti*.

In Lavra (tenth century) the arms of the cross are very short and the transeptal apses are round on the exterior. The narthex is flanked by two chapels which are like miniature cross-in-square churches and is preceded by an exo-narthex and a recent porch. In Vatopedi (end of the tenth century) the dome rests on granite columns instead of piers as at Lavra and the plan is more opened out. Vatopedi has valuable treasures, including a cup given by Manuel Cantacuzenos which has a jasper bowl on a silver-gilt octagonal stem. Iveron (124), founded in the eleventh century, was rebuilt between 1453 and 1560; it has the usual chapels flanking the narthex. Chilandari, the Serbian monastery, founded in the thirteenth century by the famous monarch of that country, Stephen Nemanya, possesses a considerable amount of brick ornamentation on its exterior; it has a six-bayed narthex preceded by an exo-narthex of similar dimensions. In its long proportions, its lofty drum, its undulating roof, its many doors and the designs of its sculptured plaques, the church clearly betrays its Serbian origin. Many churches like those of the Pantocrator (fourteenth century) (125), Koutloumousiou and Dionysiou (both sixteenth century) have domes with drums over the prothesis and diaconicon. These little domes show how much the love of the picturesque, the striking, the fanciful was characteristic of the period. The churches also tended to assume higher proportions as time went on—another indication of the wish to create striking effects. This tendency is particularly evident in the Church of Docheiariou, which was rebuilt in 1568 by Moldavian generosity and under the supervision of a Moldavian bishop. The nationality of its benefactors is revealed by its external buttresses, and its slender, elongated drums. Among the other monasteries are those of Stavronitika, Xenophontos and Esphigmenou. Owing to the smallness of the courtyard the sixteenth-century Church of Stavronitika consists only of sanctuaries and nave. The little Church of Xenophontos has columns with Corinthian capitals. The Church of Esphigmenou with its numerous domes dates only from the beginning of the nineteenth century.

It will have been seen, therefore, that the churches belonging to the monasteries of Mount Athos follow the traditional plan of the Greek cross-in-square church with local peculiarities such as the transeptal apses and the spacious nartheces. In the external features of their elevations they remained faithful after the Turkish conquest to the custom of earlier centuries and were enabled to continue their Byzantine tradition in the days of the Ottoman Empire. The drums of their domes as a rule follow a model common in other areas, with bold arched cornices projecting over the windows in the sides of the polygon. The interiors of the churches on Mount Athos were covered with frescoes arranged in accordance with the stereotyped iconographical scheme, unrolling the events of sacred story in a vast series of pictured scenes. Both the Cretan and the Macedonian schools have left their impress on the character of these works. Some of the artists' names have been preserved, among them those of Manuel Panselinos, Theophanes of Crete and Frangos Castellanos of Thebes. It was Panselinos who was so admired by Dionysios of Fourna, a monk of the seventeenth century, whose celebrated "Painters' Guide" was, as we have seen, discovered by Didron on Mount Athos. It gives the most minute instructions about the character, composition and technique of the paintings which were to cover the walls of a church, and the traditions which it embodies go back far beyond the period of the life of Dionysios. Most of the frescoes of Mount Athos are later than the sixteenth century and many of them have been repainted, but their iconographical interest is of permanent importance. In Ottoman days the sacred mountain with its numerous monasteries was the real metropolis of Orthodox Christianity, and for many centuries drew artists and scholars to its rocky shores. A flourishing school of art developed and the painter-monks were always ready to paint the icons of the saints and adorn the walls of the churches. In the great Church of Vatopedi, the cycle of paintings constitutes in the words of Mr. Byron and Professor Talbot Rice, "without doubt, the greatest extant memorial of the Macedonian school". The scenes of the Entry into Jerusalem and the Crucifixion, with their life-size figures and subdued colouring, are splendidly composed and inspired with deep religious feeling. These paintings belong to the fourteenth century. The Cretan school, which took its rise in the early sixteenth century, is represented in the churches of Docheiariou, of Dionysiou in the Chapel of S. George in the

Monastery of S. Paul and other buildings. Natives of Crete, which remained for long a Venetian possession, painted on Mount Athos; the work of the school became popular over the whole of the eastern Mediterranean area, and it gave birth to the art of Dominico Theotocopulo, himself a Cretan, the famous El Greco.

This account of Mount Athos may be concluded by mentioning that the oldest church on the peninsula is the tenth-century church in the village of Karyes. It is barrel-vaulted and in plan resembles a flat-roofed ninth-century church on the island of Scyros.

THE ARCHIPELAGO AND CRETE

A few churches on some of the Greek islands may be singled out for mention. The Church of Our Lady of the Hundred Gates at Paros, which probably goes as far back as the sixth century, is the finest in the Cyclades. It really consists of three churches, the largest of which is a cross-domed basilica with transepts and galleries. The columns are finished with carved Ionic impost-capitals and the apse is occupied by seven tiers of marble steps leading up to chairs. The altar rests under a ciborium in the space in front. The south-east angle of the cross is occupied by a sacristy and chapel and the north-east one by another church dedicated to S. Nicholas. The Church of S. Nicholas, originally a galleried basilica earlier in date than the great church, was later transformed into a cross-domed basilica. The third church is a baptistery.

The Church of Nea Moni on the island of Chios is an oblong building with its dome buttressed by semi-domes in the thickness of the walls. Pairs of columns formerly supported the dome, which was restored after an earthquake in 1881; as seen by a Russian pilgrim in the eighteenth century, it rested on a high drum. The apses derived their horseshoe form from the neighbouring mainland of Anatolia. The church was adorned with eleventh-century mosaics of high quality of which many still survive, and which include the Great Festivals of the Church.

There are cross-in-square churches in Crete, one of which is of special interest as it has been alleged to belong to the late sixth century. Situated at Gortyna, it is in a ruined state but appears to have been of cross-in-square plan. The bema had niches and side-chambers, and there were apses at the ends of the north and south arms of the cross. The church was visited about the

124   MOUNT ATHOS: Iveron

125   MOUNT ATHOS: Pantocrator

126　Sopoćani

127　Dečani

middle of the nineteenth century by Spratt, who described it as "the best preserved as well as one of the most interesting ruins now seen at Gortyna" and as "a plain but well-built and very early church . . . constructed of closely fitted squared blocks". The "northern sacristy" was "almost entire", and formed a chapel still used in his day "by the Greeks of the neighbourhood".

CHAPTER XI

Yugoslavia, Bulgaria, Roumania and Russia

EDIEVAL Serbia had an independent existence of between two and three hundred years' duration, when able and ambitious monarchs endowed their country with prosperity and power. Taking full advantage of the weakness of the Latin and Byzantine Empires they aggrandised their territories and consolidated their realm. They exercised a supreme authority in the Balkan Peninsula and they were patrons of culture and of art. They even dreamt of a day when they might become the heirs of the ancient but enfeebled Empire and establish their throne in the Palace of the Byzantine Caesars. The consolidation and growth of the Serbian state was intimately associated with the fortunes of the Church. Before Stephen Nemanya had welded the Serbian tribes into a political entity in the second half of the twelfth century, it was Christianity which had linked them together. In the Serbian kingdom the Church occupied an unchallengable position of prestige and authority. Imbued with a strongly national spirit, it was upheld and enriched by the generosity of the monarch. The first of its archbishops, the saintly and venerated Sava was the son of Stephen Nemanya, and many of his successors were scions of the princely house. Of S. Sava it is written that he endowed his country with all kinds of monuments of piety: where he could not erect churches he planted crosses "that the name of God might be glorified". Most of the important churches were attached to the monasteries, which played a great part in the life of medieval Serbia. Founded by royal decree, endowed with fertile lands, and built on frequented routes, they did much to civilise and develop the country. They became the sepultures of their princely founders, whose relics, credited with a miraculous power, added a further sanctity to their shrines. The generosity of the sovereign provided churches stately in their architecture and lavish in their decoration. The wealthy and powerful aristocracy was eager to emulate the royal example, and it was to the zeal of the nobles that some of the most beautiful churches in Serbia owed their existence.

The first centre of church-building in Serbia lay in Raška, a mountainous district watered by the Ibar, which formed the nucleus of the growing state. Roughly speaking, the region containing these churches lies between the forty-fourth and forty-second parallels of latitude. In the Raškan group of churches Byzantine elements blend with Western. While the Serbian Church belonged to the Eastern Orthodox family, Raška geographically looked towards the West. Serbia extended to the shores of the Adriatic and maintained a close connection with Italy. Italian artists and goldsmiths were resident in the neighbouring state of Bosnia, and Lombardic features which had found their way into the architecture of the Dalmatian coast-land spread from there into the hinterland of Serbia. The plan of the Raškan church is that of a rectangle or of a Latin cross terminating in a single round apse. The placing of the narthex under the same roof as the nave lengthens the appearance of the church and adds to its Western look: yet a dome on a polygonal drum crowns the edifice.

The ruined Church of S. Nicholas at Kurshumlija (*c.* 1170) is of oblong plan with a lateral porch: it is thoroughly Byzantine in its use of thin bricks and in the shape of its windows. The Monastery of Studenica, standing in front of a tangled mass of mountains, was the earliest of the royal foundations, having been built in 1183–90 by Stephen Nemanya, "fearing the Last Judgment": he resided in the monastery for some years as a monk and granted it great privileges. The walls of its church are beautifully faced with polished white marble and it possesses many features which betray the influence of the Occident. There are engaged pilasters upon its walls and arcatures beneath its eaves, as in Romanesque churches of Italy. From the same source are derived the birds, the intertwining foliage and the lions on which the pillars of the west doorway rest. The tympanum has a beautiful relief of the Virgin with the Archangels Michael and Gabriel. The interior is rich in frescoes of the early thirteenth century. They are full of grace and movement and in scenes like the Nativity of the Virgin and the Presentation of the Virgin their picturesque and delicate charm is well apparent. They recall the mosaics of Kahrié-djami at Constantinople and the frescoes of Mistra in the Morea.

The church of the Monastery of Ziča (1207–19) was the coronation church of the Serbian monarchs and as such was held in great esteem and lavishly endowed with gifts. It is distant a few miles from the large market town of Rankocičevo. The monastery is famous for its seven "sealed gates", a new door being made for every coronation and permanently closed thereafter. Low transepts give the church the plan of a Latin cross; it has an arcature of recessed pointed arches running round its drum. The earliest frescoes of the Žiča, those which belong to the beginning of the thirteenth century, in the simplicity of their attitudes and draperies recall the style of the mosaics of Daphni, near Athens. The same can be said of the frescoes in Nemanya's church at Studenica described already.

The church with the lower transept forming a Latin cross is to be found also at Peć (c. 1263) and Gradac (c. 1290): both of these churches had three apses. The striking Gothic features in the ruined monastic Church of Gradac, its outside buttresses and its pointed doors with receding arches, were due to the presence of French monks, who were brought by its foundress, Helena, widow of King Stephen Urosh I and daughter of Baldwin II, Latin Emperor of Constantinople. Domed churches of Latin cross plan exist also at Podi and Blagovestenje. At Sopoćani (c. 1275)(126) and Arilje (c. 1300) the eastern angles of the cross are occupied by chambers; each angle-chamber, unlike those in a typical Byzantine church, is roofed along with the corresponding transept under the same lean-to roof. Sopoćani contains some of the most beautiful frescoes in Serbia; among which a great "Dormition of the Virgin" is worthy of especial mention. The dome in these churches is constructed on a system which also prevails elsewhere in Serbia; the drum of its dome rests on four engaged arches set in the walls of a square tower which is carried upon the main arches of the church.

The church of the Monastery of Dečani (127), near the Albanian frontier, belongs to a date somewhat later than the other Raškan churches which have been described. Founded by Stephen Uroš III, to whom it gave the name Dečanski, it has always been reputed as "a gem of Serbian Architecture". The late Sir Arthur Evans described his impressions of Dečani: "the view of this church, rising from the solitary glen with its alternate bands of black and white marble and rosy quartz could never be forgotten". Built in 1327–48 by Vita, a Franciscan from Cattaro on the Dalmatian coast, it contains many Western features. Its western façade, the slopes of the central ridge-roof and the two lean-to roofs remind one of churches in Pisa. The arcatures beneath its eaves, and its arched doorway with clustered columns and sculptured tympanum are familiar to Italian Romanesque: but the construction of the dome and essential features in the plan are Byzantine. The interior is covered with frescoes, the pillars being appropriately painted with stylite saints. One other church in the area is deserving of attention, the so-called "royal church" at Studenica, not to be confused with Stephen Nemanya's building previously described. It was built in 1314. With an elevation that closely follows Byzantine lines, it contains some splendid frescoes of the so-called Macedonian school.

The beauty of the churches of Raška lies more in the richness of their material and of their detail than in their general architectural outline. The dome upon its square tower does not always look satisfactory, and there seems sometimes to be a want of proportion between the east and western ends. But the play of fancy, the delicate richness of detail, the wealth of frescoes, reach a high level of artistic achievement and the builders showed a power of adaptation which they employed with brilliant effect.

In the late thirteenth century, Serbia began to extend rapidly towards the south. Stephen Milutin (1282–1321) had occupied the Upper Vardar valley and the reign of Stephen Dušan (1331–1355) beheld the great Serbian Empire, the frontiers of which extended from the Danube to the Duchy of Athens and the shores of the Gulf of Corinth.

Elated by his victories over the Imperial arms and his absolute ascendancy in the Balkans and Thessaly, Dušan imitated the pomp which for centuries had been the prerogative of his defeated enemy. He styled himself "Tsar and Autocrat", and as such was crowned at his capital of Skoplje. He wore the tiara and assumed the double-headed eagle as his badge. He secured the title of Patriarch for the head of the national Church, who gathered round him all the additional prestige which was associated with so famous a title. The reigns of these sovereigns were marked by a great architectural activity in the territory captured from the Empire, especially in the neighbourhood of the River Vardar in Macedonia. The churches which were erected in this area are Byzantine in style: as the Serbs imitated the Empire in their ceremonial, so did they imitate it in their architecture. At the same time these churches possess their local and national peculiarities and derive their elements from different sources. Constantinople, Macedonia, Salonica and Greece all seem to have had a share in moulding their style. The common plan is the four-column cross-in-square without an extra bay before the apse (128). The majority of the churches follow the general Serbian tendency to accentuate the height and lessen the breadth. The northern and southern arms of the cross are proportionately short and the angle-spaces are narrow. Generally speaking, only the central apse projects to the exterior, the side-apses being niches in the thickness of the wall. The drums of the domes are polygonal in plan and like the walls imitate the later architecture of the Empire in the richness of their brick ornamentation. The exterior walls are plentifully varied with round-headed arches, but these are more arbitrarily placed than in Constantinople. In Constantinople they are usually employed, except on apses, to mark the interior line of vaults: in Serbia they are often but surface decoration.

The important monastic churches of Nagoričino and Gračanica have features which distinguish them from other representatives of their class. The Church of S. George at Nagoričino, which was built in 1312, has the additional bay before the sanctuary and its single projecting apse is planned on the curve outside. It has a western arm in two bays and four little domes on drums over its extreme corners. Its frescoes, which belong to the Macedonian school, are of high merit: great architectural scenes, crowded with figures and set out in long friezes, recount the events of the Gospels. They are signed with the name of their artists, Michael and Eutychios, and have been acclaimed by M. Gabriel Millet as the most precious of Serbian art.

The Church of Gračanica (c. 1320) (130) is one of the most original monuments of Serbian architecture and has been called "the Queen of Serbian Churches". It is situated to the north of Macedonia proper, in the district known as Kosmet, an autonomous area within the Serbian Republic. It is a striking building with a lofty dome towering over its centre, surrounded by a multitude of archivolts with sweeping curves. Unfortunately a squat narthex and a later exo-narthex detract considerably from its appearance. It might be described as an expansion of the cross-in-square plan, each arm of the cross being extended to two bays, vaulted and roofed at different levels. There are domes on elegant drums over the angle-spaces, and brick decoration is plentifully employed. Of the frescoes which cover the interior, the most celebrated is that of Milutin: clad in gorgeous robes and wearing a bejewelled crown, the long-bearded monarch holds in his hands a model of his five-domed church. The Church of the Virgin of the Black Mountain at the Monastery of Matejić, built in 1355, is another fine five-domed building of the cross-in-square plan. The monastery was a royal foundation, was once rich and prosperous; it is now abandoned but steps have been taken to repair the church and preserve its damaged frescoes.

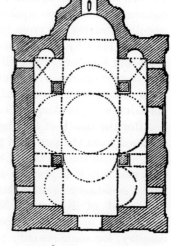

128 Ljuboten, Serbia

Many of the churches of this group, once so plentiful, have only a central dome. The ruined Church of Ljuboten (1327) is a typical example of the familiar plan (128). It is beautifully adorned with thin bricks, set in chequered and diapered patterns. Cučer (1307) has its walls panelled with niches. On the apse of Štip there are niches extending almost to the coping, each of them containing another arch of half the height. Lesnovo is another church where this system of arch within arch occurs. The Monastery of Marko near Skoplje, which is one of the few monasteries still inhabited by monks, has a beautiful fourteenth-century cross-in-square church: the arms of the cross to east and west terminate in pointed gables and the building seems to have been affected specifically by Greek influence from farther south. Marko was a petty prince who established himself at Markovgrad, where many ruins and churches attest his power: he became a heroic figure in Serbian legend.

Macedonia is rich in ruined churches: something has been said to indicate their leading features and the influences which were brought to bear upon their style. Before concluding a summary of the group mention may be made of some plans other than the cross-in-square. The domed square occurs at the Matka Monastery (1372) and at S. Nicholas on the Treska (131). The tiny Church of S. Andrew, built in the same mountainous defile in the year 1389 and adorned with frescoes, is of cruciform plan. The elegant little

Church of the Archangel at Kucevicte (123) is a trefoiled cross-in-square with a large square narthex. Nor should one forget a peculiarly attractive cross-in-square church at Nerezi near Skoplje, built in 1164 by the Emperor Alexius Comnenus when the surrounding territory was still a part of the Byzantine Empire. A five-domed church, very picturesque and admirably proportioned, it is richly decorated with archivolts of radiating bricks. It contains wall-paintings of exceptional importance.

After the death of Stephen Dušan the Serbian Empire rapidly declined from the powerful position which it had attained. Intestine feuds in the royal and noble families hastened its disintegration and left it a prey to the external enemy, until in 1389 its heroic resistance against the Turks was broken on the memorable battlefield of Kossovo. Nevertheless, a Serbian state, sadly diminished in extent, lingered on in the northern part of the country, for some seventy years. The Despot Stephen Lazarević (d. 1427) attempted to consolidate his realm. Cultured and pious, he patronised literature and erected stately churches. But the flame of learning and of art leapt up only to flicker down and die away: in 1459 Serbia became part of the Ottoman Empire. During this epoch architecture flourished in the northern area, which comprised the Serbian Despotate of Lazarević, the new churches being erected in the neighbourhood of the Morava, a tributary of the Danube. Their design is the result of an interpenetration of Byzantine and other elements. The main body of the churches takes on the form of one or the other of two plans—the trefoiled square or the trefoiled cross-in-square; in both plans a large narthex placed under the same roof as the nave draws out the square externally to a rectangle. The rectangular plan owed its inspiration to earlier churches in Raška, which lies no great distance to the south-west of the Morava area where the new churches were built. The trefoil idea came from Mount Athos, where, as we have seen, it was in vogue and where large numbers of monks from Serbia dwelt. (The possibility of a more direct Armenian influence has been suggested, but the intimate connection between Serbia and Athos was so constant as to make the direct Athonite influence far more likely.) The Morava churches of the trefoiled cross-in-square plan have narrow transepts and angle-spaces and tend to assume the proportions of the trefoil churches. Both varieties are distinguished by their loftiness, which is usually increased by the drum being elevated on arches set in a tower over the crossing.

129 Kruševać

130 Gračanica

131 SKOPJE:
S. Nicholas on
the Treska

132 MANASIJA

The exteriors of the buildings display a rich sculptured decoration derived mainly from Oriental sources. The trefoiled square plan is represented at Smederevo, the capital of the last medieval Serbian state, the ruins of whose great fortress show how strong was the determination of the Despots to preserve their realm. It is situated some eighteen miles farther down the Danube than Belgrade, the capital of Yugoslavia. The church, which is in the cemetery of the town, was built by the Despot about the middle of the fifteenth century.

Smederevo is decorated simply with arcades on high columns, but the monastic church at Kruševać (1380–5) has been profusely adorned by the sculptor's hand(129). Interlaced bands, enwreathed foliage and cable mouldings enliven its windows and its doors; curving archivolts mount up from its trefoils to the base of its elegant drum, which is rivalled by a strong but delicately adorned bell-tower above its narthex. Coloured faïence adds other notes of charm to its walls. Built as a palace chapel by Lazar, and known as Lazarica, it was long used as a store-house by the Turks.

The church at Rudenica (1490) is in a state of ruin but preserves zigzag and other geometrical ornamentation around its windows. The rich decoration on the outside of the walls of the Church of Kalenic (1410) is mostly of Eastern origin and it is strange to see how much the contact with the Moslems affected the adornment of a Christian church. Its narrow two-light windows, of Islamic pattern and set within pointed arches, are surrounded with intertwining strands and twisting stems of foliage, lacelike in their effect. The tympana are occupied by sculptures of griffons and dragons, of a centaur playing on a violin and a man struggling with a lion.

The trefoiled cross-in-square type of church is represented at Ravanica, Ljubostinja and Manasija. The church of the Monastery of Ravanica, erected in 1388, is a five-domed building with a triple apse at its eastern end. The outer decoration of its walls is of interest and beauty in its combination of brick and coloured faïence and sculptured marble. Ljubostinja dates from 1405 and is a one-domed church which has been much restored. It has a square narthex almost as large as the main body of the building. This kind of narthex, so different from the narrow one of the typical Byzantine church, passed into Roumania, where it became a customary feature. The Church of Manasija, sometimes called Reseva, and built after 1407, is one of the most celebrated monuments in Yugoslavia. The monastery, once an important centre of the arts, stands inside a lengthy fortified wall, modelled by the Despot Stephen, it is said, on the walls of Constantinople. To build the church, the Despot brought an architect from Herzegovina, telling him that no other church must be found to have surpassed it in beauty or in height. A five-domed church, it is faced with stone and has a simple exterior, being decorated only with arcatures running around the walls below the cornice(132). Tall thin columns connect some of the arches of the arcature with the ground. Everything in the structure tends to accentuate its height—its columns, its composition, its tall vertical lines, its soaring domes. Manasija, perhaps more than any other church in Yugoslavia, illustrates the difference in style between the Byzantine Architecture of medieval Serbia and that of Greece and Constantinople. In the southern countries the dome gathers the clustering elements of the edifice around it, in the northern country it abandons them and soars aloft. It seemed as if the princely founders of these churches were determined to impress the spectator, and did so by emphasising the note of verticality. In other ways the style of the Serbian churches as a whole differs from that of the Greek. In the typical Greek church there exists a sense of completeness and restraint, a feeling of contentment and repose. The structure of the Serbian church seems different. In its lines there is a greater play of fancy, an urge to break away from the rigid demands of the type, a certain restlessness and a search for new adventure. Not only are elements from alien sources freely welcomed but the essential features of the type are modified. As at Gračanica, aisles are doubled, arches are backed by arches, roofs are freely curved, drums are elongated and raised still higher on lofty towers. The result can be inspiring and beautiful. The fact simply reveals a difference in spirit, but it is significant of the truth that Byzantine Architecture for all its adherence to essentials could blossom forth into many varieties of form.

Several churches of the last period of Serbian architecture also possess notable frescoes. Painted in great detail, picturesque in their style and refined in their execution, they mostly belong to what is called the Cretan school. The paintings of the Miracles of Christ at Ravanica and Kalenić and those of the Communion of the Apostles at Ravanica and Manasija may be singled out for special mention. Not the least interesting pictures are those of the royal or noble founders of the monasteries, holding a model of their church in their hands. It is well to remark that the Yugoslav Government is exercising care over all the ancient buildings and frescoes and doing much to preserve these fine examples of medieval Serbian Art.

A few churches on the Adriatic coast of Yugoslavia, in Dalmatia, have been connected with Byzantine influence, though some authorities would rather derive them from Croatian wooden architecture. S. Nicholas near Nona (Nin) is a small trefoiled square. The dome, which rests on squinches, is marked with a battlemented tower (133). S. Croce, also at Nin, is a cruciform church with three low apses at the east

133   S. Nicholas, Nona

and with a dome supported by squinches. Though less than thirty feet in length this little sanctuary was a cathedral in Byzantine days. Nin was a town of great antiquity, famous in Roman times, and in the Middle Ages one of the residences of the kings of Croatia: now it is only a small fishing village on an island off the Dalmatian coast.

At Kotor (Cattaro) there are two churches of the domed oblong plan, the dome being supported by pendentives on pointed arches. One of them, La Collegiata or S. Maria Infunara, was rebuilt in 1220. It has three bays, the middle one being covered by the dome: an apse projects from the east end. S. Luca, though much smaller in size, is of the same type of plan. The pendentives are poorly formed: built in the fourteenth century, it may have followed an earlier model. These churches or their prototypes may have had much to do with the early plan of the Raškan churches in old Serbia.

In the very south-west corner of Yugoslavia, on the frontier with Albania, the picturesque little port of Ochrida lies upon the shores of its mountain-girt lake. It has been ruled by many different races and was an important stopping-place on the Via Ignatia of the Romans. The famous Serbian saints Clement and Naum preached in its environs, and from its associations with the early days of Christianity in the Balkans it has always been an important religious centre. It was credited with possessing a church for every day in the year, and a number of ecclesiastical remains witness to its ancient fervour. The Basilica of Santa Sophia was founded by the great Tsar Samuel of Bulgaria in the eleventh century, but its narthex dates from 1317. The church was originally a cross-in-square, but was altered by the Turks. For centuries used as a mosque, it is now under process of restoration, and some valuable frescoes are being brought to light. The same process has been carried out at S. Clement (135), where great areas of splendid fourteenth-century frescoes have been uncovered. The church, which is of cross-in-square plan, was built in 1295. The walls are profusely decorated with brick patterns, all most rich and varied but thoroughly appropriate to the structure. The whole character of the building is thoroughly Byzantine. The church possesses a notable series of icons, among which may be mentioned a picture of Our Lord with an expression of grave and tender compassion. S. John (fourteenth century) in a picturesque situation overlooking the lake has the windows of its drum crowned with pediments which in characteristic Byzantine fashion cover little brick arches flanked by half-arches. S. Nicholas possesses notable wooden doors of the thirteenth and fourteenth centuries, carved with horsemen, fantastic animals and birds which betray an influence coming probably through Byzantium from the East.

BULGARIA

In the course of the ninth century, Boris, the ruler of Bulgaria established Christianity as the national religion. As he received the faith from Constantinople, where he sent Simeon, his son and successor, to be educated, a strong current of Byzantine influence swept rapidly across Bulgarian soil. Simeon did his best to propagate and advance the knowledge of Byzantine culture in his realm. While Clement the missionary was busy with his Christian activities at Ochrida, at that time under Bulgarian control, Simeon the Tsar occupied himself busily with his school at Preslav. "There," says Mr. Steven Runciman, "translations were being made on all

134　Curtea D'Arges: S. Nicholas

135　Ochrida: S. Clement

136 Cozia

137 Curtea
D'Arges:
the Cathedral

sides. Simeon himself even superintended a collection of explanatory extracts from the Fathers: and the Preface paid a flattering tribute to his patronage, calling him 'the new Ptolemy, who, like the industrious bee, gathers the juice of all the flowers to spread it over the boyars'." Establishing his capital at Preslav, he adorned it with palaces and churches, and in his pomp and ceremonial strove as far as he could to imitate the pageantry of Constantinople. The sudden show of splendour and luxury was a marvel to astonished visitors and panegyrists sang the praises of Simeon's court and buildings in grandiloquent terms: "but", as Mr. Steven Runciman says, "it is doubtful if beneath this surface gorgeousness there was what to the eyes of Constantinople would have seemed a respectable standard of civilisation and comfort". A church of Simeon's excavated from the ruins of Preslav had marble panelling and mosaic decoration. According to a MS. in Moscow it was built in the year 907. In the tenth century, Bulgaria was severed into two portions. In the western division, where Ochrida was the capital, a considerable architectural activity was in evidence during the reign of the Tsar Samuel (976–1014): the Monastery of Santa Sophia, as has already been said, was founded by this monarch. Eastern Bulgaria had succumbed in 972 to the Greeks, who in 1018 conquered the western tsardom also. Regaining its independence in 1186, Bulgaria presently reached the apogee of its power, and under the Tsar John Asen occupied the leading position in the Balkans. The Tsar dwelt in a princely residence at the rocky hill of Tirnovo, "the Hill of Thorns", where he surrounded himself with courtiers and officials bearing grandiloquent Byzantine titles. But dissension and decay soon followed his death, and a renaissance of art and letters under Ivan Alexander (1331–71) arrived too late to endure. Already the power of the Turk overshadowed Bulgaria, which in 1393 was annexed to the Ottoman Empire.

A number of churches were built in the indefinite area before it was occupied by the Bulgarians and when it formed a part of the Byzantine state; some of them were wooden-roofed basilicas, but there is a variety of plans. There are domed basilicas at Sofia, the present capital of Bulgaria, and at Pirdop. The cruciform plan is to be found at Kilisse-Kjoi. It is clear that influences from the East penetrated the country at an early date, for the horseshoe apse exists in a ruin at Tchoban-dere, while the ruined "Red Church" at Peroushtitsa (Philippopolis) was a quatrefoiled square:

fragmentary frescoes in the "Red Church" have pronounced Oriental traits. The churches of the earlier period in Bulgaria are affected by Anatolian types. It is in the later period—that of the second Empire—that the cross-in-square plan became common and Byzantine influence was strongly felt.

There were many churches built in the royal city of Tirnovo, where one inconsiderable area preserves the ruins of eighteen chapels, mostly cross-in-square, painted with frescoes. The churches of S. Demetrius and of the Forty Martyrs at Tirnovo are larger in size. They have been subjected to alterations, but the apse of S. Demetrius is interesting for the red-and-yellow faïence with which it is enlivened, while the impost-capitals of the Forty Martyrs are worthy of notice for their resemblance to those of S. Vitale at Ravenna. The Church of SS. Peter and Paul at Tirnovo suffered greatly in 1913 from a disastrous earthquake; its frescoes included a fine enthroned Christ, clad in the robes of an Eastern bishop. The same earthquake damaged the Church of S. John beside the harbour at Mesemvria on the Black Sea coast. Its exterior was elaborately decorated with brick patterns in the true Byzantine style. The mausoleum Church of Asen II, on a high peak at Stanimaka, comprises two stories, the lower one forming the crypt, the upper the church. There is another example of the two-storied mausoleum church at Batchkovo (tenth century), which has well-designed frescoes.

Mention may here be made of the Church of the Pantanassa at Melnik on the Struma (1289), built when the district still belonged to the Byzantine Empire. It had good frescoes on the outside of its walls. The Church of S. Charalambos at Melnik has interior and exterior frescoes of sixteenth-century date.

The cross-in-square and two-storied mausoleum plans are to be found in combination in the Church of S. Nicholas and Panteleimon at Boiana, to the south of Sofia: the small cross-in-square portion was built in the eleventh century and the mausoleum church was added to its west end in 1259. The frescoes (1259), which cover older work, are of considerable merit; the scenes are not overcrowded, the figures are graceful and dignified, the composition is harmonious, and the expressions are individual. Warrior-saints predominate on the lower part of the walls. The grand robes of the Tsar, Constantine Asen, and of the Tsarina show how the Bulgarian sovereigns sought to imitate the majesty of the Byzantine Emperor. Many frescoes in Bulgarian churches have perished. Surviving examples at Zemen and Liutibrod are marked by strong Eastern traits, but those in the rock-cut churches of northern Bulgaria are more picturesque in style and seem to carry on the Hellenistic tradition. The Turkish conquest of the country had a profound effect upon Bulgarian Architecture. The Christians were allowed to build only churches of a humble description, and even the erection of a dome was often prohibited. In the monasteries situated in outlying districts in the mountains they had greater scope, but even there the churches are simple in their design. The brick decoration at Poganovo (c. 1400) is reduced to a minimum. This small church, belonging to a mountain monastery, has transeptal apses, the result of influence from Mount Athos. The larger church at Batchkovo (1604) is of the same type, but during the Ottoman régime the plan generally adopted in Bulgaria was of the simple hall type. The interiors, however, continued to be profusely adorned with frescoes. Those of Poganovo date from the sixteenth century. Most of the saints depicted are monks, and in some of the details, such as the head-dresses, a Western influence is apparent.

ROUMANIA

The provinces of Wallachia and Moldavia, which today form part of Roumania, were for a long period an appendage of the Ottoman Empire. Towards the end of the fourteenth century, Mirtchea, the Duke of Wallachia, decided to become tributary to the Sultan, to whom, in 1512, the ruler of Moldavia also made voluntary submission. The result was that these provinces were allowed a considerable measure of independence. They retained many of their institutions, and it was not until 1711 that their native princes were displaced. The country, consisting of fertile plains which stretched to the foothills of the Carpathians, carried a population of serfs who tilled the land for powerful nobles. Monasticism flourished throughout the land, and it was to the monks that Roumania was indebted for the cultivation and development of art during the Ottoman régime.

The earliest important church in Wallachia is Byzantine in plan and elevation. The second Church of S. Nicholas at Curtea d'Arges (134), it was built by a Greek, Hyacinthos of Vitzina, who was the first Roumanian metropolitan. It is a cross-in-square church with a dome on a polygonal drum over the crossing. Built of brick and stone in courses, it is adorned with bricks arranged in saw-toothed bands and radiating arches. Tall recessed niches encircle the bold drum, and the cross-arms terminate in archivolts, like churches in Constantinople. It has noteworthy frescoes characterised by picturesqueness, realism of expression and dramatic quality. Arranged after the usual Byzantine plan, and belonging to the "Macedonian school", they bear inscriptions of which some are in Greek and some in Slavonic. The cross-in-square type, however, was not common in Roumania. The usual plan takes the form of a trefoiled square, with a dome on a drum over the centre and a large square narthex at the western end. The plan appears to have been transmitted from Serbia. In Wallachia it is represented at Cozia (1386)(136) with its tall soaring dome over the church itself and its two more slender ones above the narthex. While the Byzantine element is manifest in the basis of the plan, in the domes and in the niches in the drums, other features, like the broad eaves and applied ornament on the upper story, show how different a character was being assumed by Byzantine Architecture in this region beyond the Danube. Churches of the same plan are to be found at Dealu (early sixteenth century), Caluiu (sixteenth century) and other places. There is a ruined church of domed square plan at Nicopolis (fourteenth century). It also has the familiar twin domes above its narthex.

The trefoiled square plan with a large narthex is also represented in Moldavia, the province which lies to the north of Wallachia on the Russian frontier. It is well exemplified at Voronets (138). This church was built in 1488 and the exo-narthex added in 1546. The ultimate influence on the basis of the plan is Byzantine, but the appearance has been completely transfigured by alien elements (140)—the broad uniform roof, the deep projecting eaves, the stepped buttresses outside, the decoration on the drum, the Gothic window, the curving spire. Other examples of the trefoiled-square plan in Moldavia are to be found at Siret (1373–93), Baia (1467), Harlau (1492), Jassy (S. Nicholas) (1492–7) and other localities. These churches possess other interesting features. The façades of the earlier ones are often gaily decorated with coloured bricks and plaques carved with fantastic monsters. The exteriors of later ones were often clad with frescoes of Byzantine style. Rich and varied in their colouring, these frescoes lend a unique and beautiful appearance to their aspect. Arcading is also used as an adornment. In the construction of the dome, the drum is set on a high tower above the arches of the crossing.

On the outside it is often placed on a star-shaped base and covered with a pointed roof. Thus it is that, while some primary characteristics of the Moldavian churches are traceable to a Byzantine origin, many others have been assimilated from different sources. Doors are square-headed and are recessed in Gothic arches in several orders; windows are pointed and are adorned with trefoils and rosettes; stepped buttresses support the walls. In course of time the buildings became higher and extra rooms lengthened the

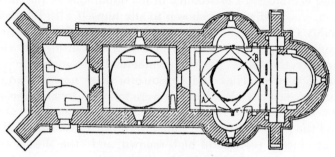

138   Voronets, Moldavia

western end. Masons' marks betray the employment of Gothic masters. Russian, Oriental and Renaissance influences all become pronounced in later years, as in the Church of the Three Hierarchs at Jassy (1638), the most celebrated monument of Moldavian Art. After a long interruption, an attempt was made in Wallachia to revive old traditions in the royal church at Targoviste, a sixteenth-century building of the cross-in-square plan with a dome over the centre and two domes over the narthex.

The most famous church in all Roumania is the Cathedral of Curtea d'Arges, called the "crown of architecture in the Balkans" (137). Built in 1517 as a royal mausoleum, it consists of two parts —a trefoiled square with an extra bay before the apse and a large narthex. Over the church the high drum of the dome soars aloft. The narthex contains the royal tombs and is crowned with three domes on twelve columns which mystically represent the twelve apostles. The drums of the side-domes have their panels and windows twisted round obliquely, producing a most peculiar effect. The external decoration is rich and intricate. The windows are surrounded with Renaissance and Mussulman

229

ornament. There are also recollections of Georgian decoration as seen in the Cathedral of Mszkhet. Cable string-courses run around the walls.

U.S.S.R.

Although some churches were built in the south of Russia at an earlier date Byzantine Architecture made its definite entrance into that country towards the close of the tenth century. It was then that Vladimir, Prince of Kiev, overthrew the idols of paganism and established Christianity in his dominions as the national religion. As Vladimir had chosen to ally himself with the Eastern Orthodox Church and to accept the Patriarch of Constantinople as religious superior, it was natural that Byzantine Art should accompany the faith. To the commercial intercourse that had subsisted between Kiev and Byzantium there now was added a religious movement. Missionaries were followed by architects and artists, so that in receiving its faith Russia adopted the artistic style of the Eastern Empire. Under Jaroslav, the son of Vladimir, Kiev attained a position of high renown, and "the Mother of the Cities of Russia" with its royal palace, its sumptuous cathedral and its crowded markets, excited an astonished admiration among its numerous visitors. One traveller descants on its four hundred churches, while another compares it to Constantinople, whose envied splendour it eagerly sought to reflect. Jaroslav, imbued with religious fervour, did his utmost to glorify and strengthen the Christian faith throughout his realm. He built churches and monasteries, he translated portions of the Scriptures into Slavonic and he enriched his cathedral with "golden images" and many sacred objects. But the brilliance of Kiev faded. Sporadic pillage hastened its decay, until at last the devastating invasion of the Tartars in 1239 shattered its broken power.

The cathedral which was erected by Vladimir at Kiev fell a victim to this invasion, but excavations, undertaken in 1926, prove that it must have been a worthy edifice, embellished with mosaics and marble. The Cathedral of Santa Sophia (139) was erected in 1037 by Prince Jaroslav, and, though its exterior was altered out of recognition, the core of its structure was left, and the outside of its apses preserved their original aspect. The cathedral is one of the most famous buildings in Russia and set the style of ecclesiastical architecture in the country in brick or stone, however much that style may have been modified throughout the

139 KIEV:
Santa Sophia

140 VORONETS

142   Moscow: Cathedral of the Archangel Michael

141   Ouvroutch: S. Basil

centuries. During the course of its long history it suffered much damage and by the seventeenth century its western end had become a heap of fallen masonry. Thereafter it underwent a drastic restoration and regained its eminence as a great place of worship. Originally it was a cross-domed basilica with an extra aisle to north and south and five round apses. The extra aisles were finished with galleries, and beyond these aisles, on north, west and south, there ran an open portico. Various alterations were made on the building at widely separated periods, until it assumed the aspect of a church with four aisles on each side of its central nave, the three outer aisles on each side having galleries. Nine apses terminate the eastern end and two western towers give access to the galleries. At the beginning the cathedral was crowned with thirteen domes the number being symbolical of Christ and His twelve apostles; eight others were added about the eighteenth century when the whole twenty-one were masked with roofs in the style of the Ukrainian Baroque. The mosaics of the interior, in their hieratic and rigid style, resemble those in the Church of S. Luke of Stiris in Greece (p. 203). The Byzantine custom was followed in the portrayal of Christ Pantocrator in the central dome, surrounded by angels and prophets. On the east wall stands the Virgin Orans, wearing purple sandals and a mantle with dark blue sleeves. Below her the Communion of the Apostles is represented. The numerous frescoes show a predilection for events in the life of the Virgin. In the western towers—which were originally entrances to palaces—there is a remarkable series illustrating the games and fêtes of Constantinople. Emperor and Empress view the hunting scenes of the Hippodrome; one acrobat holds another upon a long pole; actors clad in skins of bears perform the "Gothic Game" at the Palace.

It seems certain that the plan of Santa Sophia was derived from Constantinople. Resemblances have been pointed out between it and the Church of Mokwi in the Caucasus, and attempts have been made to derive it from a Georgian source. When the close religious associations between Constantinople and Kiev are taken into consideration it will be thought much more probable that the capital of the Empire was the real source of inspiration: the plan of the Church of the Panachrantos in that city bears a strong resemblance to that of Santa Sophia at Kiev.

Kiev remained true to the Byzantine plan, the complex plan of Santa Sophia giving way to the simple cross-in-square. The pressure from enemies became so great and the sources of wealth so diminished that only simpler churches could be erected. Many churches in Kiev have been destroyed and many have undergone great alteration. Among them were S. Michael of the Golden Roof (1018), which has retained its apse with some mosaics, S. Cyril (1140) with its round apses and S. Saviour (eleventh century) with such typical Byzantine features as alternate courses of brick and stone and radiating tiles.

The Cathedral of the Transfiguration at Chernigov, a town to the north of Kiev, was built about 1031 by its prince, a brother of Jaroslav. It is a cross-domed basilica with a short western arm and with its side galleries supported on columns between the central piers. The narthex is flanked by two round towers, and three round apses project from the eastern end. With the four central piers goes the additional bay before the apse, a feature so common in Greek medieval churches and indicative of the fidelity with which the Russians followed the Byzantine model. The church has five domes and drums; the roofs follow the extrados of the vaults—another Byzantine feature, and one which, as we shall see, was later abandoned by the Russians for climatic reasons. The Church of S. Paraskeva (1118) at Chernigov is of similar general type. The walls of these and other churches at Chernigov were elaborately decorated with sculptured plaques and formed a distinguished group. The Church of S. Basil at Ouvroutch, some sixty miles north-west of Kiev (141), underwent a complete restoration in the first decade of the twentieth century, but its present appearance is said to give an excellent impression of that of the early Russian churches. Round towers flank the façade; tall thin colonnettes extend from the ground to the wallhead; the single drum over the crossing is decorated with blind arcades, the roofs follow the curves of the vaults, and the tympana are filled with windows arranged in Byzantine set-out. The appearance of the church also indicates Georgian influence.

Another artistic centre in Russia was Novgorod. The northern town was an important commercial centre and held regular connection with distant Constantinople. Year by year the traders, wending their way southwards with their freights of amber or of furs, sailed down the Dnieper and across the Euxine to their destination on the Golden Horn. There they dwelt in special quarters and plied their trade in the crowded markets, and thence they carried back the precious luxuries of the East to their northern home. Pilgrims and travellers followed in their wake, and two such wanderers, the Novgorod Pilgrim and Stephen of Novgorod, wrote valuable accounts of their impressions in the imperial city: Stephen recounts that in the Monastery of Studion he talked with monks who had come there from his own native city. It was, however, chiefly from Kiev that the Byzantine influence came which moulded the architecture of Novgorod. The two cities had close dynastic connections with each other and lay on the same commercial highway. At the same time other currents flowed from a different direction, and while Byzantium and Kiev played an important part in the formation of the architecture of Novgorod, these totally distinct influences differentiated it from the regular Byzantine style. Engaged in a busy and flourishing trade with the Baltic towns, with Scandanavia, even with Bremen and Cologne, Novgorod borrowed architectural features from the Germanic West. Local conditions also played their part. The simplicity of the churches is in part a reflection of the political and social outlook of the community. The climate, most potent factor of all, transformed the outer structure, and there is a vast contrast in appearance between the exterior of a Byzantine church in Novgorod and that of its ancestor on the equable Mediterranean shore. The churches of Novgorod are cross-in-square or cross-domed basilical in plan, but the prevalence of heavy rain and deep falls of snow in this northern climate completely altered the shape and disposition of the roof. The undulating type of roof, already mentioned, which followed the curves of the vaults beneath it, was the original form of roof in Novgorod. It was derived from Kiev, but it was discovered that climatic conditions rendered it unsatisfactory. Another type of roof was therefore substituted for the undulating variety: it consisted of four slopes, which could throw off the snow. For the same reason the domes, resting on high cylindrical drums, assumed a bulbous form. The actual source of the bulbous dome is uncertain but it was in use in Novgorod by the middle of the twelfth century. The bulbous domes, in different varieties, assuming fantastic forms and multiplied in profusion at varying heights, became one of the most striking features of later Russian architecture. The churches of Novgorod were plastered and painted white; apses were round and the side-apses were often half the height of the central one; windows were narrow but deeply splayed.

As has been already stated, it was through the medium of Kiev that Byzantine Architecture first passed into Novgorod. The Cathedral of Santa Sophia (1045–52), though smaller in size and simpler in treatment, is based on the cathedral of the same name at Kiev. The original core of the building had only three apses instead of five and there were fewer domes. The interior is somewhat encumbered by the number of heavy piers, and the sense of spaciousness characteristic of a large Byzantine church is minimised at Novgorod even to a greater extent than at Kiev. There is a feeling of loftiness, a tendency to verticality in the exterior. The tapering bulbous domes on their high cylindrical drums rise picturesquely above the plain white walls. Quadrant arches over the galleries and arcatures round the drums are of Western origin. The twelfth-century Byzantine frescoes have all been repainted. The Pantocrator in the dome is of unique interest in having the right hand closed: thrice, says the legend, the artist tried to paint it in the attitude of benediction but thrice it closed again; then a voice was heard saying that in His closed hand Christ held the destinies of Novgorod. The plan of Santa Sophia was not imitated; the other churches are of the cross-in-square type and tend to curtail or eliminate one element after another as time went on. Simplification and economy of labour seem to have been the rules. The cross-in-square churches of S. George (1119–30), two or three miles to the south of Novgorod and of the Nativity of the Virgin (1113), have three round apses of equal height, a central dome on a cylindrical drum and two towers on the façade. They are four-pier churches with an extra bay before the apse, but the walls between the narthex and the naos are reduced to piers of the same dimension as the others. The north and south walls are decorated with simple panels formed of pilasters and arched heads and articulating the three interior compartments. The churches of the Annunciation on Lake Miatchine (1179) and of Nereditsi (1198)(144) exemplify the trend towards elimination and simplification by their omission of the extra bay before the apse. The church at Nereditsi was of singular interest. The roof originally followed the line of the vaults: on the outside walls the arches corresponding to the vaults were carried down as three panels separated by pilasters. The vaults of the angle-spaces being lower than those of the cross-arms the panels were relatively lower. At a later date a pavilion roof was substituted for the original roof. At the beginning of this century this was taken off, and an undulating roof brought back its pristine nature, greatly enhancing the whole appearance of the structure. It should be noted that the side-apses were only half the height of the central apse—another illustration of curtailment. The frescoes of Nereditsi were notable in Russian Art. Though not arranged in the regular order, they followed the Byzantine style. As in S. Mark at Venice, the dome was occupied by the Ascension. On the arch of the chief apse there was a bust of Christ. He held sceptre and orb and was designated in Slavonic "Jesus Christ the Ancient of Days". Unhappily the Church of Nereditsi with its long memories of over seven hundred years, its noble architecture and its precious art, was totally destroyed in the Second World War.

Probably in the fourteenth century another type of roof made its appearance in the architecture of the Novgorod churches. Consisting of four high ridge-roofs forming a gable on each wall, it was derived either from German architecture or from the local wooden buildings. The same century brought other developments. The heads of the niches in the walls are of trefoil or half-trefoil shape, instead of being round, as in the earlier churches. The number of apses is reduced from three to one. The ring of little arches or angular indentations round the drum which appears only in some of the earlier churches is now ordinarily employed.

Among churches of this type are S. Theodore Stratilates (1360) and the Transfiguration (1374). Both of these were erected in the "Commercial Quarter" of Novgorod by the river's bank, where many wealthy merchants lived, both native and foreign. Plain but dignified buildings, they seem to express the spirit of the traders who built them and worshipped within their walls. The arcading on their single apse shows German influence. Other churches of the same class are SS. Peter and Paul (1406) and The Twelve Apostles (1450). Some seventeenth-century churches revive previous forms; the Myrophores (1510) and S. Procopius (1520) revert to three apses.

The town of Pskov, situated between Novgorod and Riga, threw off the suzerainty of Novgorod in 1348. Pskov was smaller than the latter city, but it carried on a brisk trade with the West, and its proximity to the Gulf of Riga afforded it a ready outlet for its products. Its architecture was modelled on that of Novgorod, though Novgorod, in its turn, seems to have borrowed some features, such as the bell-towers, from Pskov. The churches of Pskov are small and squat and are furnished usually with three low apses. The same types of dome, of plan, of roofs and of decoration are to be found in Pskov as in Novgorod, but the construction and details are more primitive and crude. S. Sergius, S. Athanasius and SS. Cosmos and Damian, all belonging to the fourteenth century, may be chosen for mention out of a number of churches in the town and district. In the Church of S. Sergius (143) such familiar features may be observed as the bulbous dome, the decoration around the high cylindrical drum, the triple apse with the decoration under the eaves, and the panels with half-trefoil heads. In the fifteenth century some diminutive churches were built in Pskov and environs without central piers. Such is the Church of S. Nicholas at Pskov and that of the Annunciation at Gdov. The method by which the domes of such churches were supported is of considerable interest in view of its use and elaboration in later Russian Architecture. A series of arches was corbelled out from the walls and upon the extrados of the final ones the drum could rest. In Moscow at a later date these tiers of arches were made to show outside and became a decorative feature of Russian Architecture.

After the decline of Kiev as a political power the position of importance was assumed by a region which lay in the very middle of Russia, between the rivers Volga and Oka. Moscow later became its political and religious centre, but the earliest churches are to be found in other places within the area. Numerous immigrants fled to the forests of this new region from the harassed territories of Kiev, and they brought their architectural knowledge and conceptions to their new homes. So the Byzantine cross-in-square plan, derived from Kiev, forms the basis of the new structures, though other influences left their impress upon them. Built of a white sandstone, the churches usually have one bulbous dome on a cylindrical drum over the crossing and three high round apses at the eastern end. In the second half of the twelfth century the capital of the province was fixed at Suzdal and later on at Vladimir. It is in these towns or their neighbourhood that the cultured princes of Suzdalia erected their most important foundations. One of the earliest churches was that of SS. Boris and Gleb, beautifully situated on the river bank near Suzdal and erected in 1152 by Prince Yuri as a royal chapel. It is of cross-in-square plan. The roof and upper front have been restored but it is possible to see the denotation of interior divisions on the outside of the walls. This was a prominent characteristic of the churches of this district. The sculptured corbel-tables which decorate the walls of the Church of the Intercession of the Virgin outside Vladimir (1165) and the Church of S. Demetrius within the city (1195) have emanated from Western Romanesque sources: the round-arched doorways recessed in several orders and the deeply-splayed windows have the same origin. The expression of the interior divisions on the outside by clustered shafts supporting arches is also reminiscent of the West. (Documentary evidence shows Western architects to have worked in the Upper Volga region.) The Church of the Intercession has great harmony of line and beauty of proportions. The Church of S. Demetrius follows the same plan of a four-pier one-domed cross-in-square church, but the general effect is more massive. The Cathedral of Vladimir was rebuilt after a fire in 1183, and in its restored form was modelled on Santa Sophia at Kiev. With its sweeping curves and balanced drums, its variety of outline and decoration of corbel-tables and its sparkling white stone, it is of considerable beauty. It was the largest church in all the Principality and with its rich interior, replete with silver and gold, evoked the admiration of all the chroniclers.

The exteriors of the churches in this area were sometimes sculptured richly. S. George at Jouriev-Polski (1230) is covered with low bas-reliefs representing saints, interlacing foliage and fantastic monsters, designs which are due to Georgian and Armenian influence. Owing to rebuilding the sculptures are not in their original positions.

In the fourteenth century Ivan I transferred the residence of the Metropolitan from Vladimir to Moscow, which thus became the religious centre of the country. S. Saviour, a small cross-in-square church which replaced a wooden edifice in a quadrangle of the Kremlin, belonged to his time but assumed its later form in 1527. The buildings of Ivan III in the Kremlin were on a more elaborate scale. Ivan, surnamed "the Great", who reigned from 1464 to 1505, married a Byzantine princess who had been educated at Rome. Attracted by the reputation of the West, he encouraged the immigration of European traders and brought to his capital Italian and German craftsmen who could instruct the Russian workmen. His architectural achievements were great, and he devoted himself especially to the improvement of the Kremlin, the fortified area where a wooden palace and other timber buildings occupied most of the sites. The Cathedral of the Dormition (or Assumption) of the Virgin, built in 1475–9, was constructed by a distinguished Italian architect whom Ivan had summoned to his aid. Faithful to his instructions, Aristotle of Bologna adhered to a five-domed cross-in-square plan based on the Cathedral of Vladimir. But he reduced the aisles to three, and he divided each side-apse into two. Here too the walls are divided into round-headed panels marking the interior space, and here too the projecting arcade runs midway along the walls. The influence of the West has left its impress on the structure, and the balanced proportions and harmonious symmetry of the southern front breathe the spirit of the Italian Renaissance. The second of Ivan III's churches within the precincts of the Kremlin was the Cathedral of the Annunciation (1482–90). Built by architects who were specially summoned for the purpose from Pskov, its roof may derive features from wooden architecture. The old relationship between outside and inside characteristic of Vladimir begins to be lost. This cathedral—the church in which the Tsars of Russia were baptised—follows the plan of the Cathedral of Vladimir, being a cross-in-square church with three round apses and five bulbous domes. In the sixteenth century it was encircled, except at the east, with a veranda, surmounted by further domes. The third church in the Kremlin is the Cathedral of the Archangel Michael (142) erected between 1505 and 1509. Its architect was an Italian, Alevisio Novi, of Milan, and his origin is expressed in the profusion of Renaissance ornament with which he decorated the exterior. The plan is, however, that of a cross-in-square church with five domes. In this church and others mentioned the eastern end of the building takes on the form of the two-column plan, the dome resting on the antae of the apse. The walls between the narthex and naos are reduced to piers, so that the church has four piers and the antae. The contrast between the upper and lower stories of the exterior is most striking. Above the roof rise the typical Russian domes with their high cylindrical drums; the façades of the walls are enriched with all the favourite details of the later Renaissance, with great scallops in the tympana, with entablatures and pilasters and composite Corinthian capitals. A church of a typical and classic Byzantine plan is displayed in the fantastic and incongruous trappings of medieval Russia and Renaissance Italy; the age-long architecture of Byzantium has assumed a strange new guise.

143 PSKOV: S. Sergius

144 NEREDITSI

146   Palermo: S. John of the Lepers

145   Palermo: La Martorana

In the sixteenth century, Russian Architecture underwent a change. The dome was replaced by a pyramidal tower, a characteristic borrowed from the wooden architecture of the country. As a result of ecclesiastical decree the dome reasserted itself in the seventeenth century. Many churches of this period are of Byzantine plan, but they are so surcharged with other features as to demand classification in a separate style.

It should be noted that some of the Russian churches which have been described were destroyed or damaged by the Germans in the Second World War.

CHAPTER XII

Sicily, Southern Italy and Venice

SICILY

I N the course of the twelfth century, when the island was ruled by Norman kings, art in Sicily, during a brief season of singular life, blossomed forth into a splendid efflorescence. Byzantine, Arab and Norman influences intermingled to form this art. Sicily, after having formed part of the Byzantine Empire for three hundred years was conquered in the ninth century by the Saracens, who established their capital at the seaport of Palermo. Under Arab rule the island attained a great renown, and Palermo is described as having been one of the richest and most beautiful cities in the Moslem world. For their constructions the Arabs were largely dependent upon the skill of architects belonging to the conquered race, and when the Normans captured Palermo and became firmly established in their dominion they fused elements from their native France and their southern Italian possessions with the composite local style.

It was in the second half of the eleventh century that Roger, the youngest son of Tancred of Hauteville, left his castle in the Cherbourg peninsula to join his brother, Robert Guiscard, Duke of Apulia, in the assault on Sicily, and, as Gibbon wrote in his *Decline and Fall of the Roman Empire*, "After a war of thirty years, Roger, with the title of great count, obtained the sovereignty of the largest and most fruitful island of the Mediterranean; and his administration displays a liberal and enlightened mind, above the limits of his age and education." Count Roger was succeeded on the throne by his son Roger II, who reigned from 1101 until 1154, taking the title of King thirty-eight years after his accession. Roger II's son, William I, surnamed the Bad, reigned until 1166, and William II, William I's son, known as the Good, wore the crown until his death in 1189. The Norman dynasty came to an end in 1204. During the century of its existence, Norman Sicily became one of the richest and most famous kingdoms of Europe. It was a cosmopolitan state, where Christianity, Mohammedanism and Judaism enjoyed an equal toleration and where representatives of many lands clad in their distinctive garb met together on the busy wharves of Palermo. The Norman rulers accepted and developed the architectural inheritance which had fallen into their hands, and in so doing they kept true to their general attitude as sovereigns in Sicily. Greeks and Orientals, as well as Norman knights, held office at their court. In the fair surroundings of the Mediterranean city, the descendants of the vikings lived lives of Eastern luxury and magnificence. The remains of their palaces at Palermo attest their wealth and their surrender to Arab and Byzantine tastes. The stream in the hall of the Palace of the Zisa flows down from beneath a stalactite roof, while above its place of issue is a Byzantine-Oriental mosaic depicting palms between peacocks, and archers shooting birds in the spreading branches of a tree. The Palace of the Cuba carries an inscription which designates William II by his Arabic title of "desirous of glory". Among the squalid ruins of the Favarah, which was perhaps a Moslem foundation rebuilt by Roger II, there is a chapel of Byzantine plan. The Cubola (155), now situated in the quiet lemon-grove of a private garden, was one of the kiosks or pavilions which enlivened the grounds of the palaces, and beneath which the king and his courtiers might rest in the heat of a summer day. It is formed of four open Saracenic arches supporting a dome and is altogether Oriental in its aspect. The fountain beneath its dome has ceased to play, but is depicted in all its freshness in one of the fine coloured lithographs in Gally Knight's *Saracenic and Norman Remains in Sicily*.

In the midst of such surroundings, when not engaged in foreign wars, the Norman sovereigns passed their days. Poets, philosophers, artists and scientists enjoyed their patronage. It was written of Palermo by the Arab geographer Edrisi that "it has buildings of such beauty that travellers flock there, attracted by the fame of the marvels of architecture, the exquisite workmanship and the admirable constructions of art".

SICILIAN CHURCHES

The earliest Palermitan church built under the Normans seems to have been S. John of the Lepers, in the suburb of Romagnolo (146). It is said to have been founded in 1072 by Count Roger and his brother, when their besieging army lay encamped in the neighbourhood. It consists of a four-bayed nave with aisles, a domed space with cross-vaulted arms in line with the aisles, and three round apses. The nave arcades have round arches, but the dome-arches are pointed and are derived from Saracenic sources. There are round-headed windows in the clerestory and pointed windows in the aisles. The dome is carried over squinches of a type which in two varieties is characteristic of the Sicilian domed churches. These squinches are of a narrow niche-like form and in the variety here exemplified are in their lower courses of angular plan; a shaft in the angle is flanked by a round-headed panel on each wall. Above, over all, projects the pointed head of the niche, which is recessed in two orders. Pointed windows on a level with the squinches pierce the dome, and pendentives between, bring the octagon to a circle. The angles of the apse-walls are cut away for colonnettes, some of which are restorations but one of which possesses an original capital carved with acanthus basket-work and a rope band, and having an Arabic inscription above. Angle-colonnettes are a characteristic feature of these churches. Characteristic also is the external appearance of the dome with its smooth unbroken surface plastered over and coloured a deep red. Like others at Palermo, the church is built of squared stone. Its ground-plan is better considered a Latin and Byzantine combination than one of Eastern origin. Its interior was restored in 1925, but the Renaissance belfry still remains.

Of a similar type of plan is the famous Cappella Palatina (1143) within Roger II's palace at Palermo (151); it has been called the most exquisitely adorned palace-chapel in the world. The nave has five bays, and both the dome-arches and nave-arches are highly stilted and broad-pointed. The dome is supported by squinches of the type already described above. The west dome-arch rests on coupled columns and three apses finish off the east end. In his monumental book on Norman mosaics in Sicily, Professor Otto Demus emphasises the dynamic quality to be found in the Chapel. It is caused by the rise from west to east and by the staggering of the socles and capitals. "Thus," he says, "the dynamism of Western architecture, after all, is the outstanding quality of the building, realised, it is true, not so much in the functional structure but by means of optical devices." Yet, as we shall see, how strangely do the Byzantine and Saracenic elements mingle with the sentiment which Western Europe had provided!

The Cappella Palatina is magnificently adorned with marble and mosaics throughout (148). Contemporaries sang paeans in praise of this lovely shrine, "glittering with light, glistening with

147 PALERMO: La Martorana and S. Cataldo

148 PALERMO: Cappella Palatina

150   PALERMO: S. John of the Hermits

149   MONREALE: Apse Mosaic

gold and resplendent with jewels", and in spite of the grievous
restorations which the mosaics have endured, it still remains the
most superb expression of the eclectic genius of Norman Palermo.
The columns are of marble and granite some being fashioned out
of rare peach-flower marble. The pulpit and sanctuary parapet
are richly inlaid with glass mosaic and porphyry. A revetment of
marble relieved with marble mosaic bands forms a dado, and the
walls above are encrusted with mosaics. Events in the life of
Christ are commemorated in the sanctuary. The mosaic of the
Entry of Christ into Jerusalem has suffered some maladroit
restoration, but the animation in the figures, the stately grouping

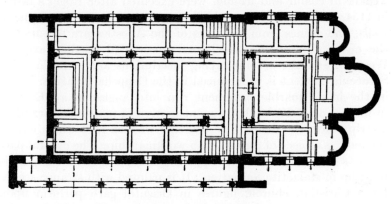

151   Cappella Palatina, Palermo

and well-planned composition still mark it out as an effective
work. The Nativity, the Flight into Egypt, the Baptism, the
Transfiguration, and the Raising of Lazarus, complete the cycle
of scenes in the south arm of the transept. The Flight into Egypt,
which has suffered little from restoration, is distinguished for its
fine sense of rhythm and the grace of its figures. The Ascension
and Pentecost are portrayed on the vaults. These mosaics derive
ultimately from the Daphni tradition (p. 204), but Islamic influence has affected their setting-out. The mosaics in the dome
are managed with consummate skill(7). In the centre is the
Pantocrator, while below Him stand the four archangels, clad in
Byzantine court and military costume, and four angels, each one
designated "the angel of the Lord". In the squinches are the
evangelists: David, Solomon, Zacharias and John the Baptist are
in niches between them; prophets occupy the spandrels. The aspect

of the brilliant dome from the dim nave is of the greatest beauty, and the golden background and richly coloured robes gleam with the utmost splendour in the glowing light with which it is suffused.

There is also a figure of Christ in the apse, and among the saints which accompany Him may be mentioned S. James, who is clad in the robes of a bishop of the Greek Church. It would seem strange to find such a representation in a Western church and it may have been specially commanded by the King as a concession to the Orthodox. The majority of the mosaics in the eastern part of the church are the work of Byzantine Greeks: some of the scenes in the transepts and all of those in the nave, which are weaker in colour and feeling, were executed after Roger's death in 1154, by Italian pupils. Old Testament scenes occupy the nave walls, and scenes from the Acts of the Apostles are pictured in the aisles. The saints which are represented in the nave are Western, and the accompanying inscriptions are in Latin. The Saracenic element is pronounced in the Cappella Palatina: bands in the inlaid marble pavement run into angles in an Eastern fashion and an Arabic battlement motive in marble is carried in a strip above the dado. The amazing wooden roof which covers the nave is a piece of purely Arab workmanship. The central part consists of rosettes with eight-pointed stars, and the lower part is built up in stalactite formation. It is painted with strange scenes for a Christian church: figures in Oriental garb perform upon instruments, dance, drink and play games; a giant bird carries away a man; legendary tales from the East are close neighbours to Scriptural narratives like Samson and the lion; and Kufic inscriptions celebrate the virtues of the Sicilian king.

A short distance from the Palace stands S. John of the Hermits (1132–48). Its tall yellow walls, fronted by the foliage of its garden, and its rich red domes silhouetted against the blue of the sky, combine to form a picture of rare and exotic charm (150). It has a nave in two bays, a choir with transepts, and a shallow apse. The side-apses are mere niches in the east transept walls. Each bay of the nave is covered with a hemispherical dome on squinches, and smaller stilted domes are set over the choir and south transept. The choir squinches belong to a variety described below (v. p. 247). The north transept is surmounted by a domed bell-tower. The arches and windows are pointed. The latter are small except in the highest story of the belfry, which has large pointed windows set in broad shallow orders within a square moulding, this setting-out being derived from Arab sources. The south transept projects into a hall of earlier date, and the south wall of the church formed the wall of a court also of this date. The picturesque cloister on the north has coupled columns with pointed arches.

The Baroque façade at the western end of the Church of La Martorana (147), with its curving lines, its scrolled buttresses, and its broken pediment, would completely conceal from the passing stranger the true nature of the edifice and the wealth of Byzantine Art which it contains (145). Originally known as S. Mary of the Admiral, it was founded in 1143 by George of Antioch, at one time a servant of an Emir in Tunis and later the Admiral of King Roger of Sicily. George was deeply devoted to the worship of the Virgin, and he richly endowed the church he founded in her honour. Built for a convent of Greek nuns, it was served by Greek clergy, who, until the thirteenth century, celebrated the Greek rite within its walls. In 1433 it became attached to the neighbouring Monastery of Martorana, whose name it has since retained. Both artistically and practically it has undergone strange vicissitudes. The Sicilian Parliament met in it after the famous Massacre of the Sicilian Vespers in 1282, and before it was scheduled as a National Monument in 1869 it served the purpose of a post office.

Originally the Martorana was a cross-in-square church with four columns, but without prolongation of the eastern arm. It may be mentioned, in passing, that the cross-in-square plan may have reached Sicily from the East through the medium of southern Italy, where, as will be seen later, the type is to be found. In 1588 the narthex of the Martorana was altered and the church extended farther to the west, and in 1685 a large square chancel was substituted for the central apse in the east. The arms of the cross have pointed vaults and the angle-spaces have cross-vaults. The squinches are of the type already described but are round-headed. The dome follows the Byzantine fashion of being elevated on a polygonal drum. The apses have angle-colonnettes of porphyry and verd-antique and the pavement, inlaid with marble and porphyry, displays the angular Saracenic twist.

The mosaics which adorn a portion of the interior hold high rank among the surviving examples of Byzantine Art. The Pantocrator, in the centre of the cupola, appears as a full-length figure seated upon a throne. Around Him bend the four arch-angels, in an attitude of adoration, clad, not in the customary habiliments of the Byzantine court, but in simple robes. Prophets, holding scrolls, stand in the sides of the drum, and the evangelists occupy the squinches. Below the cupola there runs a quotation from a Byzantine hymn in Arabic lettering. Numerous saints and apostles are depicted throughout the church. Of the various scenes, the Nativity and the Dormition of the Virgin are especially worthy of attention, charged as they are with a deep emotional expressiveness and a simple dignity in treatment. In the latter picture (153) Christ stands beside the bed, holding the soul of the Virgin. S. Peter stands at the head swinging a censer, and S. Paul is at the foot. Along with the mourning apostles are two saints in episcopal vestments, while women weep under the roof in the background. The non-representational art of the church, showing stars on a deep blue surface and twisting wreaths of foliage, is singularly effective. At the west end of the church there are two mosaics which are of much historical interest. One of them shows Christ, a stately figure in blue, placing the crown on the head of King Roger: in the other, George of Antioch kneels at the feet of the Virgin. The gaily coloured frescoes by Borromans which decorate the western portion of the church, and the ornate Baroque adornment of the chancel, are in striking contrast to the simplicity and solemnity of the Byzantine mosaics.

Beside the church stands a tower, perfectly proportioned in four stories and beautifully enriched with decoration. Over the two-light windows of typical Byzantine form are orders consisting of billets laid lengthwise upon each other. The same type of adornment is seen on La Cubola and also at the entrance and over the windows of the Church of the Holy Sepulchre at Jerusalem. Black basaltic inlays pattern the stonework of the tower, and the angles of two upper stories are rounded into turrets on slender colonnettes. Of the Martorana, Ibn-Jubair wrote at the end of the twelfth century:

> One of the most remarkable works we have seen at Palermo is the Church which they called the Antiochean. . . . The interior walls of the temple are gilded or rather all of a piece of gold. One notes the tablets of marble in colour of which none has ever seen the like. . . . The belfry is one of the most marvellous constructions that could be seen.

Beside the Martorana stands S. Cataldo (1161), a cross-in-square church (24) of a very Eastern appearance, with a pierced battlement, much restored, and three smooth-surfaced domes along the

246

153 PALERMO: Death of the Virgin Mosaic

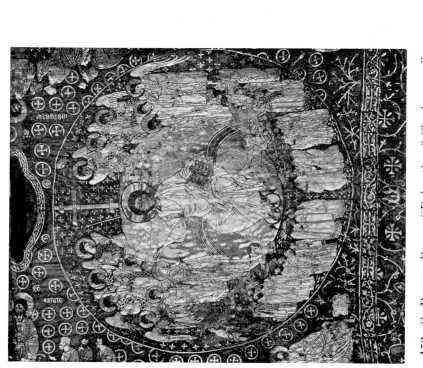

152 S. PETER, ROME: "Dalmatic of Charlemagne"

154　Castelvetrano

155　Palermo: La Cubola

longitudinal axis (147). The upper part of the walls is entirely carried forward in Saracenic fashion to form flat-pointed niches in shallow orders, which serve as a wide frame for the small pointed windows. Only the central apse projects. It shows round outside. Saracenic influence appears in the pavement and in the angular twists of a capital. The pointed arch reigns throughout, the angle-spaces being groin-vaulted. The squinches are of the second variety of the Sicilian type: in this variety the plan is semicircular right up to the springing of the arch. The same variety of squinch appears in the already mentioned Chapel of the Favarah and in that of the Zisa, part of which now forms the baptistery of the Church of S. Spirito a la Zisa.

The method of placing three domes in a row probably came over from southern Italy, where, as will be shown later, it was employed to a considerable extent.

The cathedral which overlooks the picturesque little seaport of Cefalu, on the north coast of Sicily, is a Romanesque church with a timber roof over its nave. Built by King Roger II between 1131 and 1148, it still possesses some splendid Byzantine mosaics (156). A noble bust of the Pantocrator in a blue and golden robe dominates the church from the conch of the apse. Below Him and between the four archangels stands the Madonna with outstretched hands. Still lower down there are apostles and evangelists: Mark, Matthew, Peter, Paul, John, Luke, Philip, James, Andrew, Simon, Bartholomew and Thomas. Tiers of saints and prophets adorn the walls of the choir, those on the lower zones being named in Greek. The pictures of the four Fathers of the Church on the south wall of the choir are among the finest examples of Byzantine Art. Standing full face on and with their vestments falling in vertical folds, they are dignified in bearing and rich and harmonious in colour. The warrior-saints, patriarchs and prophets are named in Latin, and Professor Demus has shown that the two latter groups along with the mosaics of the vault are the later work of Sicilian pupils. The strongly ribbed vault contains an angel in each of its four compartments, those in the west and east being designated cherubim and those in the north and south seraphim; the cherubim—as well as the seraphim—have six wings. Regarding this fact, Professor Demus says "the distinction between Seraphim and Cherubim was never very clear from the iconographical point of view. On the vault of Cefalu where the two orders are identified by inscriptions the only difference is in the positions of their wings." By their picturesque composition, their statuesque quality, their emotional expressiveness and their harmonious colouring, the oldest mosaics of Cefalu connect with those of Daphni. It is true that the Cefalu mosaics show less organic growth in the figures but they possess more intensity of religious sentiment, and it is thought that Roger must have imported Byzantine mosaicists from Constantinople to initiate his work of decoration. The same procedure seems to have been adopted for the adornment of the Cappella Palatina and the Martorana. These immigrants from Byzantium trained a number of Sicilian workmen in the knowledge of their craft and at later stages in the decoration of the churches the work was continued by these Sicilian pupils and their successors. It is this change of craftsmen which explains the marked difference in style which is to be found in the mosaics of the churches of Palermo. But it was Byzantium which was the ultimate source and inspiration of the mosaics of Sicily.

There is no church in Sicily which has attained a greater degree of general popularity than the Cathedral of Monreale, the whole of whose vast interior is encrusted with mosaic and marble (149). It crowns a hill some short distance from Palermo, and commands a magnificent panorama across the Conca d'Oro, the Golden Shell, to the city stretched along the shore and the bold mass of Monte Pellegrino jutting out into the Mediterranean. The Monastery of Monreale was a royal foundation erected in 1174 by King William II near an estate of his grandfather "in monte regali"—Monreale. William was lavish in the gifts and honours he bestowed upon his new foundation: lands were granted to it in abundance, and its abbot was elevated in 1382 to archiepiscopal dignity. On that occasion Pope Lucius III congratulated William on his church, "so wonderful a temple, so richly endowed and so nobly ornamented with gold and silver and costly fabrics". The plan is of a curiously composite nature, the western portion having nave and aisles, the eastern part being influenced to a certain extent by the Byzantine cross-in-square, though roofed in wood. (The same conjunction of plans may be seen in the Church of the Sicilian Vespers founded by Walter of the Mill, the Englishman who was Archbishop of Palermo.) The immediate effect which is created by the sumptuous and magnificent decoration in Monreale is very powerful. A colossal portrait of the Pantocrator with outstretched arms fills the whole conch of the apse (149). The enthroned

Madonna, guarded by archangels and saints, occupies the middle zone, and other saints adorn the lowest range and the antae of the arch. Scenes from the life of Christ are set in the transepts and from the Old Testament in the nave. The miracles of Our Lord are in the aisles. Yet, though the general effect is one of undoubted splendour, the individual mosaic pictures are inferior to others in Sicily. The inferiority is especially marked in the mosaics of the nave, where the design of the figures is weaker, the style poorer and an excessive preponderance of white shows in the colour.

Monreale cannot be left without a mention of its lovely cloister with its pointed arches on coupled columns with richly carved capitals. The bronze doors of the cathedral display figures of centaurs and animals within enwreathed foliage in Byzantine style and some of the gospel scenes depicted closely follow, as M. Diehl says, the Greek iconography.

The Church of the Trinità di Delia near Castelvetrano (154), a village in south-west Sicily, is a twelfth-century example of the Palermitan type. It stands among a few trees on a ridge overlooking a wide plain. With its solid appearance and smooth round dome it is a striking sight from afar, and looks like an alien intruder in the western landscape. It is a cross-in-square with three round apses. The windows, doors and vaults are pointed and the upper part of the walls brought forward in Saracenic fashion. The dome is set above squinches of the first variety. The church, which is well built of squared stone, was carefully restored about seventy years ago and now serves as a mausoleum.

Some small ruined chapels in eastern Sicily date from the Byzantine period. Two at S. Croce in Camerina are cruciforms and have their domes supported by being set back behind the angles of the square. Churches at Maccari and Malvagna are trefoiled squares, with drumless domes above squinches of the Byzantine type. The little Chapel of S. Theresa (fifth century?), concealed beneath a tower among the orchards south of Syracuse, is of trefoiled-square plan with a dome on pendentives.

SOUTHERN ITALY

There are some domed churches in that part of southern Italy which had been Byzantine before the Norman occupation in the eleventh century. They were built by the inhabitants after the Norman Conquest, the new rulers granting toleration to the

Orthodox Church. In Calabria are the Cattolica at Stilo and S. Mark at Rossano, two cross-in-square churches with three round apses. Each has five domes on pendentives. The domes at Stilo rest on high cylindrical drums decorated with tiles arranged in diamond pattern. A baptistery at Severina has a plan analogous to that of S. Vitale, Ravenna, and the Basilica of the Roccelletta at Squillace has tiles over niches in the apses.

Apulia was a great monastic centre in Byzantine days. The country abounds in grotto dwellings and rock-cut chapels which preserve innumerable frescoes. Among these are the frescoes in the Chapel of S. Biagio (S. Blaise), north of Brindisi (c. 1200), which was attached to a monastery where both Greek and Syrian monks dwelt, and the frescoes in the Chapel of S. Margaret at Melfi (twelfth to fifteenth century). Some domed churches built by the Latins after the Norman occupation show an admixture of local tradition and Eastern influences. The builders imitated Byzantine models, but, as a rule, adopted a native system of dome-construction in stone, the stones being laid in horizontal courses like those of the *trulli*, the little domed structures of the countryside. The domes are covered with low pyramidal roofs. The cross-in-square plan is exemplified in S. Pietro, Otranto, S. Margarita, Bisceglie (1197), and in S. Andrew at Trani. SS. Nicholas and Cataldo at Lecce (1180) develops from the same plan; it is one of the finest works of the Normans in Apulia and reveals many Western traits. The nave is so prolonged that the western angle-spaces form aisles. The arches and high narrow vault of the nave are pointed and the cross-arms are short. The doorways show an admixture of Byzantine and Arab motives. The Baroque façade is of early eighteenth-century date. With this church may be compared S. Joseph at Gaeta in Campania. A church near Melfi consists of two cross-in-squares placed longitudinally beside each other. The three-domed plan, as in S. Cataldo, Palermo, is seen in the former Cathedral of Molfetta (twelfth century)(157). The narrow cross-arms and angle-spaces are roofed all at the same level with a sloping roof outside. Two tall Lombardic-featured towers stand at the west end and the exterior of the church has little of Byzantine appearance about it. S. Francis, Trani (1184), built by the Benedictines, is of the same three-domed plan. The domes are covered with pointed roofs. The Benedictines had also a three-domed church at Conversano. The three domes of a ruined Church of All Saints some miles from Bari were masked

157   MOLFETTA

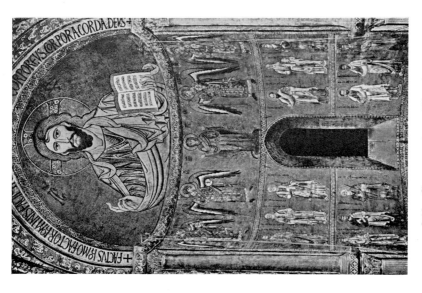

156   CEFALU: Apse Mosaic

158, 159 VENICE: S. Mark

by a flat roof outside. S. Leonardo, near Siponto, which belonged to the Teutonic Knights, had two domes (only one is preserved) and a vaulted bay between; it shows intermingled Byzantine and Northern influence on a doorway beautifully carved with foliage, centaurs, lions and other devices.

Mention may here be made of the Church of S. Mary of the Five Towers near the famous Benedictine Monastery of Monte Cassino, to which many Byzantine mosaicists went in the eleventh century. S. Mary's Church appears to have been of an earlier date. It was of cross-in-square plan, but instead of domes had five low square towers.

In Sardinia, for several centuries under the Empire, a few Byzantine remains still exist. S. Giovanni in Sinis has a dome on pendentives before the apse. S. Saturnino at Cagliari is a domed cruciform with aisles and "transeptal apses". S. Giovanni, Assemini, is a small domed cruciform with the angle-spaces filled in as late as the end of the nineteenth century. These churches probably date from the ninth or tenth century.

VENICE

It is a far cry from buildings such as these to the great Byzantine church of northern Italy. As Santa Sophia at Constantinople is the supreme glory of Byzantine Architecture in the East, so is S. Mark at Venice in the West (159). The fugitives who had settled on the islands of the lagoons had gradually consolidated their strength until in 811 the Rialto of Venice had become the seat of government. Under the protection of the Eastern Empire, Venice continued to prosper. Secure in her impregnable lagoons, she developed her far-flung trade and became the chief depot for the commerce between East and West. Her traders travelled into all the ports of the eastern Mediterranean, and she was permitted to occupy her special quarter in Constantinople. Her ambition grew with her wealth, and after the Fourth Crusade, in which she took a leading part, she established many colonies in the islands and ports of Greece. For long she had striven to emulate and imitate Byzantium, and the intercourse with that city fascinated her gaze. The influence of Byzantine art and culture permeated that of Venice and left its impress upon her life. It is not surprising that, when the rich commercial city desired to rebuild its cathedral, it was to the age-old city on the Bosphorus that it went for inspiration.

The body of S. Mark the Evangelist had been conveyed from Alexandria to Venice in the first half of the ninth century and was interred in a basilica erected on the same site as the existing cathedral. This church was partially burnt in 976 and thereafter restored. About the middle of the eleventh century preparations were made for its reconstruction on a scale of magnificence commensurate with the pride and wealth of the Republic. Orders were issued that voyagers should bring materials from the East for its enrichment, and the result is seen in the multitude of coloured marble columns which bear aloft its arches. In the late eleventh century the walls began to be clad with mosaics, continuing for many centuries to receive their rich adornment. The Byzantine element at first prevailed, but waned with the passing years, until finally the sixteenth century saw the replacement of many old mosaics by new ones based on the drawings of Renaissance artists. Despite the wide difference between the Byzantine and Renaissance work, the effect of this dim bejewelled shrine is superb, and with its great portrayal in gleaming mosaic of the Sacred Story, S. Mark is indeed in the words of Ruskin "a vast illuminated missal, bound with alabaster instead of parchment, studded with porphyry pillars instead of jewels, and written within and without in letters of enamel and gold". The plan (160) is that of a Greek cross, part of the walls of the old basilica having been used in its formation. It was modelled on that of Justinian's Church of the Holy Apostles at Constantinople, which it followed in having a dome over the crossing and another over each arm of the cross. The domes are drumless but are encircled by low walls which, with other external features, are the product of a later age (158). The arms of the cross are furnished with aisles, from which they are separated by beautiful arcades with galleries above. The domes rest upon pendentives, short barrel-vaults span the spaces between dome and dome, and barrel-vaults cover the aisles. The massive piers of the central dome are pierced with arches in two stories, each of them thus forming into four small piers on the ground-plan. Pointed arches divide the bays of the porch which runs around the western arm of the cross; most of these

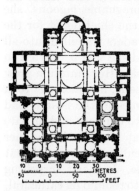

160 Plan of S. Mark, Venice

252

bays are covered by low domes. All three apses have their inside walls broken by niches, but only the central apse projects externally.

The mosaics of the three domes on the longitudinal axis, of the vaults over the arms, and of the upper walls, are Byzantine in style and belong to the eleventh or twelfth century: Pentecost is portrayed in the west cupola with the Holy Ghost in the form of a dove, the twelve apostles below, and figures representing the nations yet farther down; in the central dome there is the Ascension with female figures personifying Christian virtues between the windows; Christ Emmanuel with sixteen prophets occupies the eastern dome; the vaults and the upper part of the walls display the Feasts of the Church, the miracles of Christ and episodes from the life of S. Mark. In the narthex there are thirteenth-century mosaics, depicting scenes from the Book of Genesis. Byzantine in style and characterised by picturesque detail, they have affinities with the sixth-century manuscript in the British Museum known as the Cotton Bible. S. Mark is the possessor of many exquisitely fashioned capitals (30), which crown the columns of its interior and of the great recesses of its façade.

But there are over five hundred Byzantine capitals in S. Mark, some of them brought from overseas, some of them transferred from the old basilica and some of them fashioned for the new cathedral. Some of the numerous marble slabs which form the parapets and balustrades also came from the old basilica. The designs are often of the familiar Constantinopolitan type—interlacing bands and rosettes, animals and birds. S. Mark is rich in treasures, the acquisitions of many periods. Chief among them is the celebrated Pala d'Oro, sumptuous with its gold and silver, its enamels and its jewels. A composite work, it contains plaques and ornaments of different periods, but predominantly Byzantine in character.

Such is S. Mark. It was a glorious expression of many sentiments. It expressed the spirit of emulation which gripped the soul of the rising commercial city, as she cast her gaze towards the east. Her cathedral was not the product of a western tradition, but must imitate the plan of an imperial foundation in the famed city of Byzantium. It expressed her pride and opulence, rich as it must be in all the glowing colour of mosaic and of marble. It expressed her faith, for with its golden domes and storied walls it breathes the spirit of a solemn and mystical religion.

In a charming and sequestered spot among the broad lagoons to the north of Venice there lies the little island of Torcello. It contains two churches side by side, one of them a basilica with a tall campanile, the other a small, central-planned church called S. Fosca (161). A vast representation of the Last Judgment, Byzantine in treatment and iconography, occupies the west wall of the basilica, while the Virgin above with apostles is portrayed in the main apse and Christ with angels in that of the southern aisle. On the beautiful marble parapet the forms of animals and birds are fantastically shaped. Some of the designs are thoroughly Oriental in spirit and had their origin in the patterns on fabrics imported to Constantinople from Iran. Such a one is that which is illustrated in Fig. 162, a magnificent design with two affronted peacocks stretching up their bodies and bending down their heads into a vase upon a lofty column.

S. Fosca was transformed into a Greek cross-plan in the year 1008. The central square was brought to a suitable base for a dome by means of squinches, but the dome was never constructed and the church is covered by a timber roof. A portico runs round part of the outside. The apses are decorated with arcading and flat niches and with saw-tooth archivolts and bands. A broad round drum supports the roof outside and the central apse is of polygonal plan externally. It may be said of S. Fosca that Byzantine influence inspired its builders both in plan and in detail, but that they found the problem which faced them too difficult for them to solve. But in its quiet site beside its cathedral its attraction is undeniable.

Only mention can be made of the twelfth-century mosaic of the Virgin in the apse of the basilica at Murano, near Venice, which is completely Byzantine in character.

161 TORCELLO: S. Fosca

162 TORCELLO
CATHEDRAL:
Slab of Chancel
Parapet

163   PÉRIGUEUX: S. Front

164   PÉRIGUEUX: S. Stephen

CHAPTER XIII

Aquitaine

DORDOGNE AND LOT

IN the south-west of France, in the region which once formed the Duchy of Aquitaine, there exists a number of domed churches for which a Byzantine origin has been alternately claimed or rejected for over a hundred years. They belong, often in a reconstructed form, to the twelfth century and are to be found mainly in the departments of Dordogne and Charente. Chief among these buildings, so remote from the Byzantine homeland, is the Cathedral of S. Front at Périgueux, capital of the hilly and richly wooded department of Dordogne (163). Seen from close at hand it appears somewhat confused, but when viewed from beyond the Tarn it looks strangely fascinating with its amazing campanile and its fantastic domes towering above the whitewashed red-roofed houses that cluster down the slope to the river's bank. Yet the interest of S. Front of Périgueux is not confined to the strangeness of its architecture, so alien to the country in which it stands. It has other claims on our regard; for there can be few churches in Europe which have aroused a controversy that has so persistently endured.

Built as an abbey church, S. Front became the cathedral of the diocese in 1649. Faced with ashlar masonry both within and without, it is in plan a Greek cross, with five domes—one over the centre and one over each arm (165). The five domes are supported by pendentives on broad arches resting on massive square piers. These central piers are pierced on the ground-level by arched passages and have chambers in their upper stories with openings looking into the nave. The lower part of the walls of nave and transepts so projects as to form a passage resting on blind arcades with pilasters, a feature to be found again in churches later described. The transepts, spacious and lofty, have apses flanked by niches projecting from their eastern walls. The main apse dates only from the nineteenth century; ringed with interlacing arcades, it is impressive in itself but is disproportionally large to the church as a whole. It replaced a medieval chapel which

255

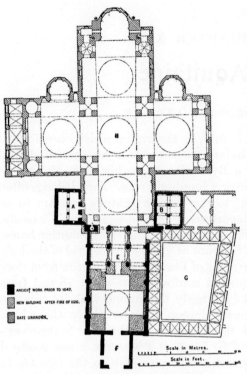

ANCIENT WORK PRIOR TO 1047.

NEW BUILDING AFTER FIRE OF 1120.

DATE UNKNOWN.

Scale in Metres.

Scale in Feet.

165   Plan of S. Front, Périgueux

in its turn took the place of the original apse. From about 1856 the Cathedral of S. Front underwent a considerable amount of reconstruction at the hands of Abadie, a distinguished architect of his day. He made alterations to the upper part of the church, changing the curve of the great arches, and he confused the external appearance by the addition of colonnaded lanterns to the domes.

In spite of Abadie's alterations, the interior of S. Front (166) is noble and majestic. The unencumbered nave and transepts, the sparseness of decoration, the lofty arches, the great curving pendentives, the solid grey stone, combine to form a grand and impressive structure. Only the domes are disappointing. They are set back, and several courses separate their bases from the arches below them. They seem like little caps, puny coverings of a massive substructure which deserves to be crowned by something satisfying and grand.

The controversy connected with S. Front was begun in 1851 by Félix de Verneilh, a young archaeologist of Périgord, who died in the 1860's and whose bust occupies the place of honour in the entrance hall of the museum of Périgueux. He pointed out the close resemblance of the plan to that of S. Mark at Venice, and it was this resemblance which prompted him to assert the Byzantine origin of S. Front. His book, L'architecture byzantine en France, beautifully furnished with engravings, contained two parts: "Monographe de Saint Front" and "Eglises à coupole de l'Aquitaine". In them he tries to prove his double thesis: that S. Front

256

of Périgueux was a Byzantine church, deliberately modelled on
S. Mark of Venice; and that the domes of S. Front were the
prototype of those in the other domed churches of Aquitaine.

166   Interior of S. Front, Périgueux

De Verneilh assumed that the date of S. Mark was 984 and that
S. Front was consecrated in 1047. But subsequent research proved
that the domed Greek cross Church of S. Mark dates from 1053.
It seemed evident that de Verneilh's first thesis was untenable.

However, it also became evident that S. Front must also be assigned a later date. A previous church was destroyed in 1120 by a memorable fire, a fire which was so fierce that the very bells were melted and which caused much loss of life. Of this earlier church—the one which was consecrated in 1047—portions remain at the west end. These remains consist of an open court, the walls of the area around the bell-tower and two confessionals: these were incorporated into the present church, which was begun shortly after the great conflagration of 1120. In the open court there are four massive piers which have aroused much discussion. They are subsequent to the existing church. So is the enormous campanile with its arcaded stories and its crowning member of a circular colonnade supporting a cone.

The present Cathedral of S. Front was therefore begun a year or so after the completion of S. Mark, which took place in 1120. It is quite likely to have been modelled on the Venetian building. The resemblance between the plans is too close to permit of any other opinion. There are of course differences; in S. Mark the galleries are brought forward, there is a triple apse, the arches are round, and the domes are not all of equal size. The sumptuous and glittering walls of S. Mark are very different from the cool grey stone of S. Front. Yet the similarity of plan is obvious even in details; the great piers are even cut by passages in both the buildings. S. Mark had a reputation which had spread far and wide; there was constant traffic with the great commercial city on the Adriatic; the descendants of Venetian colonists were settled at Limoges, to the north of Périgueux. It is easy to see how the idea of adopting the plan of S. Mark entered the imagination of the builders of the new abbey church in Périgueux.

De Verneilh's second thesis, as has been said, was that the domes of S. Front were the prototype of those of other domed churches in Aquitaine. These churches are of aisleless plan and are covered by domes on pendentives set out in a row down the nave.

In a wide open square in the lower part of Périgueux stand the truncated remains of the former cathedral—S. Etienne de la Cité, S. Stephen of the City (164). Its outward appearance is that of two great blocks of different elevation and style and differently constructed material, covered each with a dome. The absence of any documentary evidence precludes a definite date being assigned to its foundation. It may be placed in the first quarter of the twelfth century. As the result of excavations which were carried out in 1927 by the Société historique et archéologique de Périgord it was proved that the cathedral originally consisted of three domed bays and a bell-tower, to which a fourth—the present east bay—was added before 1160. During the wars of religion in the sixteenth century the bell-tower, the two west bays and the cupola of the easternmost bay were destroyed. For many years they lay in ruins, but in 1625 an endeavour was made to restore the edifice. A new dome crowned the easternmost bay and the two west bays were rebuilt. But the latter two domes collapsed soon after their erection and by closing the arch the cathedral was reduced to its now truncated state. About forty years later it surrendered its dignity as cathedral to the Abbey Church of S. Front. The interior has a certain sombre grandeur and the domes crown the areas more satisfactorily than in some other churches of the type. In the earlier—the west—bay the dome-piers are massive, in the later bay they are lighter and have engaged columns.

The walls of both bays are decorated with blind arcades (partly destroyed) supporting a passage, but those on the east bay are, with the windows above them, treated in a much richer and more elegant fashion than those of the west bay. The points of contrast and resemblance between the two bays are a clear indication of the development of the style. The same may be said of the blind arcades which adorn the exterior of the church. An interesting relic is a broken pendentive of the third dome on the outside of the west wall. The arches in the interior are pointed and the piers supporting the domes are engaged to the side-walls.

Before proceeding to a description of the other domed churches of Aquitaine, it might be well at this stage briefly to point out some of their leading characteristics and to indicate how they differ from the true Byzantine churches of Eastern lands. It must not be assumed that the characteristics here enumerated occur equally in all the churches: the classification is a general one though of a wide application. The domes of the French churches are ovoid in section and instead of showing externally are concealed by a roof. They are set back from the rim of the circle which supports them and which may be enriched with a decorated moulding. The pendentives are of a peculiarly indigenous form. They are laid in horizontal beds and are set out from the intrados instead of from the extrados of their arches: the face of the voussoirs of the arches slopes to the inclination of the pendentive of which the voussoirs may be said to form a part. Sometimes the slope of the voussoirs extends right up to the apex of the arch. Sometimes it stops short when a curious twist in the arch is formed. After some courses the pendentive projects, and then recedes, forming a "counter-curve". It is therefore not like the Byzantine pendentive, a curved triangular portion of a hemisphere. In some cases, however, the voussoirs of the arches are vertical and the beds of the pendentive are normal to the curve. The arches are to a greater or less degree pointed. The domes rest on piers engaged to the side-walls. These piers are tied together by transverse arches across the nave and by arches engaged to the side-walls. Most of the churches have a column or columns attached to these piers carrying an additional rib below the arch. Arcades, sometimes supporting a passage, run along the nave walls: the tower and west façade may be characterised with typical Romanesque arcading. Lighting is provided by round-headed windows in the upper walls of the nave and in the apse. The village churches are high and narrow: they are admirably suited for their main purpose, the celebration of Mass at the altar in the apse. Thither the vision of the worshippers is immediately and easily directed. Aesthetically, their height and narrowness are apt to give them a somewhat depressing effect, but this is relieved by the arcading which breaks the walls. The larger churches gain by comparison with their wide free spaces. The domes on the smaller churches somewhat interrupt the vista and aesthetically are inferior to a Romanesque or Gothic vault. They better suit the wider churches, which are often solemn and impressive. However, even in the larger churches the system of dome construction falls short of the Byzantine in aesthetic effect.

The vineclad walls of Tremolat stand in a fertile countryside where the broad and placid Dordogne curves round in a majestic arc. The village, long called Tremolac, has reverted to its original name of Tremolat. The church, in the village square, an austere building with a lofty western tower and a neo-classic door, once belonged to an abbey and dates from the twelfth century. It is a long, high, narrow building of cruciform plan, with four bays in the nave, three of them with domes on pendentives (169). The piers, attached to the side-walls, have engaged columns only in the most westerly domed bay. Their capitals are sculptured with faces or foliage. The arches in the nave are round and appear to be

168 SOUILLAC

167 CAHORS

170   ANGOULÊME: the Cathedral

169   TREMOLAT

weakened and depressed at the keystones. The pendentives are of a peculiar formation and give the impression of hesitation and experimentation on the part of the builders: the transverse arches and the engaged arches do not touch at the springing, the result being that the pendentives do not rise from a point. Pointed arches appear in the lofty crossing covered also by a dome.

The embattled gateway of a famous medieval castle and of a stately Renaissance château faces the incline which leads to the Church of Bourdeilles. The church itself has a Renaissance chapel built on to its southern side which once served as a place of sepulture for the barons. The church has been excellently restored in modern times and displays in a more or less renovated form the main aspect of its original design. The nave has three domes on pendentives with engaged columns on the projecting piers. The western façade is simple, its chief feature being a doorway recessed in several orders. Shallow buttresses flank the walls, and the restored apse, semicircular in plan, is richly adorned with external arcading. The large tower with its three openings in each side of its upper story and with its pointed spire rises prominently from the church.

The Church of Brassac-le-Grand, standing on a lofty platform above the village street, is said to be the latest of all the domed churches of the Périgord countryside. The eastern end dates from the twelfth and the western part from the early thirteenth century. The nave, which originally had a barrel-vault, is covered by three domes on pendentives: there are engaged columns to the supporting piers, the arches are pointed, and the faces of the arches follow the inclination of the pendentives. The late date of the nave is evidenced by the Gothic feeling in the capitals and by the general sense of height in the proportions. The chancel finishes off square. There is a fine Romanesque sculpture at the entrance doorway on the north wall. It shows, on an archivolt on corbels, Christ in the act of benediction with figures on either side, and, on the tympanum below, the Virgin with kneeling figures. This rich and beautiful work dates from the fourteenth century.

The Church of S. Jean-de-Cole has an unusual plan. From a sort of apse there project three polygonal chapels decorated externally with pointed arches on storied capitals. The church was built at the end of the eleventh century, but in the following century four great piers were built in the "apse", with four arches and pendentives carrying a dome. In 1787 the dome collapsed on an evening after vespers and has never been rebuilt. De Veneilh, who makes much of this church, lamented the presence of the wooden planks which occupied the place of the dome: wooden planks cover the space today. The pendentives, however, look well. Records disclose that the dome, which was conical or ovoid in shape, showed externally. It was of much ampler dimensions than the usual cupolas of the village churches in Périgord. The intended nave seems never to have been added to S. Jean-de-Cole, or with the monastic buildings has perished.

The little village Church of Paussac, some four miles from Bourdeilles, has three bays all covered with domes on pendentives. It ends square in the east, and the easternmost bay, whose dome is surmounted by the tower, forms the chancel. The domes are supported by transverse arches on engaged piers with projecting shafts and on arches engaged on the side-walls. The face of the arches follows the inclination of the pendentives. The arches on the south wall enclose an arcade. This decoration is repeated with differences on the south wall outside; pointed arches enclose a narrow window, a string-course and triple arches enriched with dog-tooth mouldings on double colonnettes. This part of the church was altered about the thirteenth century. The main part dates from the mid-twelfth.

The parish Church of Agonac stands on a gentle eminence not far from the railway station on the line from Périgueux to Limoges. It is a severe and massive structure of a defensive nature with a broad tower pierced by three openings high up beneath the eaves. It belongs to the latter part of the twelfth century. Unlike others of its class, it has no domes over its nave, but it has one over the chancel and one beneath its tower. The pendentives of the chancel dome are almost flat in inclination. The barrel-vault of the nave is supported by massive projecting piers connected by pointed arches, and pierced with openings at ground-level, forming narrow aisles.

Other domed churches in the Dordogne are to be found at S. Avit Senieur and Le Vieux Mareuil. If S. Astier ever had domes they have disappeared.

The church, which is the pride of the pleasant little resort of Souillac (171), south-east of Périgueux, was once attached to a very influential monastery sequestered in the Revolution. It is famous for the sculptures which have been assembled inside its western wall and which rank among the masterpieces of Romanesque Art.

Among the sculptures treated are the Legend
of the Monk Theophilus, a subject derived
from Eastern sources; others depict the Sacrifice of Abraham (where a Byzantine influence
is discernible in the posture of the heads) and
the prophet Isaiah, a striking portrait full of
life and vigour. The church was completed
about 1150, and restored in the seventeenth
century. It has the plan of a Latin cross with
an apse and chevet of three polygonal apses,
and apses on the east walls of the transepts.
Two domes surrounded by a ring of corbels
cover the nave(168). The massive engaged piers
have no engaged columns and the arches are
pointed. The wall-passage is carried on an

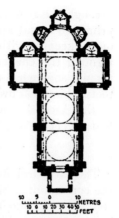

171   Souillac

elegant arcade. The voussoirs of the arches are splayed to the
inclination of the pendentives part of their way. A lofty dome
"pressed in" at the sides covers the crossing, and the transepts
are barrel-vaulted. The two domes over the nave were formerly
concealed by a roof whose removal in 1932 greatly added to the
outside appearance. Souillac is a fine church of noble proportions,
simple and dignified in its interior. The domes agree with the substructure far more than usual, and the view, especially from the
crossing, is quite Byzantine in look.

Cahors, capital of the department of Lot, is celebrated for its
medieval bridge, perhaps the finest in Europe, with its tall
fortified towers rising nobly above its arches. In a great curve the
river sweeps round the hill on which the cathedral stands in the
principal square. It is a remarkable building. A high amorphous
façade, the product of different ages, occupies the west end; a
lofty Gothic window looks out between buttresses on the east;
but between west and east the nave is covered by two cupolas on
drums strangely Eastern in their appearance(167), each fifty feet
in diameter. They rest on pendentives and arches supported by
huge piers engaged into the side-walls. The usual passage runs
along the walls on a simple arcade and the wall-space is utilised
for altars. Great arches rise above the arcades to carry the domes.
One of the tympana which they form, with its setting-out of its
three windows, is strongly reminiscent of Byzantine design, though
the resemblance may be only accidental. Cahors Cathedral was
consecrated in 1119 by Pope Calixtus II during a journey he made

through the region. The high Gothic choir was substituted for a primitive round apse; though quite good in itself it is altogether out of keeping with the rest of the building; two of the little apses forming the chevet are said to be original. The whole church, though somewhat crude and clumsy in design, is of great architectural interest owing to its style. A fine Romanesque tympanum of the Ascension and angels in the north door is an additional feature (1130) of great interest.

CHARENTE

The Cathedral of Angoulême(170) occupies a prominent site upon the commanding hill which contained the nucleus of that historic city. Close beside it are the ramparts which encircled the medieval town and from which so magnificent a panorama extends over the wide valley of the Charente. The cathedral was begun, it seems, in 1110, by Bishop Giraud II and completed by him about twenty years later. An important and impressive example of the Byzantine-Romanesque style, it has the plan of a Latin cross, with a chevet jutting from its deep apse and chancel. There are small apses on the east walls of the transepts. It was subjected to considerable reconstruction by Abadie in the nineteenth century, but the work was in part a restoration of ancient features which had been altered in the Middle Ages. The interior is dignified in its spatial conception, restrained in its appropriate decoration and admirable in its harmonious proportions. The three cupolas which cover the aisleless nave rest on pendentives and piers which are of special interest because they show a development in the method of constructing these members. Building operations were begun at the west end, so that the first bay of the nave from the west is the oldest part of the church. Abadie altered this bay by adding engaged columns to the massive piers supporting the dome, but originally these piers were plain. In the second and third bays the piers are considerably reduced in area, and a column is engaged to each of them to support a rib beneath the transverse arches. Moreover, in the first bay the construction of the pendentives is hesitating and maladroit, revealing makeshifts and deformities. In the second and third bays the true form of the typically French pendentives has been achieved, where the courses rising from a "tas de charge" in the angle are corbelled out and then recede into a backward curve. The faces of the supporting arches are splayed to a greater height in the later bays to follow the

173 ROULLET: Exterior

172 ROULLET: Interior

174 Solignac

175 Germigny-des-Prés

inclination of the pendentives. The arches are pointed. A passage resting on an arcade and going through the piers runs along the nave walls. Only the dome over the crossing, rebuilt by Abadie, appears externally. The beautiful northern campanile, a typical Romanesque structure with its tiers of elegant arcades, once had a counterpart over the south transept. The western façade of the cathedral is renowned for its rich Romanesque decoration. Ranges of arches enclose designs of various kinds: figures, medallions and patterns. There have been restorations and additions, but the general effect is very fine and the individual details are often characterised by grace and life.

A short bus drive from Angoulême takes one to the pretty village of Fleác, where in a characteristic and commanding site facing the green stands the church. It is a simple rectangle terminating in a semicircular apse. One dome on continuous pendentives lies beneath the tower and two other domes on independent pendentives cover the rest of the nave. The arches which support the domes are almost round and the splay by which they follow the plane of the pendentives is very clearly discernible. The western façade is not distinguished by that wealth of arcading which adorns some other churches of its type, but contains some interesting grotesque sculptures in its capitals. Fleác belonged to the chapter of Angoulême Cathedral. The existence of small external buttresses is thought to indicate that the original roof was a barrel-vault, and that the cupolas were substituted for it in the middle of the twelfth century. The idea of the domes would be derived from the parent Cathedral of Angoulême. The builders of this and the other domed churches would also realise that by roofing the church with domes a greater guarantee of stability was assured than if a continuous barrel-vault, with its strong lateral thrusts, had been employed. Larger buttresses were added in the seventeenth century. The domes do not show externally.

The Church of Roullet (172) stands in the main street of a somewhat dreary village, about a quarter of an hour's distance from Angoulême. It is of aisleless oblong plan with a semicircular apse and three domes on pendentives over its narrow nave. The pointed arches, which rise transversely and against the walls, rest on a cluster of five shafts projecting from the nave walls. The arches are in two orders, the upper of which is splayed to follow the inclination of the pendentives. A fourth dome beneath the tower rests on squinches, and the deep chancel has a barrel-vault. The façade (173) is of a typical Romanesque character. The door has round arches in several orders and is flanked by blind arches. There are five arches above, and the façade as a whole is divided into three vertical divisions by three tall arches containing those below. The church has capitals carved with animals, foliage and interlacing strands. It is thought that a part of the walls belongs to the eleventh century. Before 1162 it was attached to the Cathedral of Angoulême, and in imitation of that building the church was roofed with cupolas.

A short distance on either side of the road which runs through an extensive vine-clad plain from Jarnac to Cognac in western Charente, there stands a domed church of considerable charm and interest.

On the south side is the attractive Church of Gensac la Palue: it faces an open green shaded with trees and set in a scattered village of picturesque farms and rich orchards. It dates from the third quarter of the twelfth century, its Romanesque façade being a fine example of its period and style. The central doorway, recessed in several orders, is flanked by arched recesses with sculptured tympana. Two mandorla, one of them containing S. Martin, the patron of the church, decorate the wall above. Two ranges of blind arcades on coupled columns run along the upper part of the wall, which is terminated by a triangular gable, flanked by two open lanterns. The nave of the church, which is a long and narrow oblong, is covered by no less than four domes on pendentives roofed over by a ridge-roof and a lofty tower and spire. The transverse arches which carry the domes approach the round, but those engaged to the side-walls are strongly pointed. The arches are splayed to follow the curve of the pendentives. These arches are supported by pilasters projecting from the side-walls with engaged columns. As in the Cathedral of Angoulême and elsewhere a passage runs along the walls piercing the pilasters and resting on engaged pointed arches. The choir is a late thirteenth-century addition and has pointed ribbed cross-vaults. Gensac underwent some restoration in the eighteenth and nineteenth centuries but remains a fine example of the village church of the Charente, with its interesting combination of Romanesque, Byzantine and Gothic elements.

A short distance to the north of the road from Jarsac to Cognac stands the church of the tiny hamlet of Bourg-Charente. It was once attached to a priory. Rebuilt in the third quarter of the twelfth century, it is of aisleless cruciform plan with a small apse on the east wall of each transept. Two domes on pendentives cover the nave, appearing only internally. There is a somewhat experimental appearance in the construction of the domes and their supports, the builders employing their native methods to interpret an idea emanating through Cahors and Angoulême from the East. The domes themselves are not true circles on plan but are flattened at the sides. The arches which support them are clearly pointed. The whole interior of the church is extremely simple and has plain pilasters for dome-supports. A further dome on pendentives covers the crossing. The western façade, very attractive in its old grey stone, has a fine doorway in four recessed orders. On the first story a bay separates fourteen narrow arches on richly carved corbels, and there are six blind arches above. The familiar Romanesque chevron device is conspicuous in the decoration of the façade.

The Church of Champmillion is also an apsed oblong with domes, but the original apse has disappeared and only two of its three domes remain. It dates from the late twelfth century. It was a fortified church and a corbel table at the wall-head supported machicolations. With its high bare walls and its massive buttresses it looks gaunt and powerful on its little eminence. The west front is, however, decorated with arcading and the capitals of its doorway, sculptured with affronted animals and birds, reveal an unmistakable Oriental influence.

Two other churches both near Cognac may be mentioned which show features like those already mentioned. One of them belonged to the ruined Abbey of Châtres near S. Brice. Of cruciform plan, it has three domes on pendentives over the nave and one beneath the tower. It has a richly arcaded façade. That of Cherves-de-Cognac has three domes on pendentives over the nave, and one beneath the tower. Both churches date in a rebuilt form to the later twelfth century.

SOLIGNAC

The beautiful church at Solignac (174) in the department of Haute-Vienne was connected with a famous abbey, the halting-place of throngs of pilgrims to Italy and the East, who stopped to venerate the numerous relics which it possessed. Solignac is not far from Limoges where Urban II preached the First Crusade in 1043, and its church was consecrated about 1145. It has the plan of a

Latin cross, with three small apses projecting from its central polygonal apse and two from the east walls of the transepts. The broad nave is covered by two domes in a row: there is also a dome over the crossing and one over the north transept. The south transept has a barrel-vault. A roof conceals the domes, which are carried by pendentives and pointed arches on great piers tied to the walls. The pendentives, unlike most in Aquitaine, are set out from the extrados and not the intrados of the arches. The domes are flattened at the sides, but have rounded angles. A course or two rises above the arches before the base of the dome is reached. Passages run along the walls, supported on arcades with pilasters and corbels. The interior of Solignac is characterised by a solemn and spacious beauty. The wide nave, simple and well proportioned, looks towards the broad apse so beautifully terminated by the arches of its radiating chapels. The domes look better than in some of the other churches, but even here do not sit satisfactorily on the building. Arcading adorns most of the exterior, and the chevet apses are beautifully decorated with an arcature below the eaves and arches farther down. The whole east end looks most attractive as viewed from the lower level of the slope which mounts towards it. A crypt, built up as a little church, lies beneath.

THE PROBLEM OF THE DOMED CHURCHES OF AQUITAINE

After having considered the nature and date of the domed churches of Aquitaine we are now in a position to examine de Verneilh's second thesis—that S. Front of Périgueux was their prototype. We have already seen that S. Front was modelled on S. Mark at Venice. Did S. Front spread the influence it derived from Venice throughout the adjacent district of Aquitaine? As has been said above, the present Cathedral of S. Front was commenced some time after the fire of 1120. But the Cathedral of Angoulême was in course of erection before that date, while that of Cahors was consecrated in 1119. The oldest part of S. Stephen at Périgueux appears to date from about the same time. It is therefore clear that S. Front was not the first domed church in Aquitaine and that de Verneilh's second thesis is untenable.

From where, then, were these French domes upon pendentives derived? The domed churches of Aquitaine have often been bluntly called Byzantine. Those in the Charente, in virtue of their domes and their Romanesque arcading and detail, have been classified as "romano-byzantine", Romanesque-Byzantine. How far are these appellations accurate? To what extent, if any, can Byzantine influence be detected in their structure? Some French scholars have denied any Eastern influence at all. To them the domes on their pendentives are either indigenous, a product of local endeavour, or else they were the successors of domes derived from Italy at an earlier period without any contact with Byzantium. These scholars point to churches where a dome on squinches or even on pendentives has been employed for the base or roof of a tower over the crossing. Its employment, they say, in these towers led to its use in the naves of the churches of Aquitaine. But these domes of towers, when of earlier date, are of small dimensions and their pendentives are more often like corbels with splayed faces—as at Vigen, a twelfth-century village church, near Solignac. There is no small domed church in Aquitaine which can with certainty be assigned an earlier date than Cahors Cathedral, and the leap is too great from the small cupola of a tower to the great domes, fifty feet in diameter, which span the nave of Cahors.

The dome had certainly long been familiar to the French builders but this fact does not explain how they conceived the idea of covering a broad nave with great domes on pendentives. It is well within the bounds of possibility that the idea was brought to their minds in the late eleventh century by travellers who had returned from the Orient. For long years pilgrims had journeyed over land and sea to visit the scenes which had been hallowed by their association with Christ. Did they halt in Cyprus they would even see churches with domes set down the axis of the nave. Many of these pilgrims were men who would be ready to describe in detail the impressions they had received on their travels and to transmit to their hearers conceptions which they would be eager to adopt. It is on record that a Bishop of Cahors itself spent some years in the East at the beginning of the twelfth century. Nor should we rule out the possibility of a direct contact with Constantinople itself. As M. Ebersolt has pointed out, one of the routes which pilgrims took to Palestine was by the Balkans and Constantinople. In the course of their sojourn there they would visit and admire the domed churches which filled the city. Mercenaries in the imperial army, students at the famous university, traders who sought the products of the Orient, could all return to their native West and describe the great domed churches which they had seen.

Once the idea came to the French builders of covering a broad area with a dome on pendentives, they would carry out the conception by their own methods and with their own inventive skill. Hence the ovoid domes set back from the rim, the pointed arches, the pendentives with horizontal beds set out from the intrados of the arch.

It is true that some of these features are also to be found in the East, but it is simpler to think that the French builders, following general ideas which had ultimately been derived from Byzantium, fashioned their own methods of construction. But the basic inspiration was from the East. Full of Western and native elements though the domed churches of Aquitaine may be, it is with justification that they are brought within the orbit of Byzantine Architecture.

GERMIGNY-DES-PRÉS

The final church to be described lies not in Aquitaine but considerably farther to the north. Moreover, it antedates the other buildings by three hundred years. The Church of Germigny-des-Prés (175) is said to be the oldest church in France in which services are regularly held. It stands at the cross-roads of the little village near the Loire some miles from Orléans, with its round apses and pointed gables and sturdy tower rising in stages above the dark green foliage of its garden. As one passes through the rose-festooned portico into the eastern part, it is with amazement that one discovers oneself in a building of such a plan in central France. For it is that of the Greek cross-in-square, so familiar in the Byzantine East. The Church of Germigny-des-Prés was built as an oratory between 805 and 811 by Theodolphus, Bishop of Orléans, an intimate friend of Charlemagne who wielded great influence upon the Emperor. It was thoroughly restored in 1869. From the central square, barrel-vaulted arms extend to the outer walls. They terminate in four low apses of horseshoe plan. The eastern apse was formerly flanked by two small apses which have been destroyed. The western apse has also disappeared, but its ground-plan is marked out on the floor. It gave place in the twelfth century to a broad plain nave, rebuilt in 1869. Over the centre of the cross-in-square rises the tower, in three states which diminish in area, owing to the presence of blind arches on the walls. Between the highest arches spring four pendentives, carrying a little dome. This tower was rebuilt in 1869 but it is said that

270

traces of an original pendentive were discovered during that reconstruction. The broad arches which carry the tower and vaults are of horseshoe plan. The angle-spaces of the cross are roofed at a lower level than the arms, and blind arcades decorate the eastern apse. The whole plan bears a close resemblance to the quatrefoiled cross-in-square type of Armenia, and Stryzgowski would trace a definite influence emanating from that distant land. Charlemagne had commercial and diplomatic contacts with the Emperors of the East, and Constantinople housed many Armenians, some of whom would travel to Western Europe. Indeed, Theodolphus is said to have employed an architect who was of Armenian origin. Other scholars trace a Byzantine influence through the intermediary of northern Spain. The plain late nave, though an unfortunate addition, forms an interesting contrast to the original eastern end, with its complex construction, its varied perspective, its receding arches and its fascinating optical effects. The church retains only one of the mosaics with which it was once so richly adorned. The subject is the Ark of the Covenant and a careful investigation of the style and material made some years ago has shown the mosaicist to have been a Byzantine.

The design closely follows the description given in the Book of Exodus, "And thou shalt make an ark of shittim wood . . . and thou shalt overlay it with pure gold . . . and shalt make upon it a crown of gold round about." The rings at the corners are visible and the staves projecting from the ends, while the two cherubim are standing on the mercy-seat with outstretched wings. At the sides are two angels in robes of gold and silver, red, blue and green. They point to the ark. Between the angels on a blue background with golden stars extends the hand of God.

BYZANTINE ORNAMENT IN FRANCE

A brief note should be added on the influence which was exerted by the East upon the carved ornament which so profusely enriched the façades, the mouldings and the capitals of the churches of France.

From early Christian days there was constant intercommunication between southern Gaul and the lands of the eastern Mediterranean, and the Church soon came to play a dominant role as the importer of artistic objects from the Orient. As Mr. O. M. Dalton pointed out, there was a continuous trade in works of art between Gaul and the Levant right up to the time of the Arab conquest of Syria and Egypt in the seventh century. The famous Monastery of S. Vincent was established on the island of Lérins at the beginning of the fifth century and there were constant exchanges of visits between the monks and their brethren in Egypt. During the Carolingian epoch, the ninth century, the monasteries grew in power, and important episcopal sees were filled from the cloister. Refugees from the Iconoclastic persecution still further disseminated the artistic culture of the East. At a still later date the wonderful Romanesque movement was touched by Eastern contact through the Crusades and by means of the steady commerce which flowed through Venice from Byzantium.

The figure-sculpture showed Eastern traits. In the seventh century they appear on the famous cross in Ruthwell near the shores of the Solway Firth in Scotland. At a later period they are to be found in the Christ which, as already mentioned, is carved on a tympanum of the cathedral at Cahors. There is a Madonna in the cloister of S. Trophime at Arles in Byzantine style. Tympana at Vézelay and Moirssac, which have been described as paintings translated into stone, are ultimately derived from Byzantine miniatures.

These are but a few examples of the figure-sculptures where that influence has been felt. Far more numerous are the capitals and friezes whose non-representational devices have borrowed, in whole or in part, from the East. The palmette and the Eastern acanthus, the affronted animals and birds, the enwreathed foliage, are repeated in the sculptures of the West. Many capitals look like imitations, sometimes crude imitations of Byzantine originals.

The objects which conveyed a knowledge of these designs to the Western craftsman might be ivories, textiles or illuminated manuscripts. The manuscripts played a great part in moulding the iconography. The rich fabrics were woven with patterns of strange animals which the medieval masons loved to reproduce in stone, decorating their buildings with the fabulous monsters of the Orient. But it was, above all, the delicate and enduring objects in ivory which most readily attracted their attention and impelled their skill. A bishop might receive from Constantinople the relic of a saint, housed in an ivory casket whose beauty of workmanship was worthy of such a treasure. An abbot may have been given an ivory diptych where the figures of Christ and His apostles were standing in arcades and with a border of twisting foliage.

272

The artist who was shown it felt the impulse to bring something of the design into the stone which he was carving, and in his creation his native genius mingled with that of the far-off city on the Golden Horn. Thus it was, as the ivories were carried far and wide, they affected the sculptures of some little town in France.

The craftsman in the medieval town or abbey in Western Europe, hearing only with wonder about the marvellous city of Byzantium, sees an ivory reliquary which has been brought home to the abbey by a wandering pilgrim, and uses some device on its carven sides to modify his native art. So the influence of the glittering metropolis of the Empire spread to the shores of the Atlantic, and left its record on the grey stones of the West.

CHAPTER XIV

The Spirit of
Byzantine Architecture

ALL throughout the Christian East and far beyond its confines Byzantine churches rear the domes which proclaim
the sovereignty of God. In the streets of crowded cities
they invite the stream of worshippers within their doors. In the
market-places of distant villages they tower above the humble
dwellings. In the courtyards of ancient monasteries they summon
the black-robed monks to daily prayer. Some of them belong to
the early centuries when councils were formulating the dogmas of
the creeds. Others were the bequest of empires that were hastening
to their dissolution. Within many of these churches the worshipper still hears the Liturgy in the very words in which it was
heard by his forefathers centuries ago. Others have been adapted
to the needs of an alien faith, and yet more have been shattered
by war or earthquake or slow decay. Their abandoned ruins
crumble on deserted hill-sides and vacant plains, silent witnesses to
the devotion of a distant age. The splendour of mosaics gleam
on the vaults of imperial cathedrals and the dim hues of frescoes
fade on the walls of village shrines. Their masonry may be stern
and unadorned or rich in the polychromatic decoration of brick
and stone. Their external outline may display the soft and
swelling curve or the hard and elevated angle. According to the
resources, the materials, the climate and the sentiments of the
places and regions where it flourished, Byzantine Architecture
took on many different aspects.

Yet, in spite of all its variety of form, Byzantine Architecture
evolved around an essential nucleus, and that nucleus was the
dome upon the square. It was from this primary feature that
almost everything essential in the building ultimately sprang.
Employing and developing the device of the spherical pendentive
to set the dome upon the square, the Byzantines, constructing
their light vaults of brick, developed the nucleus into complex
articulated structures. They extended the supporting arches and
formed a cruciform plan, whose symbolic shape made a fitting

274

sepulchre for martyrs of the Christian faith. They combined the cruciform martyrion with the vaulted basilica whose wide nave and aisles could accommodate a congregation. Otherwise, by filling in the angles of the cruciform church, they provided more space for worshippers in a building which was completely central-planned. The requirements of the ritual added three apses and the need for more room for the clergy extended the sanctuary. A narthex was required for catechumens at the western end, and it was later combined with an exo-narthex for monastic offices. Side-chapels with their own apses were built along the lateral walls, and porches and porticoes were added. In these and other ways the building was extended and enlarged and complicated, but the true Byzantine church retains its original and essential feature, the dome upon the square, its centre and its core.

But we must go far beyond the thought of utilitarian needs when we consider the structure of the Byzantine church. The Byzantine church had its own aesthetic qualities and its own religious atmosphere, and these were created chiefly by the presence of its crowning feature, the dome with its subsidiary vaults. It was this which helped to give the structure its spiritual content. In the large churches of the earlier epoch, the spectator who stands within the ample nave is profoundly moved, and the primary cause of his emotion is simply the wide outstretching space which envelops him on every hand. Great open space extends around him, free and unconstrained: great open space soars above him into the lofty hemisphere of the superincumbent dome, poised above the nave with the majesty of heaven and holding all the space together in its splendid curve. Moreover, the component parts of the building are so adjusted that its spaciousness has the quality of the infinite. For the dome, lightened and etherialised with its ring of windows, and resting on its open arches, does not weigh upon the building or hem it in, but seems rather to float above it without heaviness and without constraint. How different is the impression created by such a building as the Church of S. Bernardo in Rome, a rotunda connected with the Baths of Diocletian and converted into a church in the early seventeenth century. The deeply coffered ceiling weighs down upon the heavy mouldings, and all the plastic decoration only adds to the feeling of constraint! In the Byzantine church it is the very reverse. Majesty is combined with freedom and the soul rises to the sublime. Space flows upwards to the dome and vaults and penetrates through arches on the ground floor to lose itself in shadowy recesses. All is untrammelled and opened out, while the dome gathers the component elements together with its unifying power. While this spirit is uniquely felt in Santa Sophia in Constantinople, it is characteristic of all the larger Byzantine churches, like S. Irene, and is continued in such later types as Daphni and S. Luke of Stiris.

Now this spirit of majesty and serenity and unity is a true expression of the Christian belief in God. Unlike the pagan religions of Greece and Rome with their multitude of deities, Christianity believes in one God, the Creator of the Universe, dwelling eternally in the heavens, the same from everlasting to everlasting, infinite in wisdom, power and love. All the curving lines of a great Byzantine church and all its spatial elements combine to embody that idea. The Byzantine church is a sublime expression of the Christian belief in the Almighty.

But the structure of the Byzantine church embodied far more than that idea, just as Christianity was far more than a bare monotheism. The complementary element in Byzantine Architecture is most clearly to be seen in the type of church which became so popular and so enduring, the cross-in-square. Christianity asserted that God Almighty became incarnate in the person of Jesus Christ His Son. He did not remain aloof from the world, indifferent to its needs, but came down to earth and dwelt among men. The Eastern Church was constant in its reiteration of that truth.

> We believe in one God, the Father Almighty, Maker of heaven and earth, and of all things visible and invisible: and in One Lord Jesus Christ, the only-begotten Son of God, begotten of His Father before all worlds, Light of Light, Very God of Very God, begotten, not made, being of one substance with the Father, by whom all things were made: who, for us men, and for our salvation, came down from heaven, and was incarnate by the Holy Ghost of the Virgin Mary, and was made man. . . .

So ran the so-called Nicene creed as it was accepted in 381 at the Council of Constantinople. It was on the doctrine of the Incarnation that many of the great divines of the Eastern Church expended most of their energy and learning, and the theology of that Church was primarily incarnational. It is possible to see this attitude of mind reflected in the very structure of the cross-in-square church. Once the type had been evolved and built, did not the

Byzantine churchmen with all their love of symbolism behold this doctrine expressed in the very system of its construction?

Let us enter within a cross-in-square church and strive to apprehend its spirit. It is of moderate, perhaps even of modest, dimensions, and the wide extent of unbroken floor space is much diminished. Yet the majestic and transcendental spirit and the sense of spaciousness and freedom are indubitably present. The presence of the infinite and eternal God is still expressed. If we stand beneath the dome and look upwards we realise it. The arms of the cross are high in proportion to their width, and the gaze roams freely over the surfaces of their smooth and frescoed vaults and over the open spaces which they contain. There is a serenity and sublimity in these lofty but simple vaults. But it is the dome which chiefly contributes to the sense of the infinite and the sublime. It has been thrust upwards, for it rests upon an elevated drum, and above us, as we stand in the centre of the church, there rises a cylinder of space, completed in its dome. It lifts itself above us, illuminated by the windows which surround it, and as the gaze rests within it, the mind feels the sense of the majestic and sublime. Moreover, by the insertion of the cylindrical drum, the portrait of Christ the Almighty is thrust into a remoter distance. Dwelling in light inaccessible, He looks down from His lofty height and the sides of the drum are utilised to furnish Him with the guard of bejewelled angels to signalise His glory.

Nevertheless, as we have said, there is another impression to be conveyed by the cross-in-square church. It emphasises the idea of the Incarnation. When the vision rests upon the rounded surface of the dome and vaults, it does not lose itself in endless aspiration as when it follows the pointed ribs of a Gothic vault into the mysterious recesses of distant shadows. The dome is not a spire. The spire points incessantly upwards, leading the vision to unknown regions: the hemisphere of the dome, however light it seems, covers and completes; the soul finds rest and peace within, and returns to earth again. The connection between the dome and the floor is so obvious in the four-columned cross-in-square Byzantine church. The vision passes from the dome down the drum to the pendentives and the arches on which they rest; it reaches the columns which support them and bound the central space. Isolated and prominent, the columns thrust themselves on the attention and their intimate connection with the dome is at once apparent. The heavenly is related to the earthly; Christ the Pantocrator is in closest contact with the world of men. As we have seen in an earlier chapter, the Byzantine theologians looked upon the dome as the vault of heaven, and upon the nave as the worshipping church below. They saw the pendentives as the links between heaven and earth, and they painted the evangelists on their curving surfaces. On one of the central pillars they depicted Jesus who dwelt among men. They must have realised in a still deeper emotional sense the relationship of open vaults and dome with the pillared and complex base. Not only symbolically but aesthetically does the structure show forth the connection between heaven and earth, the revelation of God to man through Christ. Byzantine Architecture is the architecture of the Incarnation.

There is, moreover, a quality about the cross-in-square church which distinguishes it sharply from the great church of the earlier age. In its ground-area it possesses an intimacy, a friendliness and a humanity which mingles with the impression of majesty in the vaults and dome. It is as if one felt both the power and the love of God. Here we do not stand in the midst of great stretches of unbroken space. Just beside us rise the marble columns or the frescoed piers. The nave is no longer a vast space but a series of compartments opening the one into the other: we move from the cross-arm to the angle-chamber through an open arch and pass through another archway into the cross-arm once again. We pause to gaze upon the saints who are ranged along the walls so near us and to look upon the complex vista of arch and column. The whole area has an atmosphere of intimacy which contrasts and yet merges with the sense which the dome inspires. By means of the whole articulation of the church, the temporal and the eternal have been mingled together and become one.

As time went on and Byzantine Architecture emerged upon its final phase it was affected by a subtle change of temper. It lost in simple grandeur and became more delicate and refined. The appeal was more to the eye than to the soul. It possessed a strong dramatic quality and a desire for the creation of striking effects. There was a decline in the appreciation of the unity and majesty which could be expressed by a solitary or outstanding dome. There arose a preference for the picturesque silhouette, and cupolas on projecting cornices were multiplied over parecclesia and nartheces. Often the drums of the domes are still further heightened, and, especially in the Balkans, are raised on high square bases. They lose their original character and leap into the air like slender towers, losing their aesthetic connection with the body of the church and impairing the unity of the composition. One feels that the builders have lost both the aesthetic value and the spiritual significance of the dome. The humanistic and classical revival of the period is reflected in a weakening of the supramundane quality and in a closer adaptation of the parts of the building to the human scale. Rich and complex patterns are elaborated on the walls, and the artists of the closing centuries of the diminished Empire seem to have rejoiced to express themselves in exquisite and meticulous detail.

The majority of the churches of the closing epoch are to be found outside the limits of the Empire. Sufficient, it is hoped, has been said in previous chapters to indicate their nature. They took on many alien features, but the basis of their plan was Byzantine and the source which inspired them was Constantinople. Byzantine Architecture is rightly named. It was moulded by influences which emanated from other regions and it developed in different countries in divers ways, but it was Byzantium that created its character and sealed it with the impress of its genius.

For well over a thousand years the great Christian city on the Bosphorus was the guardian of civilisation in the East. Cultured and opulent, she proudly cherished the double inheritance which she owed to the Orient and to Hellenism. Profoundly religious, she consecrated most of her artistic activity to the service of the Church, on whose shrines she lavished all sumptuous and exquisite adornment. She did not hesitate to draw inspiration from far and wide, but in recompense she awoke a mighty influence which extended to distant regions and endured long after her own glory had passed away.

Pilgrim and merchant, prince and artist came to reside within her walls, and, fascinated by the magic of her spell, carried back the tale of magnificence to their homes and filled the souls of their countrymen with the longing to emulate her splendour. Monks and missionaries went forth from her precincts to teach their listeners not only the doctrines of their faith but their methods in raising the house of God and embellishing its walls. Warrior and wanderer carried her objects of beauty to the West, there to be imitated in sculptured stone. Her art was the forerunner of early Italian painting. The Moslem acknowledged the sublimity of her architecture, deeming it worthy for the mosques of Allah. Masters of the Renaissance accepted its features to aid them in forming their own noble style.

Many of the most important monuments of Byzantine Architecture have perished. Many others are shorn of almost all their ancient glory. The purple and the gold have grown dim. But incomparable memorials remain to witness to its impressive beauty, and the written records of the past indicate the magnitude of splendour now no more.

> The pillars of it fallen, and no clue,
> But through the ruin penetrates a blaze
> Of glory beyond glory, and of light behind
> The light.[1]
>
> [1] Lawrence Binyon

BIBLIOGRAPHY

ABBREVIATIONS

A.A.J.	Architectural Association Journal.
BCH	Bulletin de Correspondance hellénique.
BSA	Annual of the British School at Athens.
BZ	Byzantinische Zeitschrift.
DACL	Dictionnaire d'Archéologie chrétienne et de liturgie.
Pal. Exp.	Quarterly Report of the Palestine Exploration Fund.
RA	Revue archéologique.
Bull. Mus. N.Y.	Bulletin of the Metropolitan Museum of Art, New York.
J.R.I.B.A.	Journal of the Royal Institute of British Architects.
JHS	Journal of Hellenic Studies.
n.d.	no date.

A

LIST of works on Byzantine Architecture and Art, etc., which have been consulted in the preparation of this volume.

(References in square brackets [ ] are to buildings or subjects dealt with in the books named.)

1. GENERAL AND ORIGINS

Adam, R. *Ruins of the Palace of the Emperor Diocletian at Spalatro in Dalmatia* (London, 1764).

Anderson, W. J., Spiers, R. P., and Ashby, T. *The Architecture of Ancient Rome* (London, 1927). [Sedia del Diavolo: Licinian Nymphaeum, etc., Spalato.]

Bagenal, H. "Principles of Dome Design illustrated in the Historical Styles," in *A.A.J.*, vol. XLV (1929–30).

Bayet, Ch. *L'Art byzantin* (Paris, 1924).

Bréhier, L. "Orient ou Byzance," in *RA* (1907).

Bréhier, L. *L'Art chrétien: son développement iconographique* (Paris, 1918).

Bréhier, L. "A propos de la question Orient ou Byzance," in *BZ*, vol. XXII (1913).

Bréhier, L. *L'Art byzantin* (Paris, 1924).

Bréhier, L. "Byzance, l'Orient et l'Occident. L'iconographie chrétienne au moyen âge," in *RA* (1918).

Bréhier, L. *La civilisation byzantine* (Paris, 1950).

Choisy, A. *L'Art de bâtir chez les Byzantins* (Paris, 1883).

Cresswell, K. A. C. *Early Muslim Architecture*, 2 vols. (Oxford, 1932–40). [Chapters on the Pendentive and Squinch.]

Dalton, O. M. *Byzantine Art and Archaeology* (Oxford, 1911).

Dalton, O. M. *East Christian Art* (Oxford, 1925).

Davies, J. G. *The Origin and Development of Early Christian Architecture* (London, 1952).

Demus, O. *Byzantine Mosaic Decoration* (London, 1947).

Didron, A. N. *Christian Iconography*, 2 vols. (London, 1886).

Diehl, C. *Manuel d'art byzantin*, 2 vols., Second Edition (Paris, 1925–6).

Diehl, C. "Les Origines asiatiques de l'art byzantin," in *Journal des Savants* (1904).

Diehl, C. *L'Art chrétien primitif et l'art byzantin* (Paris, 1928).

Diehl, C. "Byzantine Art," in *Byzantium*, ed. N. H. Baynes and H. St. L. B. Moss (Oxford, 1948).

Durm, J. *Die Baukunst der Etrusker und der Römer* (Stuttgart, 1905). [For early pendentives in the East.]

Eusebius Pamphilus. *The Life of the Blessed Emperor Constantine.* English Translation (London, 1845).

Evagrius. *A History of the Church* (A.D. 431 to A.D. 594). English Translation (London, 1846). [Santa Sophia, Constantinople.]

Fergusson, J. *A History of Architecture. . . .* Third Edition. Edited by R. P. Spiers, vol. I (London, 1893).

Grabar, A. *Byzantine Painting.* Trans. by S. Gilbert (Geneva, 1953). [Magnificent coloured plates.]

Jackson, T. G. *Byzantine and Romanesque Architecture*, vol. I (Cambridge, 1913). [Churches in Constantinople, Salonica and Northern Italy.]

Laurent, J. "Delphes chrétien," in *BZ*, vol. XXIII (1899). [General discussion of Theodosian capitals, impost-capitals, etc., based on discoveries at Delphi.]

Leclercq, Dom H. *Manuel d'archéologie chrétienne depuis les origines jusqu'au VIIIe siècle*, vol. II (Paris, 1907).

Leclercq, Dom H. "Byzantin (Art) and Basilique," in *DACL*.

Lethaby, W. R. *Medieval Art. From the Peace of the Church to the Eve of the Renaissance* (London, 1912).

Lowrie, W. *Christian Art and Archaeology* (New York and London, 1901).

Maillard, D. *L'Art byzantin* (Paris, n.d.).

Maskell, A. *Ivories* (London, 1905). [Chair of Maximian, etc.]

Michelis, P. A. *An Aesthetic Approach to Byzantine Art* (London, 1955).

Millet, G. "Essai d'une méthode iconographique," in *RA* (1917). [Brief summary of views expanded in his *L'Iconographie de l'Évangile.*]

Millet, G. *L'Iconographie de l'Évangile* (Paris, 1916).

Millet, G. "L'Art byzantin," in vol. I, and "L'Art chrétien d'Orient du milieu du xive au milieu du xvie siècle", in vol. III of Michel's *Histoire de l'art* (Paris, 1905).

Muratoff, P. *La Peinture byzantine* (Paris, 1928).

Peirce, H., and Tyler, R. *Byzantine Art* (London, 1926).

Procopius. *Of the Buildings of Justinian.* English Translation by A. Stewart (London, 1886).

Rice, D. Talbot. *Byzantine Art* (Harmondsworth, Middlesex, 1954).

Rivoira, G. T. *Lombardic Architecture: its origin, development and derivatives.* English Translation by G. McN. Rushforth, 2 vols. (London, 1910).

Rivoira, G. T. *Roman Architecture.* English Translation by G. McN. Rushforth (Oxford, 1925).

Sisson, M. A. "Roman Architecture at Jerash," in *J.R.I.B.A.*, vol. XXXV (1927). [Pendentives in Thermae.]

Smith, E. Baldwin. *The Dome, A Study in the History of Ideas* (Princeton, 1950).

Statham, H. H. *A Short Critical History of Architecture* (London, 1927).

Stewart, C. *Simpson's History of Architectural Development,* vol. II. *Early Christian Byzantine and Romanesque Architecture* (London, 1954).

Strong, E. *Art in Ancient Rome,* vol. II (London, 1929).

Strzygowski, J. *Altai-Iran und Völkerwanderung* (Leipsig, 1917).

Strzygowski, J. *Orient oder Rom. Beiträge zur Geschichte der spätantiken und frühchristlichen Kunst* (Leipsig, 1901).

Strzygowski, J. *Origin of Christian Church Art.* English Translation by O. M. Dalton and H. M. Braunholtz (Oxford, 1923).

Sturgis, R. *A Dictionary of Architecture and Building.* Articles on "Byzantine Architecture" (Hamlin) and "Pendentive" (Babcock) (London, 1902).

Swift, E. H. *Roman Sources of Christian Art* (New York, 1951).

Texier, C., and Pullan, R. P. *Byzantine Architecture* (London, 1864).

van Berchem, M., and Clouzot, E. *Mosaïques chrétiennes du IVᵉ au Xᵉ siècle* (Geneva, 1924).

Westlake, H. M. B. *A History of Design in Mural Painting,* vol. II (London and Oxford, 1905).

Wulff, O. *Altchristliche und byzantinische Kunst,* 2 vols. (Berlin, 1914 and 1924).

2. CONSTANTINOPLE

Antoniades, E. M. *Ἔκφρασις τῆς Ἁγίας Σοφίας,* 3 vols. (Athens, 1907).

Brunoff, N. "Eine Reise nach Konstantinopel, Nicäa, und Trapezunt. I. Forschungen im Gebiete der byzantinischen Baukunst," in *Repertorium für Kunstwissenchaft,* vol. XLIX (1928).

Diehl, C. "Les Mosaïques de Kahrié-djami," in *Études byzantines* (Paris, 1905).

Diehl, C. *Constantinople* (Paris, 1924).

Ebersolt, J., and Thiers, A. *Les Églises de Constantinople.* (With Album of Plates) (Paris, 1913).

Ebersolt, J. "Une Mission à Constantinople," in *RA* (1909).

Ebersolt, J. *Sainte-Sophie de Constantinople. Étude de topographie d'après les cérémonies* (Paris, 1910).

Ebersolt, J. *Rapport sommaire sur une mission à Constantinople* (1910) (Paris, 1911).

Ebersolt, J. *Constantinople byzantine et les voyageurs du Levant* (Paris, 1918).

Fossati, G. *Aya Sophia, Constantinople, as recently restored by order of H.M. the Sultan, Abdul Medjid* (London, 1852).

Freshfield, E. "Notes on the Church now called the Mosque of the Kalenders at Constantinople," in *Archaeologia*, vol. LV (1897).

George, W. S., etc. *The Church of Saint Eirene at Constantinople* (Oxford, 1912).

Gurlitt, C. *Die Baukunst Constantinopel* (Berlin, 1913).

Henderson, A. E. "The Church of SS. Sergius and Bacchus at Constantinople," in *The Builder* (1905).

Henderson, A. E. "The Mosque of Sancta Sophia, Constantinople," in *Country Life* (March, 1915).

Lethaby, W. R., and Swainson, H. *The Church of Sancta Sophia, Constantinople. A Study of Byzantine Building* (London, 1894).

Preger, T. "Die Erzählung vom Bau der Hagia Sophia," in *BZ*, vol. X (1901).

Psellus, M. *The Chonographia of Michael Psellus*. Translated from the Greek by E. R. A. Senter (London, 1953).

Pulgher, D. *Les anciennes églises byzantines de Constantinople* (Vienna, 1878). Plates (1880).

Rice, D. Talbot. *Excavations at Bodrum Cami 1930* (Brussels, 1933).

Rüdell, A. *Die Kahrie-Dschamisi in Constantinopel. Ein Kleinod byzantinischer Kunst* (Berlin, 1908).

Salzenberg, W. *Altchristliche Baudenkmäle von Constantinopel vom V. bis XII. Jahrhundert* (Berlin, 1854).

Schmidt, T. "La 'Renaissance' de la peinture byzantine au xive siècle," in *RA* (1912). [Kahrié-djami Mosaics.]

Sheepshanks, M. "Some ruined Byzantine Churches of Constantinople," in *Architects' Journal*, vol. LXIII (1926).

Swift, E. H. *Hagia Sophia* (New York, 1940).

Toy, S. "The Church of St. Sophia, Constantinople," in *The Builder*, vol. CXXIII (1922).

van Millingen, A., and Traquair, R. *Byzantine Churches in Constantinople* (London, 1912).

van Millingen, A. *Byzantine Constantinople* (London, 1899).

3. ASIA MINOR

Ainsworth, W. F. *Travels and Researches in Asia Minor, Mesopotamia, Chaldea and Armenia*, 2 vols. (London, 1842). [Sivri Hissar.]

Bell, G. L. "Notes on a Journey through Cilicia and Lycaonia," in *RA* (1906-7).

Bent, J. T. "A Journey in Cilicia Trachea," in *JHS*, vol. XII (1891).

Bréhier, L. "Les Églises rupestres de Cappadoce et leur témoignage," in *RA* (1927).

Cronin, H. S. "First Report of a Journey in Pisidia, etc.," in *JHS*, vol. XXII (1902). [Rock-church at Kyzyl-Ören.]

Crowfoot, J. W. "Notes upon late Anatolian Art. II. The Church at Yurme," in *BSA*, vol. IV (1897-8).

de Jerphanion, R. P. G. "Deux Chapelles souterraines en Cappadoce," in *RA* (1908).

de Jerphanion, R. P. G. *Une nouvelle province de l'art byzantin. Les églises rupestres de Cappadoce* (Paris, 1925-8). [Text and Plates. Coloured Drawings.]

Hamilton, W. J. *Researches in Asia Minor, Pontus and Armenia*, 2 vols. (London, 1842).

Hasluck, F. W. "Bithynica," in *BSA*, vol. XIII (1906-7). [Churches at Triglia.]

Headlam, A. C. "Ecclesiastical Sites in Isauria," in *JHS*, Supplement (1892). [Khodja Kalessi: full description with plans, etc.]

Heberdey, R. "Vorläufiger Bericht über die Grabungen in Ephesos," in *Jahreshefte des Österreichischen Archäologischen Instituts in Wien*, vol. X (1907) Beiblatt.

Heberdey, R. (quoting Knoll, F.). "Vorläufiger Bericht über die Grabungen in Ephesos, 1907-1911," in *Jahreshefte des Öster. Arch. Inst.*, vol. XV (1912) Beiblatt. [Baptistery.]

Herzfeld, E., and Guyer, S. *Monumenta Asiae Minoris Antiqua*, vol. II. *Meriamlik und Korykos: zwei christliche Ruinenstätten des Rauhen Kilikiens* (Manchester, 1930).

Keil, J. (quoting Knoll, F.). "Vorläufiger Bericht über die Arbeiten in Ephesos, 1912," in *Jahreshefte des Öster. Arch. Inst.*, vol. XV (1912) Beiblatt. [The Double-Church.]

Langlois, V. *Voyage dans la Cilicie*. . . . (Paris, 1861).

Millet, G. "L'Asie Mineure, nouveau domaine de l'histoire de l'art," in *RA* (1905).

Millet, G. "Les églises et les monastères de Trébizonde," in *BCH*, vol. XIX (1895).

Millet, G., and Rice, D. Talbot. *Byzantine Painting at Trebizond* (London, 1936).

Ramsay, Sir W. M., and Bell, G. L. *The Thousand and One Churches* (London, 1909).

Ramsay, Sir W. "The Thousand and One Churches in Lycaonia," in *Studies in the History and Art of the Eastern Provinces of the Roman Empire* (Aberdeen, 1906).

Rice, D. Talbot. "New Light on the Round Circular Building Plan," from *VIIIth Congress of Byzantine Studies*, vol. II.

Rice, D. Talbot. "Trebizond, A Medieval Citadel and Palace," in *JHS*, vol. LII.

Rott, H. *Kleinasiatische Denkmäler* (Leipzig, 1908).

Spratt, T. A. B., and Forbes, E. *Travels in Lycia, etc.*, vol. I (London, 1847). [Déré-Aghsy.]

Strzygowski, J. *Kleinasien: ein Neuland der Kunstgeschichte* (Leipzig, 1903).

Weber, G. "Basilika und Baptisterium in Gül-bagtsche," in *BZ*, vol. X (1901).

Wood, J. T. *Discoveries at Ephesus* (London, 1877). [References to Churches.]

4. CYPRUS

Buckler, W. H. "Frescoes at Galata, Cyprus," in *JHS*, vol. LIII (1933).

Enlart, C. *L'art gothique et de la Renaissance en Chypre*, 2 vols. (Paris, 1899). [Describes some of the Byzantine churches.]

Enlart, C. "Les églises à coupoles d'Aquitaine et de Chypre," in *Gazette des Beaux-Arts*, vol. XIII (1926).

Hill, Sir G. *A History of Cyprus* (Cambridge, 1944 ff.).

Jeffery, G. *A Description of the Historic Monuments of Cyprus* (Nicosia, 1918).

Jeffery, G. "The Present Condition of the Ancient Architectural Monuments of Cyprus, 1910," in *Archaeologia*, 1910 I.

Jeffery, G. E. "The Byzantine Churches of Cyprus," in *Proc. Soc. Ant. Lond.*, vol. XXVIII (1915–16). [Especially the earlier churches, S. Hilarion, etc.]

Stylianou, A. and J. *Byzantine Cyprus as Reflected in Art* (Nicosia, 1948).

5. MESOPOTAMIA

Bell, G. L. *Amurath to Amurath* (London, 1911).

de Villard, U. M. *Le chiese della Mesopotamia* (Rome, 1940).

Guyer, S. "Surg Hagop. Eine Klosterruine der Kommagene," in *Repertorium für Kunstwissenschaft*, vol. XXXV (1912).

van Berchem, M., and Strzygowski, J. *Amida*. With a contribution, "The Churches and Monasteries of the Tur Abdin," by G. L. Bell (Heidelberg, 1910).

Wigram, Rev. T. A., and Sir E. T. A. *The Cradle of Mankind* (London, 1922). [S. James, Nisibis, etc.]

6. ARMENIA

Bunt, C. G. E. "The External Niche in Armenian Architecture," in *The Builder* (1922).

Conway, Sir M. "The Churches of Northern Armenia," in *Country Life* (February, 1916).

der Nersessian, S. *Armenia and the Byzantine Empire* (Cambridge, Mass., 1945).

Fetvadjian, A. "An Outline History of Armenian Architecture," in *J.R.I.B.A.*, vol. XXIX (1922).

Lynch, H. F. B. *Armenia, Travels and Studies*, 2 vols. (London, 1901). [A standard work, valuable on the historical and geographical side. Useful for churches at Ani and Etschmiadzin.]

Macler, F. "L'architecture arménienne dans ses rapports avec l'art syrien," in *Syria*, vol. I (1920).

Mourier, J. *L'Art au Caucase*. Second Edition (Brussels, 1907).

Rivoira, G. T. *Moslem Architecture, its Origin and Development.* English Translation by J. McN. Rushforth (London, 1918). [Includes a chapter on Armenian churches. Illustrated.]

Strzygowski, J. *Die Baukunst der Armenier und Europa*, 2 vols. (Vienna, 1918). [Exhaustive. Indispensable. Fully planned and illustrated.]

7. SYRIA AND PALESTINE

Bernard, J. H. *The Churches of Constantine at Jerusalem, being Translations from Eusebius and the Early Pilgrims* (London, 1891).

Butler, H. C. Part II of the Publications of an American Archaeological Expedition to Syria in 1899–1900. *Architecture and Other Arts* (New York, 1903).

Butler, H. C. *Syria*. Publications of the Princeton University Archaeological Expeditions to Syria in 1904–5 and 1909. Division II. Architecture. Section A, Southern Syria [Bosra, Omm-es-Zeitoun]. Section B, Northern Syria [Kasr-ibn-Wardan] (Leyden, 1917–20).

Chitty, D. J. "Excavations at the Monastery of St. Euthymius, 1929," in *Pal. Exp.* (1930).

Chitty, D. J., and Jones, A. H. M. "The Church of St. Euthymius at Khan el Ahmar near Jerusalem," in *Pal. Exp.* (1928).

Conder, C. R. *Survey of Eastern Palestine*, vol. I (London, 1889). [Kusr-en-Nueîjis.]

Crowfoot, J. W. "Jerash, 1929," in *Pal. Exp.* (1929).

Crowfoot, J. W. "The Church of St. Theodore at Jerash," in *Pal. Exp.* (1929).

Crowfoot, J. W. "The Churches of Gerasa," in *Pal. Exp.* (1930).

Crowfoot, J. W. *Early Churches in Palestine* (London, 1940).

Crowfoot, C.B.E., J. W., *Churches at Jerash. A Preliminary Report of the Joint Yale-British School Expeditions to Jerash, 1928–1930* (London, 1931).

de Vogüé, Comte M. *Syrie centrale: architecture civile et religieuse du Ier au VIIe siècle*, 2 vols. (Paris, 1865–77).

Duckworth, H. T. F. *The Church of the Holy Sepulchre* (London, n.d.).

Harvey, W., etc. *The Church of the Nativity at Bethlehem* (London, 1910).

Jeffery, G. *A Brief Description of the Holy Sepulchre, Jerusalem, and other Christian Churches in the Holy City* (Cambridge, 1919).

Mark the Deacon. *The Life of Porphyry, Bishop of Gaza.* English Translation by G. F. Hill (Oxford, 1913).

Schneider, A. M. *The Church of the Multiplying of the Loaves and Fishes* (London, 1937).

8. EGYPT

Anon. "The Coptic Monasteries of the Wady-el-Natroun, Lower Egypt," in *The Builder* (October, 1911).

Butler, A. J. *The Ancient Coptic Churches of Egypt*, 2 vols. (Oxford, 1884).

Clarke, S. *Christian Antiquities in the Nile Valley* (Oxford, 1912).

Jones, H. J. "The Monasteries of the Wadi Natrun," in *Bull. Mus. N.Y.*, vol. VII (1912).

Jones, H. J. "The Coptic Monasteries of the Wadi Natrun," in *Bull. Mus. N.Y.*, vol. VI (1911).

Kaufman, K. M. *Die Menasstadt und das Nationalheiligtum der alchristlichen Ägypter*, Part I (Leipzig, 1910).

Strzygowski, J. *Koptische Kunst* (Vienna, 1904). [Catalogue of Coptic Sculptures in the Museum, Cairo.]

White, H. J. E. "The Monasteries of the Wadi Natrun," in *Bull. Mus. N.Y.*, vol. xv, Part 2 (1920).

White, H. J. E. "The Monasteries in Wady 'n Natrun," in *Bull. Mus. N.Y.*, vol. XVI, Part 2 (1921).

9. GREECE

Bevan, B. "Byzantine Salonika. The Churches as they are To-day," in *Apollo*, vol. III.

Bréhier, L. "Les Monuments chrétiens de Salonique," in *RA* (1919).

Bühlmann, M. *Die Entstehung der Kreuzkuppelkirche* (Heidelberg, 1914). [Based on a detailed description of Paros; plans, etc.]

Comyn, H. "Church of the Ruined Monastery at Daou-Mendeli, Attica," in *BSA*, vol. IX (1902–3).

Curzon, Hon. R. *Visits to Monasteries in the Levant* (London, 1916). [References to churches in Athos, Egypt.]

Dawkins, R. M. "A Visit to Skyros," in *BSA*, vol. XI (1904–5).

Diehl, C. "Les mosaïques du monastère de Saint-Luc," in *Études byzantines* (Paris, 1905).

Diehl, C. *L'église et les mosaïques du couvent de Saint-Luc en Phocide* (Paris, 1889).

Diez, E., and Demus, O. *Byzantine Mosaics in Greece: Daphni and Hosios Lucas* (Cambridge, Massachusetts, 1931).

Enlart, C. "Quelques monuments d'architecture gothique en Grèce," in *Revue de l'art chrétien* (1897).

Fougères, G. *Athènes* (Paris, 1912).

Fyfe, T. "The Church of Saint Titus at Gortyna in Crete," in *Architectural Review*, vol. XXII (1907).

Giannopoulos, N. J. "Les constructions byzantines de la région de Démétrias (Thessalie)," in *BCH*, vol. XLIV (1902).

Hamilton, J. A. *The Church of Kaisariani in Attica and its Frescoes* (Aberdeen, 1916).

Hamilton, J. A. *A Medieval City in Greece: its Churches and its Ruins* (Aberdeen, 1921). [Mistra.]

Hasluck, F. W. *Athos and its Monasteries* (London, 1924).

Hébrard E. "Les travaux du service archéologique de l'armée d'Orient à l'Arc de Triomphe de Galère et à l'église Saint-Georges à Salonique," in *BCH*, vol. XLIV (1920).

Jewell, H. H., and Hasluck, F. W. *The Church of Our Lady of the Hundred Gates in Paros* (London, 1920).

Lambakes, G. *Mémoire sur les antiquités chrétiennes de la Grèce* (Athens, 1902).

Magne, L. "Mistra," in *Gazette des Beaux-Arts* (1897) [with coloured reproductions].

Megaw, H. "The Chronology of some Middle Byzantine Churches," in *BSA*, vol. XXXII (1931–2).

Megaw, H. "Byzantine Architecture in Mani," in *BSA*, vol. XXXIII (1932–3).

Michel, K., and Struck, A. "Die mittelbyzantinischen Kirchen Athens," in *Athenische Mittheilungen*, vol. XXXI (1906). [The Small Metropolis: detailed description.]

Millet, G. *Le Monastère de Daphni* (Paris, 1899).

Millet, G. "Les peintures de l'Athos," in *RA* (1927).

Millet, G. "Remarques sur les sculptures byzantines de la région de Démétrias," in *BCH*, vol. XLIV (1920).

Millet, G. *L'École grecque dans l'architecture byzantine* (Paris, 1916).

Millet, G. *Monuments byzantins de Mistra. Matériaux pour l'étude de l'architecture et de la peinture en Grèce aux xiv⁰ et xv⁰ siècles.* Album de 152 Planches (Paris, 1910).

Nicol, D. "The Churches of Molyvdoskepastos," in *BSA*, vol. XLVII (1953).

Perdrizet, P., and Chesnay, L. "La Métropole de Serres," in *Fondation Eugène Piot: Monuments et Mémoires*, vol. x (1903).

Schultz, R. W., and Barnsley, S. H. *The Monastery of Saint Luke of Stiris in Phocis and the Dependent Monastery of Saint Nicolas-in-the-Fields near Skripou in Boeotia* (London, 1901).

Steiner, P. "Antike Skulpturen an der Panagia Gorgoepikoos zu Athen," in *Athenische Mittheilungen*, vol. xxxi (1906).

Struck, A. *Mistra* (Vienna and Leipzig, 1910).

Struck, A. "Vier byzantinische Kirchen der Argolis (Plataniti, Chonika, Merbaka, und Areia)," in *Athenische Mittheilungen*, vol. xxxiv (1909).

Struck, A. *Griechenland. Land, Leute und Denkmäler*. Band I. Athen und Attika (Vienna and Leipzig, 1911).

Strzygowski, J. "Inedita der Architektur und Plastik aus der Zeit Basilios I," in *BZ*, vol. iii (1894). [Skripou.]

Strzygowski, J. "Die Ruine von Philippi," in *BZ*, vol. xi (1902).

Strzygowski, J. "Nea Moni auf Chios," in *BZ*, vol. v (1896).

Tafrali, O. "Sur la date de l'église et des mosaïques de Saint Démétrius de Salonique," in *RA* (1909).

Toy, S. H. "Salonica," in *The Builder* (1920).

Traquair, R. "Laconia: Medieval Fortresses," in *BSA*, vol. xii (1905–6). [Churches in Monemvasia.]

Traquair, R. "Laconia. The Churches of Western Mani," in *BSA*, vol. xv (1908–9).

Troump, E. *Quelques vielles églises byzantines de la Grèce moderne*. (Marseilles, 1896). [Description of the work of restoration at Daphni. Visits to S. Luke and Mistra.]

10. YUGOSLAVIA

Bunt, C. G. E. "The Architecture of the Southern Slavs," in *The Architect* (1922).

Jackson, T. G. *Dalmatia, the Quarnero and Istria*, vols. i and ii (Oxford, 1887).

Jackson, Sir T. G. "The Churches of Serbia," in *Proc. Soc. Antiq. Lond.*, vol. xxx (1917–18). [With remarks by Sir Arthur Evans.]

Millet, G. *L'Ancien Art serbe: les églises* (Paris, 1919).

Perdrizet, P. "Melnic et Rossno," in *BCH*, vol. xxxi (1907).

Pupin, M. J., Edited by. *South Slav Monuments*. I. Serbian Orthodox Church. With an Introduction by Sir. T. G. Jackson (London, 1918).

Strzygowski, J. *Early Church Art in Northern Europe* (London, 1928). [Nona.]

11. BULGARIA

Filow, B. D. *Die altbulgarische Kunst* (Bern, 1919) [also in English Translation].

Grabar, A. *La Peinture religieuse en Bulgarie* (Paris, 1928).

Macartney, C. A. "Architecture in Bulgaria," in *The Architect* (1927).

Schmit, T. "Die Malereien des bulgarischen Klosters Poganovo," in *BZ*, vol. XVII (1908).

12. ROUMANIA

Bengenco, M. "L'Art en Roumanie," in *La Roumanie en images*, vol. I (Paris, 1919).

Jorga, N., and Bals, G. *L'Art roumain* (Paris, 1922).

Tafrali, A. "Les Monuments roumains," in *RA* (1910).

13. RUSSIA

Buxton, D. R. "Ecclesiastical Architecture in Russia," in *A.A.J.*, vol. XLV (1929–30).

Buxton, D. R. *Russian Medieval Architecture. With an account of the Transcaucasian styles and their influence on the West* (Cambridge, 1934).

Ebersolt, J. "Fresques byzantines de Néréditsi," in *Fondation Eugène Piot: Monuments et Mémoires*, vol. XIII (Paris, 1906).

Halle, F. W. *L'Art de la vieille Russie* (Paris, 1922).

Hamilton, G. *The Art and Architecture of Russia* (Harmondsworth, Middlesex, 1954).

Loukomski, G. K. *L'Architecture religieuse russe du XIe siècle au XVIIe siècle* (Paris, 1929).

Réau, L. *L'Art russe des origines à Pierre le grand* (Paris, 1921).

Rice, T. Talbot. *Russian Art* (West Drayton, Middlesex, 1949).

Ward, W. H. "Russian Architecture," in *J.R.I.B.A.*, vol. XXIX (1922).

Zabel, E. *Moskau* (Leipzig, 1902).

14. ITALY

Bertaux, E. *L'Art dans l'Italie méridionale* (Paris, 1904).

Colasanti, A. *L'Arte bisantina in Italia* (Milan, 1923). [Plates.]

Crowe, J. A., and Cavalcaselle. *A History of Painting in Italy*. Edited by L. Douglas and S. A. Strong, vol. I, Early Christian Art (London, 1903).

Cummings, C. A. *A History of Architecture in Italy*, 2 vols. (Boston and New York, 1901).

Demus, O. *The Mosaics of Norman Sicily* (London, 1949).

Diehl, C. *L'Art byzantin dans l'Italie méridionale* (Paris, 1894).

Diehl, C. "Peintures byzantines de l'Italie méridionale," in *BCH*, vol. XII (1888).

Diehl, C. *Ravenne* (Paris, 1928).

Diehl, C. *Palerme et Syracuse* (Paris, 1907).

Errard, C., and Gayet, A. *L'Art byzantin*. III. *Ravenne et Pompose*. IV. *Torcello et la Dalmatie* (Paris, n.d.).

Freshfield, E. H. *Cellae Trichorae and other Christian Antiquities in the Byzantine Provinces of Sicily with Calabria and North Africa including Sardinia*, 2 vols. (London, 1913 and 1918).

Goetz, W. *Ravenna* (Leipzig, 1913). [Second Edition.]

Hamilton, J. A. *Churches in Palermo* (London, 1929).

Jackson, F. H. *Sicily* (New York, 1925).

Jackson, F. H. *The Shores of the Adriatic. The Italian Side* (London, 1906).

Jackson, Sir T. G. *Gothic Architecture in France, England and Italy*, vol. II (Cambridge, 1915). [Palermo.]

Knight, H. G. *Saracenic and Norman Remains to illustrate the Normans in Sicily* (London, 1840). [Coloured Plates.]

Orsi, P. "Chiese bizantine nel territorio di Siracusa," in *BZ*, vol. VII (1898). [Camerina, Maccari.]

Orsi, P. "Nuove chiese bizantine nel territorio di Siracusa. III. La Cuba presso Siracusa," in *BZ*, vol. VIII (1899).

Pagenstecher, R. *Apulien* (Leipzig, 1914). [Lecce: Siponto: Trani.]

Pavlowsky, A. "Iconographie de la chapelle palatine," in *RA* (1894).

Ricci, C. *Ravenna* (Bergamo, 1903).

Ricci, C. *Art in Northern Italy* (London, 1911).

Robinson, G. "Some Cave Chapels of Southern Italy," in *JHS*, vol. I (1930).

Rushforth, G. McN. *The Church of S. Maria Antiqua*. Papers of the British School at Rome, vol. I (1902).

Terzi, A., etc. *La Cappella di S. Pietro nella Reggia di Palermo* (Palermo, 1889). [Folio; Plates.]

van Marle, R. *The Development of the Italian Schools of Painting*, vol. I (The Hague, 1923). [Ravenna; Rome.]

Waern, C. *Medieval Sicily* (London, 1910).

Zimmermann, M. G. *Sizilien*, vol. II, Palermo (Leipzig, 1905).

15. FRANCE

Anon. *L'Église de Souillac* (Brive, n.d.).

Bréhier, L. "Les églises d'Aquitaine à coupoles et l'origine de leur architecture," in *Journal des Savants* (June 1927).

Hannah, I. C. "Eastern Influences on the Architecture of the West." (Reprinted from the *Archaeological Journal*) (London, 1928).

Daras, C. *La cathédrale d'Angoulême* (Angoulême, 1942).

de Lasteyrie, R. *L'Architecture religieuse en France à l'époque romane* (Paris, 1912).

de Verneilh, F. *L'architecture byzantine en France. Saint Front de Périgueux et les églises à coupoles de l'Aquitaine* (Paris, 1851).

George, J. *Les églises de la France, Charente* (Paris, 1933).

Mayjonade, M. le Chanoine. *Une basilique byzantine Saint Front de Périgueux* (Périgueux, 1955).

Rey, R. *La cathédrale de Cahors et les origines de l'architecture à coupoles d'Aquitaine* (Paris, 1925).

Rey, R. *L'art roman et ses originés* (Toulouse, 1945).

Roux, J. *Église Saint Étienne de la cité à Périgueux* (Périgueux, 1941).

Sharpe, E. *A visit to the domed churches of Charente, France, by the Architectural Association of London in the year 1875.* Presented as a Memorial to Edmund Sharpe (London, *n.d.*).

Spiers, R. P. *Architecture East and West* (London, 1905).

Totti, A. *Germigny-des-Prés. Église carolingienne* (Germigny-des-Prés, *n.d.*).

B

A Short Selected Bibliography of general works on Byzantine History, Social Life, and the Church.

The Cambridge Medieval History.

Adeney, W. F. *The Greek and Eastern Churches* (Edinburgh, 1908).

Baynes, N. H. *The Byzantine Empire* (London, 1925).

Baynes, N., and Moss, H. (ed.) *Byzantium: An Introduction to East Roman Civilisation* (London, 1948).

Bréhier, L. *Vie et mort de Byzance* (Paris, 1947).

Bury, J. B. *History of the Eastern Roman Empire*, 2 vols. (London, 1923).

Byron, R. *The Byzantine Achievement* (London, 1929).

Diehl, Ch. *Byzance: grandeur et décadence* (Paris, 1919).

Diehl, Ch. *Études byzantines.* Articles: "La civilisation byzantine" and "L'empire grec sous les Paléologues" (Paris, 1905).

Diehl, Ch. *Histoire de l'empire byzantine* (Paris, 1919). English Translation (1925).

Finlay, Geo. *A History of Greece from its Conquest by the Romans to the present time* (London, 1877).

Foord, E. A. *The Byzantine Empire* (London, 1911).

Fortescue, E. F. K. *The Armenian Church* (London, *n.d.*).

Hamilton, M. *Greek Saints and their Festivals* (Edinburgh, 1910).

Hutton, W. H. *Constantinople* (London, 1912).

Maughan, F. H. *The Liturgy of the Eastern Orthodox Church.* With Introduction (London, 1916).

Miller, W. *Trebizond* (London, 1926).

van Millingen, G. *Constantinople* (London, 1906).

Neale, J. M., and Littledale, R. F. *Translations of the Primitive Liturgies* (London, 1859).

Oman, C. W. C. *The Byzantine Empire* (London, 1892).

Ramsay, Sir W. M. *Luke the Physician. IV. The Orthodox Church in the Byzantine Empire* (London, 1908).

Runciman, S. *Byzantine Civilisation* (London, 1933).

Schevill, F. *The Balkan Peninsula and the Near East. A History from the Earliest Times to the Present Day* (London, 1922).

Stewart, C. *The Byzantine Legacy* (London, 1947).

Tozer, H. F. *The Church and the Eastern Empire* (London, 1897).

Zankov, S. *The Eastern Orthodox Church* (London, 1929).

INDEX

INDEX

The index is a geographic one. The numerals in **heavy type**
refer to *figure numbers* of illustrations.